VW AIR-COOLED ENGINES

HOW TO BUILD MAX PERFORMANCE

Dr. John F. Kershaw

S-A DESIGN

CarTech®

CarTech®

CarTech®, Inc.
6118 Main Street
North Branch, MN 55056
Phone: 651-277-1200 or 800-551-4754
Fax: 651-277-1203
www.cartechbooks.com

Edit by Bob Wilson
Layout by Monica Seiberlich

ISBN 978-1-61325-694-7
Item No. SA512

Library of Congress Cataloging-in-Publication Data Available

Written, edited, and designed in the U.S.A.
Printed in China
10 9 8 7 6 5 4 3 2 1

CarTech books may be purchased at a discounted rate in bulk
for resale, events, corporate gifts, or educational purposes. Special
editions may also be created to specification. For details, contact
Special Sales at 6118 Main Street, North Branch, MN 55056 or
by email at sales@cartechbooks.com.

All photos and graphics courtesy Dr. John F. Kershaw unless
otherwise noted.

Front cover photo courtesy the Dub Shop.

Title page photo courtesy Scat Enterprises.

DISTRIBUTION BY:

Europe
PGUK
63 Hatton Garden
London EC1N 8LE, England
Phone: 020 7061 1980 • Fax: 020 7242 3725
www.pguk.co.uk

Australia
Renniks Publications Ltd.
3/37-39 Green Street
Banksmeadow, NSW 2109, Australia
Phone: 2 9695 7055 • Fax: 2 9695 7355
www.renniks.com

Canada
Login Canada
300 Saulteaux Crescent
Winnipeg, MB, R3J 3T2 Canada
Phone: 800 665 1148 • Fax: 800 665 0103
www.lb.ca

CONTENTS

Acknowledgments 4
Preface...4
About the Author..4

Chapter 1: Engine Design.........................5
Air-Cooled and Liquid-Cooled Engine Basics 5
Planning 8
Increasing Performance 9
Thermodynamics..10
Engine Combustion.....................................12
Engine Fundamentals..................................13
Displacement 13
Performance Factors 14
Four-Stroke Cycle.......................................16
Valve and Port Timing 18

Chapter 2: Horsepower and Torque 20
Engine Dynamometer...................................22
Calculating Torque and Horsepower 23
Compression Ratio 26
Fly Cutting the Combustion Chamber...............31
Dynomation Simulation Software 32

**Chapter 3: Rotating Assembly
and Lubrication System Upgrades.....35**
Engine Core Selection...................................36
Stock Engine Setup 37
Cases..39
Lubrication System Modifications 43
Crankshaft and Connecting Rods 50
Flywheel..54

Chapter 4: Cylinder Heads and Camshafts 55
VW Head Castings.......................................56
Valve Grind 59
Valvetrain 61
Rocker Geometry Setting Procedure 68
Porting..71

Chapter 5: Ignition System and Upgrades 74
Detonation...74
Preignition 75
Ignition System...75
Ignition Coils 77
Self-Induction 77
Mutual Induction 77
Creating 40,000 Volts Under the Hood 77

Ignition System Selection 78
Advance Curves 79
Setting Ignition Timing on a Dynamometer............80
Coil...80
Electronic Ignition 81
Distributorless Ignition System 82
Magneto Ignition 83
Capacitive Discharge Ignition........................84
Ignition Timing 85
Spark Plugs 87
Spark Plug Wires 89

Chapter 6: Powertrain Upgrades 91
Flywheel..92
Clutch Pressure Plate 92
Clutch Disc 95
Transaxle 95

Chapter 7: Induction System 98
Carburetion 98
Carburetor Modifications 102
Volkswagen Intake Manifold 103
Carburetor Make and Model 106
Carburetor Selection 108
Fuel Pumps 110
Electronic Fuel Injection 112
Forced Induction.......................................117
Build Recommendations 122

Chapter 8: Exhaust System and Cooling System ...126
4-into-1 Merged Exhaust Systems 126
Header Size 128
Mufflers...129
Heater Boxes...129
Open Exhaust Stingers 130
Building an Exhaust System 130
Engine Cooling...133

Chapter 9: Engine Builds 135
Common Rebuild Materials............................135
Build 1: 1,600-cc Bolt-on Horsepower 135
Build 2: 1,776-cc Engine 136
Build 3: 2,110-cc Engine 137
Build 4: 2,165-cc Engine 139
Build 5: 400-bhp Engine 140

Source Guide 143

ACKNOWLEDGMENTS

Thank you to Joan, my wife, for her continued support in all of my projects.

Also, I need to acknowledge my good friend and colleague noted author Jim Halderman, who has generously provided information and support for this project along with many other projects.

Thank you to Mario Velotta Jr. of the Dub Shop for expert advice and the use of his many photographs; Stefan Rossi of ACE Performance for his expert advice and the use of his many photographs; and Tim Carnacchi of Michael Kunzman and Associates for providing a significant number of Scat photographs for this book.

Information from aircooled.net provided valuable insight for this project as well as videos from jbugs.com. I apologize if I forgot anyone who helped me on this project.

PREFACE

This book is for do-it-yourselfers (DIYers) to build high-performance Volkswagen air-cooled engines. This book fills the need for missing and forgotten high-performance information on these air-cooled engines.

I relied on my background in mechanical engineering and years of teaching automotive technology in the development of this book. When I worked for Volkswagen's Atlantic Region, I was the senior warranty case review adjuster in the engine and electrical areas. I reviewed hundreds of Volkswagen and Porsche warranty claims to learn a great deal about the workings of these air-cooled engines. I have owned seven Type 1 Beetles and two Type 2 Microbuses. I worked on them in all areas and have built many engines in the past.

In the 1970s, I worked for one of the privately owned Volkswagen distributors called Volkswagen Atlantic Inc. in Valley Forge, Pennsylvania. My boss, Karl Heinz Klimpe, had been a VW factory apprentice and was a wealth of VW design information.

In those days, there were about 16 independent distributors, including VW Atlantic. The largest distributor was Worldwide VW in Orange, New York, which Volkswagen was trying to buy back. Volkswagen wanted to control all of the distributors in those days. Volkswagen of America (VWOA) was the importer, and the rest of the organizations were the distributors at the wholesale level. The retail level consisted of the franchised dealers that sold the vehicles imported by VWOA at the time.

I worked for several Volkswagen dealers as a technician, so I have been a Volkswagen enthusiast for many years. Most of my hands-on experience occurred in the 1970s working for these dealers and also building Super Vee engines. I am writing this book because of my interest in these air-cooled engines that can be bumped up to an amazing 400 hp with the right parts and knowledge.

I assembled the most current air-cooled engine information that is needed to build a high-performance Volkswagen engine. I also researched all of the Volkswagen performance parts suppliers, which are listed in the source guide. My goal is to help those who want to build a high-performance engine.

ABOUT THE AUTHOR

Dr. Kershaw has more than 50 years of experience in automotive technology. He has provided classroom curriculum and training as an instructor.

He applies his expertise to investigate and determine the cause for claims involving automotive failures.

Dr. Kershaw also validates manufacturer defects or validates the normal operation of vehicles involved in such mechanical claims.

Dr. Kershaw is the author of 15 General Motors technical training publications and has written 6 automotive textbooks. He developed instructional materials for GM, Nissan, Fiat, Hyundai, Mazda, General Mills, Corinthian Colleges, Ohio Technical College, IntelliTec Colleges, the University of Missouri at Columbia, and Penn Foster College.

ENGINE DESIGN

The basic design of the VW air-cooled engine has not changed much. To increase power, stronger parts are required, and more displacement, supercharging or turbocharging, and nitrous oxide can be used. Ferdinand Porsche made the original Volkswagen engine design, and the car was set up to transport a family of four every day at about 60 mph. However, today's world requires something with more horsepower.

Air-Cooled and Liquid-Cooled Engine Basics

Automotive air-cooled engines require an auxiliary fan to adequately cool the engine. A shroud directs the airflow so that it circulates around the heads and cylinders efficiently. A thermostat opens and closes either the fan's air intake or outlet (depending on design) so that the engine warms up quickly and the operating temperature doesn't vary over a wide range.

Most automotive air-cooled engines require an oil cooler for extra engine heat reduction, which in the case of a Type 1 or Type 2 is under the fan shroud. These oil coolers are small radiators that the oil circulates through after being pumped through the engine before returning to the crankcase. Air-cooled engines rely on the oil supply to help maintain the designed engine temperature. When making performance upgrades, upgrade the oil cooler and filtration system.

When building a high-performance Beetle engine, upgrade the air-cooling systems to accommodate the increased engine heat that will be produced. Heat is thermal energy and cannot be destroyed; it can only be transferred. Heat always moves from a hotter object to a colder object, which is part of the second law of thermodynamics. The cooling fan in the air-cooled cooling system

The Formula Super Vee racing series ran from 1970 to 1990. It was an offshoot of Formula Vee, which started in 1959. Formula Super Vee was a promotional platform for Volkswagen vehicles.

The Volkswagen military Kübelwagen Command bucket-seat car (also called the tub car) was a light military vehicle designed by Ferdinand Porsche and built by Volkswagen during World War II for use by the German military (both Wehrmacht and Waffen SS). It was based heavily on the Volkswagen Beetle, and it was prototyped as the Type 62 but eventually became known internally as the Type 82. Volkswagen built a similar vehicle in the 1970s called the Thing. (Photo Courtesy Shutterstock)

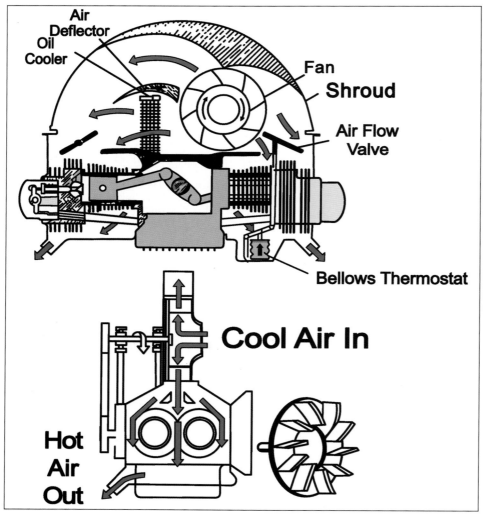

Volkswagen air-cooled engines use deeply finned heads and cylinders similar to many motorcycles. The fins provide more surface area to absorb heat and draw it away from the cylinders and combustion chambers. The fins also expose more surface area to the air to help dissipate the heat. The engine crankcases of some air-cooled engines have internal and external fins that reduce oil temperature to maintain the overall engine temperature. The internal fins speed heat absorption from the oil to the crankcase, and the external fins dissipate the heat to the air.

The Volkswagen engine cooling fan blows air inside the shroud, which is directly over the cooling fins on the cylinders and heads. This removes the heat of combustion like a heat sink. This passive heat exchanger transfers the heat generated by the engine to the air, where it is dissipated away from the engine. (Photo Courtesy Shutterstock)

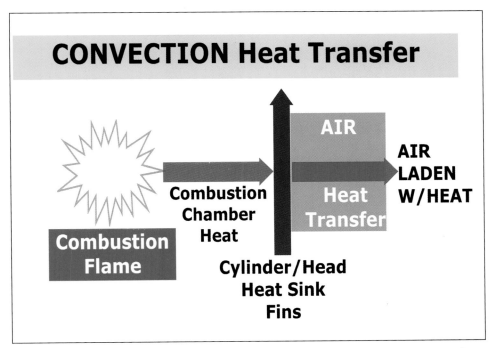

Motorcycles have used air-cooled engines for many years. However, Asian manufacturers used water-cooled engines for most of their motorcycles since the 1990s. Even Harley-Davidson engines have used liquid-cooled heads on many models for a few years now. Air-cooled engines remove engine heat by using the airflow that hits the engine when the bike is moving. This is why they have fins on the outside to create more surface area for the air to pass over. This cooling method is lightweight and simple. It usually requires no cooling fan and also has an engine oil cooler mounted in front of the engine to cool the oil. An engine-powered fan is sometimes used to send air to the fins for forced air cooling, which is similar to the Volkswagen engines. (Photo Courtesy Shutterstock)

blows cold air across the engine to remove the heat. Air is the main heat exchanger that removes the heat of combustion through convection.

Convection is heat transfer by the molecular motion within the heated substance itself. It only takes place in liquids and gases. This gas heat transfer is by the circulation of air in motion between the cooling fan and the head and cylinder cooling fins, which act as heat sinks. Combustion heat is transferred to the cylinder wall and is blown by the cooling fan into the heater boxes to either heat the vehicle or go into the atmosphere.

There are two sorts of convection heat transfer: natural convection and forced convection. Natural convection is when air motion is caused by different air densities. Forced convection is when air motion is caused by a fan, which is the method employed by most air-cooled engines. Heat transfers between the air and the fins of the heads and cylinders in relative

CONVECTION Heat Transfer

Combustion Flame → Combustion Chamber Heat → Heat Transfer → AIR / AIR LADEN W/HEAT

Cylinder/Head Heat Sink Fins

The definition of convection is the action or process of conveying movement in a gas. In this case, air in the warmer parts rises. This graphic shows the heat transfer by molecular movement in the heated substance itself and heat transfer by circulation through the air.

Porsche 911–style cooling fans are used with ultra-high-performance builds using a Bergman Porsche 911–style shroud kit. If it is a milder build, a stronger-than-stock fan is available. It has 56 welds (28 on each side in an alternating pattern), is statically balanced for higher-RPM engines, and will fit all dog-house fan shrouds. A welded race fan with a 34.7-mm inner fan width and a 36.9-mm outer fan width is shown. (Photo Courtesy the Dub Shop)

motion, and the motion is caused by the cooling fan.

The cooling fan is one of the most important parts of an air-cooled engine. Bent or cracked fins, a worn hub, or out-of-round fan hubs are issues that can cause overheating. The later-style factory fan and after-market fans are wider than the original unit.

Air-cooled engines do not provide a consistent and controllable engine-operating temperature that allows for precise fuel metering to provide lower exhaust emissions. This was one of the primary reasons that Volkswagen abandoned the air-cooled engine in favor of a water-cooled design.

Planning

When beginning a high-performance build on a Volkswagen air-cooled engine, decide what

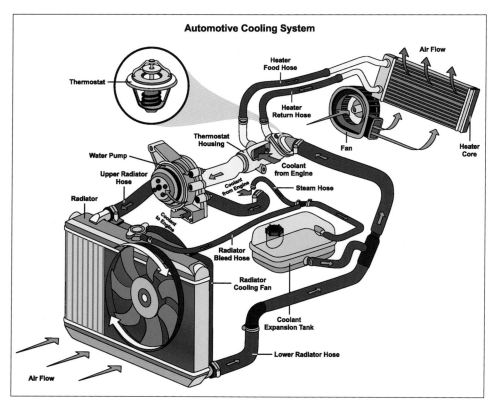

A liquid-cooled system is the most common automotive cooling system. The coolant circulates outside of the engine and is exposed indirectly to the air by a radiator. The air absorbs heat from the coolant so that the coolant can flow back into the engine and absorb more heat. The greater the difference in temperature between the coolant and the air, the more heat will be absorbed by the air. Uniform engine temperatures reduce thermal stress. The consistent temperatures also allow very precise fuel metering, which helps keep exhaust emissions low. In 1985, Volkswagen abandoned the air-cooled pancake engine in the Type 2 Microbus and Vanagan and replaced it with a water-cooled boxer pancake engine called the Waterboxer. (Graphic Courtesy Shutterstock)

Volkswagen Origins

The very start of Volkswagen and its engine begins with some politics in pre–World War II Germany.

Porsche engineers Karl Rabe and Xavier Reimspiess, under the direction of Dr. Ferdinand Porsche, designed an air-cooled, horizontally opposed, 985-cc, 4-cylinder engine to power Adolf Hitler's KdF-Wagen, which became the Volkswagen, or "People's Car." A variety of engines were tried but were shelved in 1936 in favor of the now-classic VW Beetle engine.

The 985-cc engine was replaced by the 1,130-cc engine with a 75-mm bore and 64-mm stroke. This engine was originally developed for the military Kübelwagen-Command (bucket-seat) cars, Model 62 and Model 82 that can be seen in old World War II movies.

The final decision to build the Volkswagen came after a discussion between Hitler and Porsche, where Hitler stated that the vehicle must be able to cruise at 60 mph, have fuel economy of 40 mpg, be air-cooled, have space for five people, and be priced at 1,000 Marks. Porsche felt this was unrealistic, and there was no existing plant.

In 1937, at the Berlin Motor Show, it was stated that Opel (GM owned) would build the Volkswagen. Hitler was not happy about Opel building the car and issued a command to build a factory just for the KdF-Wagen in Wolfsburg. Now with unlimited funds, Porsche built the historic Volkswagen Beetle. ∎

---

level of performance you want and assess your engine project finances. Are bolt-on options okay, or is performing a complete engine blueprint rebuild needed?

Engine performance building is a series of concessions because it likely will not be able to do everything. Decide which parts of engine building and performance are most important and prioritize them. Ask yourself the following questions:

- What is the funding for the engine project?
- What is the purpose of the engine (street vehicle, modified stock, track race car, dune buggy, etc.)?
- What level of reliability does the engine need? Do you want to remove the engine after every run? (For the range of 150 to 200 bhp, air-cooled engines need routine maintenance.)

Performance air-cooled engine building is not simple. Information regarding these old engine designs may be difficult to find online, and some of it may be misleading.

This performance kit from the Dub Shop provides complete performance-based components to install electronic fuel injection. It includes high-flow intake manifolds, the throttle body, fuel injectors, the crank pulley, controller, wiring, installation hardware, and instructions for a 1,600-cc Volkswagen engine. (Photo Courtesy the Dub Shop)

Increasing Performance

One of the quickest and cheapest ways to get more power out of an air-cooled VW engine is to make it breathe better. Larger cylinder heads, larger valves, and larger and smoother ports can be used to get more power. Another option is to replace the factory air-intake system with a higher-flow system without engine disassembly. This can increase horsepower by allowing more air to flow into the engine. A new air intake system is one of the easiest performance modifications that can be done, and it is not expensive. All of these modifications can be done without removing the engine. Although, these engines are easy to remove and reinstall. So, you may still do

---

When building an engine, complete upgrade kits are available with everything needed to build a specific engine except the external components and induction system. (Photo Courtesy Scat Enterprises)

that, especially if you are changing the cylinder heads.

To improve engine breathing, the air must exit the engine as fast as it goes in. Installing a performance exhaust system increases horsepower by allowing hot air to exit the cylinders more efficiently. Performance exhaust systems are generally bolt-on and inexpensive. A supercharger or a turbocharger can be added to improve the engine air capacity and provide a denser charge, giving a boost in power if there is a strong bottom end. These can be costly and require engine modifications. However, there are bolt-on kits from numerous aftermarket performance-parts suppliers.

Thermodynamics

Thermodynamics is the subject of the relation of heat to forces acting within the combustion chamber of an internal-combustion engine. The main thermodynamic point is energy, which is the ability to do work. Thermodynamics works with heat and temperature and their relationship to energy and work. For example, energy can move from one object to another due to a difference in pressure, volume, and temperature. When heat moves an object through a distance, work is done.

Knowledge of thermodynamics assists in the design of a high-performance air-cooled engine because enough heat needs to be generated to develop enough power for the desired performance. The science of thermodynamics developed out of a desire to increase the efficiency of early steam engines from the work of French physicist Nicolas Léonard Sadi Carnot (1824).

Thermodynamics is a broad field and includes different systems: chemical, thermal, and mechanical. The combustion of air and fuel is called a system, and everything else is called its surroundings. This internal-combustion-engine system is closed because there is no interchange of matter between the system and its surroundings. Any change within the system that it may undergo is called a process. Any process or series of processes where the system returns to its original state is called a cycle, such as the four-stroke Otto cycle.

Heat is energy in transit from one mass to another because of a difference in temperature between the two. Whenever a force of any kind acts through a distance, work is performed. Just like heat, work is also energy in transit. The early application of thermodynamics was to mechanical heat engines.

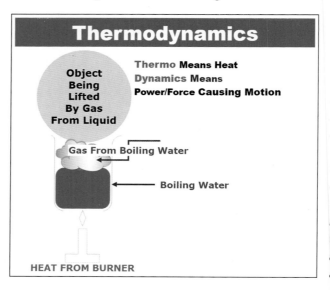

Thermodynamics

Object Being Lifted By Gas From Liquid

Thermo Means Heat
Dynamics Means
Power/Force Causing Motion

Gas From Boiling Water

Boiling Water

HEAT FROM BURNER

Thermodynamics is simply heat that is used to generate power and cause motion. It is an increase in internal energy of a closed system that is equal to the total energy added to the system. If the energy that is entering the system is supplied as heat and leaves the system as work, the heat is accounted for as positive and the work as negative.

Thermodynamic Balance
Temperature Measurement

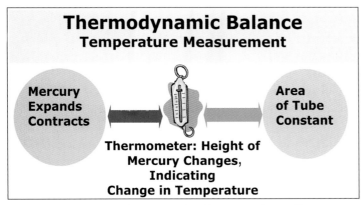

Mercury Expands Contracts

Area of Tube Constant

Thermometer: Height of Mercury Changes, Indicating Change in Temperature

Temperature is worth measuring because it predicts whether heat will transfer between objects. This is true regardless of how the objects interact. If two objects are not in physical contact, heat still can flow between them by means of radiation heat transfer. If the systems are in thermal balance, no heat flow will occur.

First Law of Thermodynamic Energy Transformation

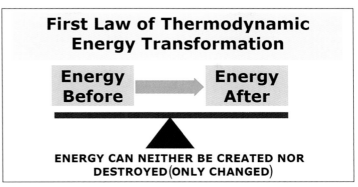

Energy Before → Energy After

ENERGY CAN NEITHER BE CREATED NOR DESTROYED (ONLY CHANGED)

The first law of thermodynamics states that when energy passes as work, as heat, or with matter into or out of a system, the system's internal energy changes in accord with the law of conservation of energy. This pertains to the internal-combustion engine as well as perpetual-motion machines of the first kind. This means that machines that produce work with no energy input are not possible.

Second Law of Thermodynamic Heat Transfer (Entropy)

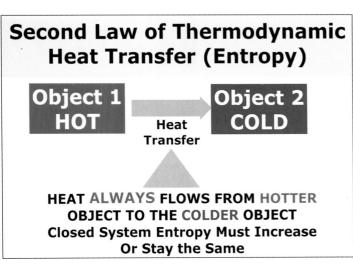

Object 1 HOT → Heat Transfer → Object 2 COLD

HEAT ALWAYS FLOWS FROM HOTTER OBJECT TO THE COLDER OBJECT
Closed System Entropy Must Increase Or Stay the Same

The second law of thermodynamics establishes that perpetual-motion machines of the second kind (machines that spontaneously convert thermal energy into mechanical work) are impossible.

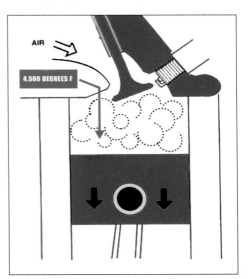

AIR

4,500 DEGREES F

The internal-combustion engine burns its fuel inside a combustion chamber. One side of this chamber is open to a piston. When the fuel burns, the hot gases expand very rapidly and push the piston away from the combustion chamber. This basic action of heated gases expanding and pushing is the source of power for all internal-combustion engines.

Temperature is a measure of the degree of heat that an object possesses. It is the measure of the speed of the molecule vibrating. An increase in temperature indicates that the speed of the molecules has increased. When heat is removed from a body, it becomes cold because heat always flows from a warmer object to a colder object. A drop in temperature means a decrease in molecular speed.

The first law of thermodynamics is part of the conservation law of energy, which states that energy cannot be created or destroyed. It can only change. Whenever energy is transformed from one form to another, energy is always conserved as stated energy. The sum total of all energy remains the same. The first law concerns the analysis of systems involving heat transfer and work.

The second law of thermodynamics states that the conversion of heat to work is limited by the temperature at which the conversion takes place. It can be roughly related to the level of disorder, the loss of information, or the amount of useless energy (energy that cannot be used to perform work). The second law is an observation of the fact that over time, differences in temperature, pressure, and chemical potential tend to even out in a physical system that is isolated from the outside world. The conversion of heat to work is limited by the temperature at which the conversion occurs.

Engine Combustion

The oldest "engine" known to man was the simple lever. Food fuels the muscle pushing the lever to move objects that the muscle alone could never budge. The automotive engine uses fuel to perform work. The Volkswagen air-cooled engine is fueled by gasoline. The automotive engine is an internal-combustion engine. It is internal because the fuel it uses is burned inside a combustion chamber. An external combustion engine burns fuel outside the engine, such as a steam engine. Fuel is burned to produce heat to make steam, and the steam powers pistons to move the vehicle.

The engine converts part of the fuel energy to useful power, which is used to move the vehicle. The chemical energy in fuel is converted to heat due to the burning of the fuel at a controlled rate, which is called combustion. Heat energy released in the combustion chamber raises the temperature of the combustion gases within the chamber. The increase in gas temperature causes the pressure of the gases to increase. The pressure developed within the combustion chamber pushes on the head of a piston to produce a usable mechanical force, which is converted into mechanical power. The trick in building a high-performance engine is to increase this explosive pressure to push harder against the piston to develop more torque or twisting force to move the vehicle faster.

In a spark-ignition air-cooled engine, a homogenous mixture of fuel and air is inducted into the engine. This gas mixes with the exhaust gas remaining from the previous cycle, which results in a slightly diluted mixture. To start combustion, a spark with a duration of about 0.001 second is discharged. A short delay of about 0.001 second follows, during which chemical reactions started by the spark produce a small flame kernel that is able to propagate across the combustion chamber. The speed with which the flame moves across the combustion chamber is determined by three main factors: laminar flame speed, turbulent enhancement of the flame speed, and the expansion ration of the burned gas.

Laminar flame speed is the speed at which a flame will burn though a calm air-fuel mixture. A laminar flame burns as a flat flame sheet as it moves through the mixture. Laminar burning velocities for gasoline range from about 3 centimeters per second for a very lean mixture up to 150 centimeters for a stoichiometric mixture at 14.7 parts air to 1 part fuel at a high temperature.

For turbulent enhancement, the flame does not propagate across the combustion chamber as a smooth flame sheet. Rather, turbulence in the gases twists and distorts the flame shape into a wrinkled sheet that greatly increases its surface area. The effect of this turbulence increases the flame spread rate by a factor of 10 at 2,000 rpm and causes further increases as the engine speed increases.

As the air-fuel mixture is burned, the gas temperature increases. This causes an expansion of the gas by a factor of 5. So, the first gas to burn near the spark plug expands and pushes the flame across the chamber. This expansion effect is greatest at the start of combustion when the cylinder pressure is low, and it is the smallest near the end of combustion. The expansion ratio is generally less than 10 meters per second.

If you were watching the top of a piston for the flame to go by, its speed would be determined by the three main factors that were just discussed. As the engine speed increases, only the turbulent enhancement component increases by a significant amount. Yet, this contribution to the increase in flame speed across the combustion chamber increases the combustion rate nearly in proportion to the engine speed. So, in a normal street engine, engine speed is not limited by the combustion rate but rather by mechanical limitations of the bottom-end components. In

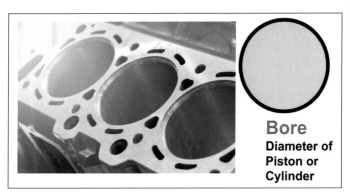

Bore is a factor in determining the displacement and power of an engine. Generally, the bigger the bore, the larger the displacement and the more torque and power it develops. The original Beetle's factory cylinder bore was 75 mm, and it progressed to 77 mm, 83 mm, and finally 85.5 mm for the 1,600-cc engine.

Bore
Diameter of Piston or Cylinder

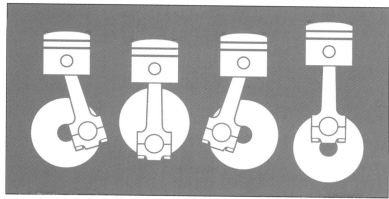

Engine stroke is determined by the length of the crankshaft crankpin that the connecting rod is connected to, which is sometimes called the big end of the connecting rod (as opposed to the small end that is connected to the wrist pin in the piston). During the original factory production, the Volkswagen engine used only two different engine strokes: 64 mm for the 1,130- and 1,192-cc engines and 69 mm for the 1,500- and 1,600-cc engines. The aftermarket offers stroker crankshafts up to an 84-mm stroke.

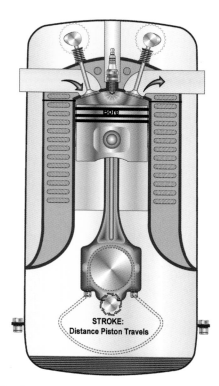

Engine displacement is the bore multiplied by the stroke multiplied by the number of engine cylinders. VW engine displacement was originally 985 cc in design. The first production engine was 75 x 64 mm. (Graphic Courtesy Shutterstock)

high-performance racing engines, high speeds can be achieved if the bottom end can support the stress.

Engine Fundamentals

Bore is the diameter of the cylinder. When the bore is larger than the stroke, the engine is oversquared and most of its power is dependent upon revolutions per minute (RPM) and generated at higher-RPM values. When the stroke is larger than the bore, the engine is undersquared with most of its power dependent upon torque.

Stroke is the movement of the piston from top to bottom (or the distance that the piston travels in the cylinder). When the piston is at the top of its stroke, it is at top dead center (TDC). At TDC, the crank journal is at a point nearest the cylinder.

When the piston is at the bottom of its stroke, it is at bottom dead center (BDC). At BDC, the crank journal is at a point farthest from the cylinder. The space between the piston and the cylinder head when the piston is at TDC is the clearance space. It is sometimes called the compression

or combustion space. The volume of this space is known as the clearance volume.

- TDC: Top dead center is the uppermost point to which the piston travels in the engine cylinder.
- BDC: Bottom dead center is the lowest point to which the piston travels in the engine cylinder.
- BTDC: Before top dead center is a point of piston travel through its upstroke.
- ATDC: After top dead center is a point of piston travel through its downstroke.

A square engine is an internal-combustion engine where the cylinder-bore diameter is exactly equal to the piston-stroke dimension. When bore and stroke values are expressed, the bore always appears before the stroke.

An oversquare engine is an internal-combustion engine where the cylinder-bore diameter is larger than the stroke dimension. An undersquare engine is an internal-combustion engine where the cylinder-bore diameter is smaller than the stroke dimension. Most truck and bus diesel engines are undersquare.

Displacement

The total (piston) engine displacement is stated as the volume in cubic inches or liters (cubic centimeters) of the space swept through by all the pistons of the engine during one complete revolution of the crankshaft. The total piston displacement is easily found by multiplying the displacement of one piston by the number of pistons. The formula is expressed as follows using English units:

Engine Displacement (Size) = 0.7854 x Bore Squared x Stroke x Number of Cylinders [x 0.001 to convert to CC].

Take a typical VW 1,600-cc 4-cylinder engine with an 85.5-mm

Most Common Volkswagen Engine Builds				
CC Displacement	Bore	Stroke	Notes	Crankcase ID
1,600 (1,584)	85.5 mm	69 mm	–	B
1,776	90.5 mm	69 mm	Same cylinder wall thickness as 85.5 mm	B
1,904	90.5 mm	74 mm	Same cylinder wall thickness as 85.5 mm	B
1,915	94 mm	69 mm	–	B

Known Bore and Stroke Combinations							
		Stroke					
		64	69	74	76	78	82
Bore	77 mm	1,192	1,286	1,378	1,415	1,460	1,527
	83 mm	1,385	1,493	1,601	1,644	1,696	1,774
	85.5 mm	1,496	1,584	1,699	1,745	1,800	1,882
	87 mm	1,521	1,641	1,759	1,806	1,863	1,949
	88 mm	1,556	1,679	1,799	1,848	1,906	1,994
	90.5 mm	1,646	1,776	1,904	1,955	2,016	2,110
	92 mm	1,700	1,835	1,967	2,020	2,084	2,180
	94 mm	1,776	1,915	2,052	2,109	2,175	2,275

Engine displacement is in cubic centimeters.

bore and 69-mm stroke, and calculate the total piston displacement.

Engine Displacement = 0.7854 x $(85.5 \text{ mm})^2$ x 69 mm = 396,161 mm x 4 cylinders = 1,584,645 cubic mm x 0.001 = 1,584 cc (1.6L).

When stated in United States English values, displacement is given in cubic inches (ci). When using metric values in millimeters for the bore and stroke, multiply the results by 0.001 or divide by 1,000 to convert from cubic mm to cubic cm. When stated in metric values, displacement is given in cubic centimeters or in liters (1 liter equals 1,000 cc). To convert engine displacement specifications from one value to another, use the following formulas:

• To change cubic centimeters to cubic inches, multiply by 0.061 (cc x 0.061 = ci).
• To change cubic inches to cubic centimeters, multiply by 16.39 (ci x 16.39 = cc).

• To change liters to cubic inches, multiply by 61.02 (liters x 61.02 = ci).

A 1968 to 1979 air-cooled engine at 96.66 ci is also a 1,584-cc engine (96.66 x 16.39 = 1,584.25) and was listed as a 1.6L engine. Metric displacement in cubic centimeters can be calculated directly with the displacement formula by using millimeter measurements and converting from cubic millimeters to cubic centimeters.

Performance Factors

The function of the internal-combustion engine is to convert chemical energy released from the combustion of fuel into useful mechanical work. Certain performance factors are used to describe how well the engine performs. These are speed, thermal efficiency, mechanical efficiency, volumetric efficiency, and atmospheric pressure.

Speed

In engine testing, speed is really angular velocity, or the rate of change of position at a particular angle. This is defined in crankshaft revolutions per minute (RPM) of time and shown in formulas as the letter N. Speed measurement accuracy depends on the combined accuracy of the revolution count and the time interval of that count. Technicians typically perform speed measurements using a dwell tachometer on these VW engines along with a timing light to measure ignition timing.

Thermal Efficiency

The thermal efficiency of an engine is a measure of the ratio between the useful work done by the engine and the thermal energy input to the engine. It is the percentage of the fuel-supplied heat energy that appears at the crankshaft as useful work. If two engines produce the same horsepower at the crankshaft, and one burns less fuel than the other, the thermal efficiency is greater for the more economical engine. The heat energy supplied by the fuel is not all converted into power for useful work. Some of it is lost in the hot exhaust gases, some is carried away in the cooling oil in the oil cooler, and some is used in overcoming friction. The remainder is available for useful work.

There are three basic efficiencies to consider to improve a Volkswagen's engine performance. They are breeding or consuming a maximum amount of air-fuel mixture, extracting the maximum amount of energy from your air-fuel mixture, and reducing the friction and pumping losses in the project engine.

The pumping losses at the pistons is a function of the throttle valve opening in the engine. This is very small when compared to the whole 4-stroke cycle in a naturally aspirated engine. Positive energy can be added when using a turbocharger or a supercharger. Yet, the number of losses from driving the supercharger needs to be taken into account if using that design. You will not have these losses with a turbocharger. Turbocharger selection is covered in Chapter 7 on induction systems.

Mechanical Efficiency

The fraction of the indicated horsepower delivered at the crankshaft is called the mechanical efficiency of the engine. Since the brake horsepower is always less than the indicated horsepower by the amount of the friction horsepower, the mechanical efficiency must be less than 1, or less than 100 percent. Dividing the brake horsepower by the indicated horsepower and multiplying the result by 100 is the mechanical efficiency.

It is necessary to understand how friction in the form of lower mechanical efficiency will cost horsepower. This can be overcome by doing some of the following:

* Keep your engine lubricated with improvements to your oil pump and sump. Chapter 3 covers lubrication system modifications that reduce friction.
* Reduce engine heat, which is a main characteristic of friction. This is an air-cooled engine, and airflow is critical. Make sure to have an adequate oil cooler and good airflow over the cylinder heads. Use the doghouse fan shroud and make sure the thermostat is working.
* Regular oil changes will keep particles of metal, dirt, fuel, and water out of the engine. The friction modifier additives in the oil will break down and friction will increase.
* Use engine oil friction reducing additives that contain Liquid Moly (Molybdenum disulfide) to reduce friction with higher temperature resistance and better overall lubricating qualities than graphite.
* Use a lower viscosity index oil, such as 5W30. Thicker oil has higher viscosity (friction between layers of oil) that creates viscous friction.

Volumetric Efficiency

Power extracted from an internal-combustion piston engine is related to the amount of air consumed and retained by the cylinders. The greater the percentage of retained air, the larger the quantity of fuel that can be completely burned. Volumetric efficiency (VE) is the ratio of the weight of air that actually enters the cylinder to the weight of air that could enter the cylinder, measured at ambient conditions, if the piston-displaced volume were completely filled. It might be better named "mass efficiency" because it is more closely related to the mass or weight of the air.

When the actual air consumption of an engine is metered at ambient conditions, the VE may be the ratio of the actual volume flow of air to the theoretical volume flow of air. Volumetric efficiency is a measure of how well an engine breathes or takes in air for combustion. Good volumetric efficiency depends on the efficiency of the air cleaner, valve timing, manifolds, porting, exhaust pipe, muffler, and turbocharger.

In naturally aspirated (NA) non-turbocharged engines that rely on atmospheric air pressure to force its way into the cylinder, the resistance to airflow is caused by the intake ducting. Factors include intake diameter, number of bends, length, and air-cleaner restriction along with intake manifold design, all of which will lower VE. The VE of an NA engine is always less than atmospheric pressure (14.7 psi) at sea level.

When a turbocharger is added to an engine, the VE can be greater than atmospheric pressure. Just because an engine has a turbocharger or gear-driven blower does not automatically mean that it is supercharged. The intake valve timing on a four-stroke-cycle engine determines whether the engine is actually supercharged. If the cylinder air pressure at the start of the compression stroke is higher than atmospheric, then the engine is basically supercharged. The amount of supercharging is directly related to the actual cylinder air pressure charge. A supercharger is an engine-driven air pump that supplies air pressure above 14.7 psi, which is all the air pressure you can have without a supercharger or a turbocharger.

Atmospheric Pressure

When a space contains a vacuum, it contains a smaller quantity of air than the space is capable of containing with atmospheric pressure in the space. Vacuum is measured in inches of Mercury (Hg) or water. Atmospheric pressure at sea level is 14.7 pounds per square inch (psi). Atmospheric pressure is available outside the engine air intake.

As a piston moves downward with the intake valve open, a vacuum is created in the cylinder above the piston. The air moves rapidly from the high pressure outside the air intake to the lower pressure in the cylinder. Vacuum is the absence of pressure or just low pressure. A complete vacuum or absence of pressure is equal to 29.995 Hg (101.06 kPa).

Atmospheric pressure decreases as elevation increases. At 5,000 feet above sea level, a 1-square-inch column of air from the earth's surface to the outer edge of the atmosphere is 5,000 feet shorter than the same column at sea level. Therefore, the weight of this column of air is less at 5,000 feet elevation than at sea level. As altitude continues to increase, atmospheric pressure continues to decrease.

Four-Stroke Cycle

The Otto cycle or gasoline engine is a four-stroke cycle. The four-stroke cycle consists of intake, compression, power, and exhaust. When all four are done, the engine has completed

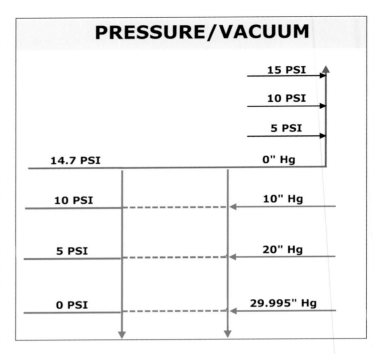

Vacuum is very low pressure or the absence of pressure. The red centerline is at the atmospheric pressure of 14.7 psi, and the baseline of Hg (inches of Mercury) is at 0. When the pressure decreases, the vacuum increases.

one full cycle.

Nikolaus August Otto was the creator of the four-stroke internal-combustion engine cycle. Otto was intrigued by the Lenoir internal-combustion engine, which was introduced in 1860 as the first commercially available internal-combustion engine. Otto spent three years and all his own money trying to improve the Lenoir engine.

In 1864, Otto formed a company with Eugen Langen called Klöckner-Humboldt-Deutz AG. It was the first internal-combustion-engine manufacturing company in the world. The first four-stroke engine was not built until 1876.

All previous internal-combustion engines were non-compression-stroke

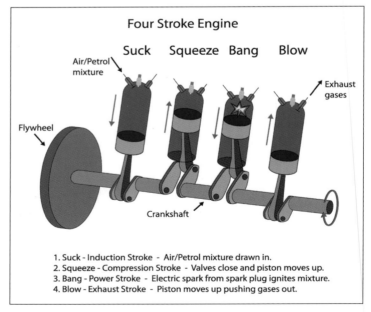

1. Suck - Induction Stroke - Air/Petrol mixture drawn in.
2. Squeeze - Compression Stroke - Valves close and piston moves up.
3. Bang - Power Stroke - Electric spark from spark plug ignites mixture.
4. Blow - Exhaust Stroke - Piston moves up pushing gases out.

The four-stroke internal-combustion engine cycle are suck (intake), squeeze (compression), bang (power), and blow (exhaust). (Graphic Courtesy Shutterstock)

engines. Fuel and air were drawn into the cylinder during part of a piston's downward stroke and then ignited. The expanding gases then pushed the piston down the remainder of its stroke. Many inventors used this design to make the pistons double-acting with a power stroke each way. Otto's new engine used a downward stroke of the piston to draw in an intake charge and a second upward stroke to compress it. It also required two more strokes to extract power and push out exhaust gases, hence the four-stroke engine cycle.

Intake Stroke

The intake stroke begins with the piston at TDC. A lobe on the camshaft opens the intake valve either directly or through a follower, pushrod, and rocker-arm assembly. The piston moves down in the bore due to the rotation of the crankshaft. As the piston moves downward, it pulls air through the air cleaner and into the intake manifold past the open intake valve and into the cylinder.

The downward movement of the piston creates a low-pressure area above the piston (as volume increases, pressure decreases). Air rushes in to fill the space left by the downward movement of the piston because atmospheric pressure is greater than the pressure in the cylinder. Actually, the piston tries to inhale a volume equal to its own displacement. The air-fuel mixture is homogeneous.

During the intake stroke, an air-fuel ratio is inducted. The throttle controls the air mass entering the cylinder. The energy needed to move the piston from TDC downward comes from either of the flywheels over the overlapping power strokes on a multiple-cylinder engine. As

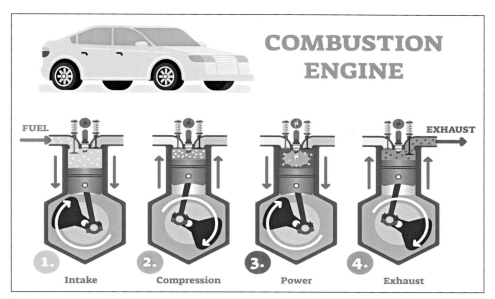

Downward movement of the piston draws the air-fuel mixture into the cylinder through the intake valve on the intake stroke. On the compression stroke, the mixture is compressed by the upward movement of the piston with both valves closed. Ignition occurs at the beginning of the power stroke, and combustion drives the piston downward to produce power. On the exhaust stroke, the upward-moving piston forces the burned gases out the open exhaust port. (Graphic Courtesy Shutterstock)

the piston nears BDC, it slows down nearly to a stop. When the piston reaches BDC, the intake valve closes, sealing the cylinder, and the compression stroke begins.

Compression Stroke

The turning crankshaft now forces the piston upward. Both valves are closed; there is no way (except past the rings) for the air to get out. The volume decreases as the piston rises, so the air-fuel gas mixture is compressed. The pressure is inversely proportional to the volume according to Boyle's law. In the compression of a gas, the volume decreases and the pressure and temperature rise as external work is done on the gas.

Compression ratio is the volume at BDC to the volume at TDC (clearance volume). A higher compression ratio means higher thermal

efficiency—that portion of the heat supplied to the engine that is turned into work. As the compression ratio increases, the expansion ratio also increases. Thus, thermal efficiency increases.

$$\text{Compression ratio} = \frac{\text{Volume at BDC}}{\text{Volume at TDC}}$$

The internal energy of the gas is increased as heat is added to the gas. Near the end of the compression stroke, a spark plug will ignite the mixture.

Power Stroke

The power stroke begins shortly after the air-fuel gas mixture is ignited by the spark plug. The high pressures in the cylinder push down on the piston. This pressure forces the piston down in the bore, which causes the crankshaft to rotate (translation to rotation).

Boyle's Law

Boyle's law states that the pressure of a perfect gas varies inversely to its volume at a constant temperature, or that the product of the pressure and volume is a constant. Pressure is inversely proportional to the volume occupied (high pressure/low volume). At a constant temperature, the pressure of a gas depends on the volume of the vessel holding it.

Boyle's law applies to compression in a spark-ignition engine. When the piston rises on compression, cylinder volume is reduced, and the pressure increases. This exerts pressure on the cylinder walls when the same number of molecules now have less space to move. ■

The pressure falls as the volume increases. The temperature falls as the gas does external work. The oxygen and fuel burn and the nitrogen expands, pushing the piston down under power. As the piston continues downward, the gases in the cylinder expand and cool as they give up their energy. The power stroke is the only stroke in which energy is used from the fuel. Cylinder pressure is the highest in this stroke.

Exhaust Stroke

As the piston nears the bottom of its travel, the exhaust valve, operated by a lobe on the camshaft, begins to open. The piston then begins to rise in the cylinder, beginning the exhaust stroke. The upward movement of the piston forces the spent gases past the exhaust valve and out of the cylinder. As the piston nears the top of its movement, the camshaft lobe again opens the intake valve, and the cycle repeats itself. The exhaust valve is allowed to close (by spring pressure) shortly after the piston begins its downward movement. This is a stroke that produces no work but expends a quantity of energy to push exhaust gases from the cylinder. In a spark-ignited gasoline-fueled engine, there is flame speed, which is nearly proportional or increases when engine speed increases. Therefore, the number of crank angles occupied by the combustion process is nearly independent of engine speed.

A gasoline-fueled engine uses intake and exhaust valves that need to be timed to provide the correct operation to develop the desired maximum horsepower. Valve timing is the time that the valves open and close with respect to crankshaft angle degrees. In this graph, the intake valve opens at 15 degrees BTDC and closes at 59 degrees ABDC. The exhaust valve opens at 59 degrees BBDC and closes at 15 degrees ATDC.

Valve and Port Timing

Valve timing is the time that the valve functions in an engine operating cycle. Valve action is stated with degrees of crank rotation about TDC or BDC piston positions in the cylinder. Moving air has inertia and allows the valves to open longer than the piston stroke in a working engine.

The piston moves at varying speeds during its stroke because it must stop at each end of the stroke, gain speed toward mid-stroke, and slow down to a stop at the opposite end.

The inertia of the air is used to keep the exhaust gas or intake air moving even though the piston may be stopped. If the valve is held open, the intake stroke lasts longer than the downward travel of the piston. The exhaust stroke also lasts longer than the upward stroke of the piston.

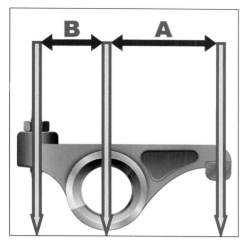

A 1.4:1-ratio rocker arm means that Dimension A is 1.4 times the length of Dimension B. Therefore, if the pushrod is moved up 0.4 inch by the camshaft lobe, the valve is pushed down or opened 0.4 inch times 1.4 (0.56 inch).

The camshaft lobe lift signifies the distance that the cam follower is moved. The amount that the valve is lifted is determined by the lobe lift multiplied by the rocker-arm ratio. The higher the lift of the camshaft lobe, the greater the amount of air and fuel that goes into the combustion chamber. The more air and fuel burned in an engine, the greater the potential power.

When the camshaft has the same lobe lift on both intake and exhaust valves, the camshaft is called symmetrical, or a single-pattern camshaft. The opening and closing ramps are the same. When the lobe specifications are different, the camshaft is called asymmetrical, or a dual-pattern camshaft, where the opening and closing ramps are not exactly the same. Some camshafts are made this way to get an opening-ramp profile with a high speed and a closing-ramp profile with a slower speed. This design will open the valve quickly and close the valve more smoothly, which also reduces seat wear.

When the amount of lobe lift increases, so do the forces on the camshaft and the rest of the valvetrain. A camshaft with a lift of more than 0.5 inch is not good for a daily street vehicle. The VW lobe-lift specifications at the valve face assume the use of the standard rocker-arm ratio. If non-stock rocker arms with a higher ratio are installed (for example: 1.4:1 rockers replacing the stock rocker arms of either 1.1:1 or 1:1), the lift at the valve is increased. Also due to the fact that the rocker-arm rotation covers a greater distance at the pivot of the rocker arm, the rocker arm can hit the edge of the valve retainer.

Camshaft duration is the number of degrees of crankshaft rotation that a valve is open. Three methods are used for measuring camshaft duration:

1. Measuring with the valve opening at zero clearance. This method refers to the duration of the opening of the valve after the specified clearance between the rocker arm and the valve-stem tip has been closed.
2. Measuring with the valve opening at 0.05 inch of the cam-follower lift. This method eliminates all valve clearances and compensates for solid lifters or cam followers, like what Volkswagen uses. It is the preferred method to use when comparing one camshaft with another.
3. The SAE–recommended practice is to measure all valve events at 0.006-inch valve lift. This method differs from the usual method used by engine or camshaft manufacturers. Whenever comparing valve timing events, be certain that the same methods are being used on all camshafts being compared.

All camshafts provide some duration overlap to improve engine performance and efficiency, especially at higher engine speeds. Less overlap provides a smoother idle and low-engine-speed operation, but it results in less power at high engine speeds. A larger valve overlap causes a rougher engine idle with less power at low speeds, but it also means that high-speed power is improved. When designing your project engine or doing a full blueprint engine, decide on the right camshaft to get the desired valve overlap.

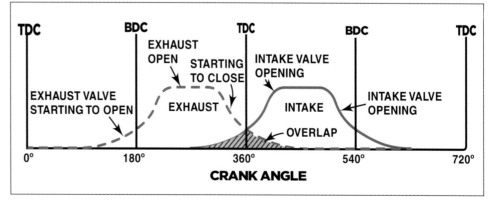

Valve overlap is the number of degrees of crankshaft rotation when both the intake and the exhaust valves are open. This action occurs at the beginning of the intake stroke and at the end of the exhaust stoke.

HORSEPOWER AND TORQUE

This chapter contains formulas for calculating several measurements, including horsepower, torque, displacement, and the compression ratio. The compression ratio is one of the most important calculations to know when performing a custom build.

Three basic deficiencies can be improved upon with engine performance: consuming maximum amounts of fuel and air, extracting maximum engine energy from the fuel, and reducing friction and pumping losses. There are important connections between volumetric, thermal, and mechanical efficiencies, and they are not separable.

Think of a VW engine as an air pump. More air and fuel need to be taken in and more exhaust thrusted out to add horsepower. The simplest and easiest way to move more air through an engine is to increase displacement by boring and stroking, but that can be expensive. It is also possible to reduce the inlet and exhaust restrictions with improved air cleaners, carburetors, intake manifolds, camshaft design, exhaust systems, bigger valves, and polished and shaped ports. As horsepower increases, engine reliability usually decreases and the cost of the engine

The VW 1,600-cc air-cooled engine is a boxer design. It is called a boxer because each set of pistons moves in and out at the same time, like a boxer's gloves. The centrally located crankshaft has the cylinders on each side. The boxer engine design allows a lower center of gravity, which aids in overall vehicle handling.

build budget increases. Balance the horsepower that is desired with what you can afford. Performance engine building is not usually low cost or easy.

Friction and pumping losses can reduce whatever power gains are made through modifications. Improving the breathing reduces pumping losses by allowing the engine to turn more freely as it sucks in the same amount of air. Getting more power from a given amount of fuel also helps because friction

is reduced to a lesser percentage of the total power being produced. The actual reduction of friction is difficult to accomplish with stock bearing clearances for both rods and mains. The reliability of an engine can be hurt by using excessive bearing clearances, so we will not be going there.

Piston rings contribute the maximum friction found in the engine but are necessary for sealing the piston. Piston clearances can be increased but there is a limit because excessive clearance can cause piston slap and

undue wear to the rings, as the piston edges can round off. A misaligned piston and rod can generate a vibration that can create power losses. Check rod alignment to reduce the possibility of unwanted vibrations.

There are other friction sources, including the valvetrain, that are helped by using roller rockers. Using a counterbalanced crankshaft can assist in reducing energy losses by providing a smooth flow of power to the flywheel. Some Super Vee builders of the past have reversed

Corvair Engine

One way to get more horsepower for a Volkswagen project is to use a General Motors Corvair engine. Many VW enthusiasts might consider upgrading to a Porsche engine from a 912 or a 911 or possibly use the transaxle from a Porsche. However, there is a less expensive alternative: using a GM Corvair 6-cylinder engine.

Clark's Corvair Parts Inc. makes a reverse engine kit that can be used to couple a Corvair engine to a VW transaxle. There are certain things that have to be done for this kind of modification, if a decent Corvair engine can be found.

The Clark Corvair parts kit includes a new camshaft that allows conversion from the counterclockwise-rotation Corvair engine to clockwise rotation that matches the Volkswagen transaxle. GM wanted to use stock powertrain components, so the automaker had the Corvair engine turn counterclockwise. If you are running a swing axle transaxle, swap over the ring gear from one side to the other, and then you will not have to modify the Corvair engine. Keep in mind that a Corvair's 6-cylinder engine is longer than the standard VW 4-cylinder, so clearance is necessary for some bodystyles. A Subaru boxer engine can also be installed into a VW, and a reverse engine kit is not needed.

In most cases, this probably won't be done because there are plenty of high-performance parts and systems from companies such as John Maher Racing, Scat, EMPI, JBugs, Summit Racing, and others to build a Volkswagen 1,600-cc series engine with significant power. However, this is just some food for thought if you're looking for some extreme horsepower from a Corvair engine, as it is an option. ∎

This Corvair engine (installed in a Corvair) has twin Weber carburetors and an upgraded performance air-cooling system. According to the owner, it develops more than 300 hp.

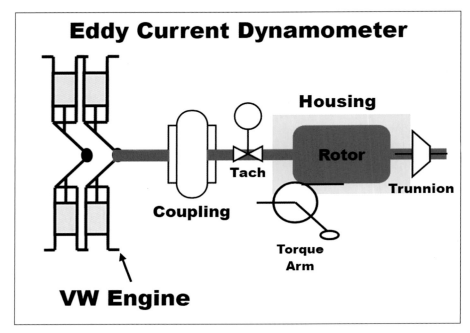

Eddy Current Dynamometer

Housing

Rotor

Tach

Trunnion

Coupling

Torque Arm

VW Engine

A dynamometer, or dyno as it is typically called, measures torque and engine speed in RPM so that its horsepower or brake horsepower (bhp) can be measured in real time. A VW engine is connected to a coupling through a shaft, and there is a sensor on that shaft that measures RPM on a tachometer. The engine is free to turn but is restrained by a torque arm. This torque arm is connected to a rotor, and a weighing scale is used to measure the force exerted by the rotor trying to rotate. Torque is the force shown on a torque arm scale or meter multiplied by the length of the torque arm. A transducer can be used instead of the scale to provide an electrical signal that is proportional to torque. The rotor is mounted on trunnions so that it can rotate.

the piston so that the offset is on the opposite side. It makes them slap for an increase of about 1 to 2 percent hp. It produces a lot of noise, and this is only for serious racers.

When improving an engine's breathing, a higher RPM value that pumps in more air to develop more horsepower is possible. The combustion-chamber shape can be improved for better turbulence so you can use higher compression ratios. This means reducing the combustion-chamber size.

Engine Dynamometer

An engine dynamometer (dyno) is very useful to measure RPM and torque to find the horsepower that your build can deliver. An engine dynamometer measures the engine's horsepower and other performance parameters at the crankshaft or flywheel. This requires the engine to be installed on the dynamometer test stand. Yet, power loss that occurs in the drivetrain is not accounted for.

The water-brake power-absorption approach uses a valve inserted into the outlet of a water pump. The pump regulates backpressure and the resulting load. In the 1970s, Harvey Stuska built a water-brake dynamometer. The pressure gauge and tachometer were mounted on a stand. The absorption unit was connected to a VW transaxle, where the engine would be mounted. These units became part of the SuperFlow dynamometer product line. (Photo Courtesy Jim Halderman)

A chassis dynamometer is used to measure the horsepower at the car's drive wheels. It is generally composed of a platform with a pair of rollers, a braking or power-absorption system, and a computer with software to calculate bhp. At an assembly plant, they are referred to as chassis rolls. (Photo Courtesy James Halderman)

There are several other types of engine dynamometer designs:

- Eddy current: The engine load is generated by eddy currents induced into a rotating metallic disk that is immersed in a magnetic field. It uses an electrically conductive core, shaft, or rotor moving across a magnetic field to produce resistance to movement. The voltage is controlled by a computer, using changes in the magnetic field to match the applied power.
- Inertial: A large spinning mass provides a load that is proportional to acceleration. Torque is calculated from the acceleration rate of the mass. Average torque can be computed from the time it takes to accelerate the mass to a given RPM.
- AC or DC motor: The load is created by an electric motor.
- Hydraulic: The load is created by smooth disk power elements that absorb power through viscous shear.

Calculating Torque and Horsepower

Work is the product of a force and the distance through which the force acts. Simply expressed, work is force (pounds/Newton) multiplied by distance (foot/meter)—hence, foot-pounds (ft-lbs) or Newton-meter. The term *torque* is derived from the principle of work.

SAE Ratings

Volkswagen rated the 1,285-cc or 1,300-cc engine (in 1966) at 40 hp, while the US SAE recourse power was listed as 50 hp. Also, the 1,500-cc engine was rated at 44 bhp in Germany, while the SAE rated it at 53 hp.

Keep in mind that the factory ratings with few exceptions come from handmade engines that were carefully assembled from selected parts. Standard production engines with shelf parts typically produce 15 to 25 percent less horsepower than the advertised readings. This is because the SAE standard allowed horsepower ratings that were not obtained by precise measuring. The ignition was set for the best power output, and there was no requirement that accessories be run. Sometimes the horsepower would actually meet the advertised figures.

Back in 1971, General Motors led the way with what it called installed horsepower ratings that considered the horsepower one might expect to get from the engine when it was burdened down with all of the power-robbing accessories. Yet, this was done primarily because cars with higher horsepower ratings would wind up having higher insurance costs.

Torque

Torque is a force that tries to turn or twist something around, and it is defined as the product of a force and the perpendicular distance between the line of action of the force and the axis of rotation. Torque is force multiplied by length. The length of the lever is the length of the throw of the crankshaft journal.

Torque is a twisting effort expressed as the engine's capacity to do work, where horsepower is defined as the rate at which the engine can do work. Engines produce torque by combustion force pushing down on top of the piston, moving a lever that is the throw of the crankshaft. Torque is generally expressed in foot-pounds or Newton-meters (1 ft-lb = 1.355 Newton-meters, and 0.737 ft-lb = 1 Newton-meter). Torque is expressed mathematically in the following formula:

SAE Standard Requirements for BHP Rating

- Net horsepower available from the engine with specified induction specifications and engine speed
- Rating guaranteed within 57 percent
- Corrected to SAE standard ambient conditions
- Air temperature 85°F (29.4°C)
- Elevation 500 feet (159.4 m)
- Dry air density 0.0705 pounds per cubic foot (11.29 g/m³)
- May be without the accessories required for the application (compressor, fan, generator, etc.)

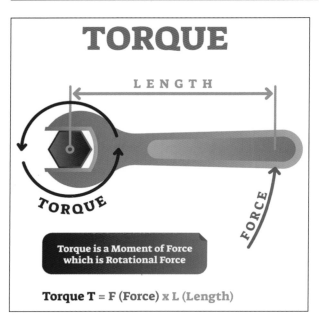

Torque T = F (Force) x L (Length)

Torque is a form of work, but it is in a circular or turning motion. In this case, the force from the work formula is the force of the engine piston pushing down multiplied by the stroke of the engine (the distance the piston travels). (Photo Courtesy Shutterstock)

becomes an electro brake measuring the power.

Horsepower

Horsepower is the rate of doing work (torque). In the metric system, horsepower is expressed in kilowatts (0.746 kW = 1 hp, or 1.341 hp = 1 kW). The raw horsepower of an engine as measured by a dynamometer is expressed by this formula:

$$HP = \frac{2FRN}{33,000}$$

HP = horsepower = 3.1416
F = dynamometer load (in pounds)
R = radius arm of dynamometer (in feet)
N = engine speed (RPM)
33,000 = conversion factor (ft-lbs per minute, to produce 1 hp)

In general, work is done whenever a force overcomes a resistance. The horsepower required overcoming resistance, or drag, is found by the following formula:

$$HP = \frac{DV}{33,000}$$

T = FR
T = torque (in ft-lbs or Newton-meters)
F = force (in pounds or Newtons)
R = radius or torque-arm distance (in feet or meters)

$$Torque = \frac{HP \times 5,252}{RPM}$$

The formula is used by most engine dynamometers. The number 5,252 is a mathematical constant derived from the horsepower formula. One can measure engine torque using either a cradle absorption dynamometer, a transmission

dynamometer, or an eddy current dynamometer.

The cradle absorption dynamometer is capable of absorbing the power output of the engine. The transmission dynamometer measures power transmitted from an engine using a torque converter, but it does not absorb any of the power. The eddy current dynamometer uses electrical resistance to measure the torque of an engine. The rotor is rotated by the engine, and the voltage is applied to the coil or stator housing. A magnetic flux is generated, and the rotor cuts off these magnetic fluxes and

D = velocity (in feet per minute [fpm])
V = drag or resistance (in pounds)

The speed of a Volkswagen Microbus is 60 mph, and the total resistance of the wind plus rolling resistance is 125 pounds. Since there are 5,280 feet in 1 mile and 60 minutes in an hour, the bus is traveling 1 mile per minute, or 5,280 fpm. In 1 minute, the truck has to supply 5,280 x 125 = 660,000 ft-lbs of work to overcome the resistance and maintain the 60-mph speed. Since 33,000 ft-lbs per minute is equivalent to 1 hp, the horsepower required at the bus's rear wheels is obtained by applying our first horsepower formula:

$$HP = \frac{DV}{33,000} = \frac{5,289 \text{ feet} \times 125 \text{ pounds}}{33,000} = \frac{66,000 \text{ ft-lbs}}{33,000} = 20 \text{ hp}$$

BHP

Brake (shaft) horsepower is the power delivered at the engine crankshaft. The term *brake horsepower* comes from the method of early engine testing. This consisted of putting a mechanical brake on the engine and measuring the force required to hold the brake from turning. The energy produced was dissipated as heat. Water or air was used to cool the friction surfaces of the brake.

Brakes of this type, called Prony brakes, were an early type of absorption dynamometer. The horse terms come from the following: 1 horsepower would be produced when a horse walked 165 feet in 1 minute pulling a 200-pound weight (165 feet x 200 pounds = 33,000 ft-lbs).

Brake horsepower may be measured with either a transmission or an absorption dynamometer. It is determined by the following formula that is the same as the one listed under horsepower but stated for brake horsepower:

$$BHP = \frac{2FRN}{33,000}$$

BHP = brake horsepower = 3.1416 (a constant)
F = dynamometer load (in pounds)
R= radius arm of dynamometer (in feet)
N = engine speed (RPM)
33,000 = conversion factor (ft-lbs per minute to produce 1 hp)

When applied to a Prony brake dynamometer, the formula becomes:

$$BHP = \frac{F \times 6.28 \, RN}{33,000} = \frac{FRN}{5,252} = \frac{Torque \, (T) \times RPM}{5,252}$$

$$BHP = \frac{Torque \, (T) \times RPM}{5,252}$$

An engine that is being tested is coupled to a dynamometer that has a radius arm of 1.75 feet. The test data shows a speed of 3,000 rpm and a load of 80 pounds. Calculate the torque and then the brake horsepower.

Torque = Force x radius arm lengths
Force = 80 pounds x 1.75 feet = 140 ft-lbs of torque

$$BHP = \frac{Torque \, (T) \times RPM}{5,252}$$
$$\frac{140 \times 3,000}{5,252} = 80 \text{ bhp}$$

MEP

Mean effective pressure (MEP) is the hypothetical constant pressure. If acting on the piston, it would produce the same work that the actual varying pressures produce. There are two mean pressure values that are normally used in engine testing—namely, brake mean effective pressure (BMEP) and indicated mean effective pressure (IMEP). IMEP generally cannot be measured directly, so BMEP is used. BMEP increases with an increase in compression ratio.

BMEP

BMEP is theoretical constant pressure that acts on the piston during each power stroke. BMEP produces a power equal to the brake horsepower of the engine. This term indicates how well an engine uses its displacement to produce work, and it is a better parameter for comparing engines than torque or horsepower. The BMEP force on the top of the piston is the average pressure exerted on each square inch of the top of the piston during the power stroke multiplied by the area on top of the piston (force [f] = area x BMEP).

FHP

Friction horsepower (FHP) represents the power needed to overcome the friction of the crankshaft and camshaft in their bearings, the friction of the pistons in the cylinders, the friction of the gearing, and the power used to drive the pumps. FHP is the variance between indicated horsepower and brake horsepower. When there is no load on the engine, the friction of the engine's moving parts is the only resistance. FHP is the indicated horsepower (IHP) when the engine runs under no load.

IHP

IHP is the power developed inside the engine at the face of the piston. The power delivered by an engine to the driveline to which it is connected is always less than the actual power developed in the cylinders. This is because some of the IHP is used to overcome engine friction. IHP is equal to the sum of the BHP plus the FHP.

Compression Ratio

Higher compression ratios produce more power from a given amount of fuel up to the point where detonation occurs. This point depends on the modifications that have been done and the octane rating of the fuel being used. Combustion efficiency is also aided by making sure that the proper air-fuel ratio is applied and that the best spark timing takes place for the ideal moment of peak power with minimum heat losses.

Do not to use too high of a compression ratio. The compression ratio is the major source of heat in the cylinder heads that can cause a failure. Volumetric or mass efficiency is also an issue to engine life and power. Any new components and compression ratio need to be correctly coordinated to your build, so the volume of the right fuel and air is what the engine needs. This will make your build run cooler and develop more horsepower than the original VW design.

Energy can be added from the fuel by polishing the piston tops, the combustion chambers, and the valve heads. Polishing reduces the heat loss in these components and ensures that more of the torque developed is able to push the piston. A lower compression ratio will allow you to run higher boost than could otherwise be run, should you choose the power-adder route.

On average, a Volkswagen air-cooled engine, if it's used strictly for transportation or as a Point A to Point B car, would have a maximum compression ratio of 8:1 to 9:1. For this type of compression, premium gasoline is most likely needed. The original standard compression ratio for a 1970s 1,600-cc engine was 7.3:1. Racing engines used for short runs may be able to tolerate compression ratios up to 11.5:1, but anything higher than this is not going to run very well on any kind of gasoline.

Running really high compression ratios most likely requires a different fuel. The reason that a racing engine can tolerate a higher compression ratio is that camshafts with lots of overlap reduce low-speed pumping capabilities of the engine. Higher compression ratios offset some of the loss of low-speed torque, which is caused by large amounts of cam overlap.

Compression ratio is calculated using the following scientific formula:

V_d = volume at BDC
V_c = volume at TDC

Computing Compression Ratio

$$\text{Compression ratio} = \frac{V_1 + V_2 + V_3}{V_2 + V_3}$$

This formula is built around calculating a VW air-cooled engine compression ratio. The cylinder volume V_1 is the volume at BDC. The clearance volume, shown as V_2, represents the volume between the head and the piston top when the piston is at TDC. Clearance volume is cylinder volume not swept by the piston and enclosed in the copper head gasket. V_2 equals 0.785

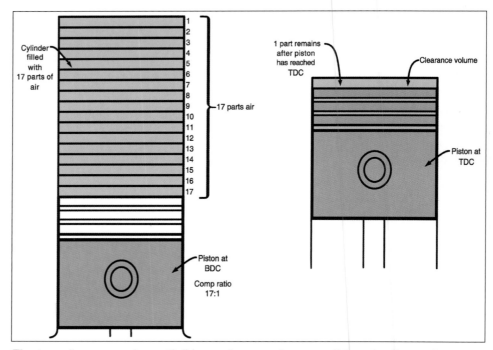

The term "compression ratio" is a misnomer because it is actually a volume ratio. In an internal-combustion engine, the compression ratio is the ratio of the total cylinder volume to the clearance volume. It is the volume of the cylinder at the beginning of the compression stroke (TDC) divided by the volume of the cylinder at the end of the compression stroke (BDC).

multiplied by the bore diameter squared multiplied by the deck clearance. The combustion-chamber volume V_3 is measured using two different processes to measure the combustion-chamber size.

Cubic inches can be converted into cubic centimeters by multiplying the cubic inches by 16.4. Calculate the cylinder volume (V_1) using the formula 0.785 x bore squared x stroke. Measure the deck clearance and calculate the clearance volume (V_2) using the formula: 0.785 x bore diameter squared x the measured deck clearance.

If the cylinder-head-measuring process described later in this chapter has been done, you will then have V_3 (clearance volume plus the combustion-chamber volume).

Remember that cylinder displacement (V_1) affects the compression ratio. Anything done to increase V_1 (such as a bigger bore or longer stroke) or to reduce V_2 or V_3 will increase the compression ratio. If you are planning to rework the cylinder heads now for use on an engine that will later be bored and stroked, use the displacement of the final engine configuration to determine the head volume so that the head work is just done once. So, it is a good idea to do piston and crankshaft work first before doing any kind of compression-ratio calculations.

Cylinder Head CC Process

Next, calculate the cubic centimeter volume of the combustion chamber, which is also called CC'ing the heads. In a Volkswagen air-cooled engine, the compression ratio can be adjusted for the intended use of the engine, taking into account the octane of the available fuel.

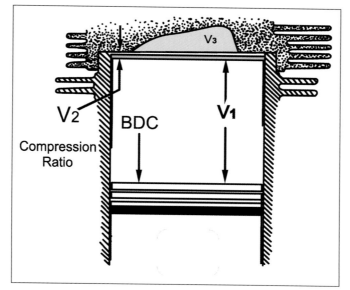

V_1 is the cylinder volume that is measured using the engine bore and stroke. Cylinder volume equals 0.785 multiplied by the diameter squared multiplied by the stroke. V_2 is the clearance volume at TDC. V_3 is the measured combustion chamber volume.

In this chapter, we will discuss engine software that can be installed on a computer and used to input the proposed engine modifications (valve sizes, compression ratio, bore, and stroke). The computer software provides a pretty good idea of how much horsepower and torque will be produced from these modifications. This software is a way of determining the outcome of the engine modifications without actually doing it. The software is called Dynomation 6. There are several different ways to compute the cubic centimeter volume of the cylinder head combustion chamber.

Cubic Centimeter Measuring Kit

This kit comes with several different-size discs: 85.4-, 90.5-, 92-, and 94-mm bore sizes. If you are using a brand-new head, there is no need for extensive cleaning. However, if this is a cylinder head that has been on an engine for some time, it must be thoroughly cleaned to nearly new-head condition before attempting any combustion-chamber measurements. Measure all four cylinders because this is a performance build, and you want all of the combustion-chamber volumes to be within 1 cc of each other.

Combustion Chamber Plaster Casts

Do a mock assembly of your engine with the crankshaft, piston, cylinder, and rod that is going to be used. Check the position of the piston at TDC and determine whether it is level with the top plane of the block. Measure the actual stroke for each cylinder and verify that the stroke is within specifications. Calculate the volume the piston displaces as it moves from BDC to TDC. Volume equals the piston area multiplied by the cylinder height from BDC to TDC, which is the stroke.

V_1	Cylinder volume: 0.785 x bore squared x stroke
V_2	Clearance volume: 0.785 x bore diameter squared x measured deck clearance
V_3	Combustion-chamber volume obtained through measurement

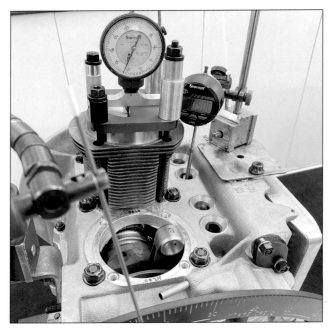

V_2 can be measured by holding the cylinders on the cases with hold-down washers and spacers under the stock head nuts. A depth micrometer caliper feeler gauge can measure the distance between the piston crown and the sealing surface of the cylinder at TDC. Be careful not to break off cylinder fins when holding the cylinders on the case. (Photo Courtesy ACE Performance Engines, Stefan Rossi)

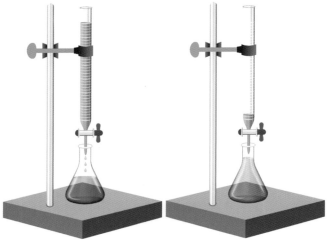

An older method is to obtain a chemist burette that is graduated in cubic centimeters. A piece of clear plastic hose is needed that is at least a 1/4-inch thick and approximately the same diameter as the spark-plug hole in the head with a plug in it to seal the head. Use a solution of engine-cleaning solvent and automatic transmission fluid as the measuring fluid. (Photo Courtesy Shutterstock)

A combustion-chamber measuring kit can be purchased from jbugs.com, Air-Cooled, Amazon, or EMPI (part number 16-9603) for about $25. This kit allows easy computing of the cubic centimeters of the combustion chamber. You need to know the same three values in the formula ($V_1 + V_2 + V_3$) to calculate the combustion-chamber compression ratio.

This plaster cast process can be used to see what the compression ratio will be as a result of changing the combustion-chamber volume. The plaster casting will be of the combustion-chamber cavity. After the casting is set, remove the casting from the head and sand the top surface with sandpaper and a flat board until it closely matches the surface of the head when the casting is placed back in the head.

Calculate the compression ratio from the volumes computed and determine how much material to remove from the head to increase the compression ratio. First, determine the density of the casting material that will be used in measuring the volume of the cylinder head cavity. A paper cup can be used to make a casting in the shape of a truncated cone. The volume of the cone can be computed from measurements of the two diameters and the height.

Any millimeter values must be converted to centimeters because our column measurements are in cubic centimeters.

Density is defined in two ways. Mass density is mass per volume or weight density is weight per volume. The density of a substance can be stated as ounces per cubic inch or grams per cubic centimeter. It is recommended that metric units of grams per cubic centimeter be used in our procedure, but other units can be used. There are two formulas that determine the volume of the cavity in the cylinder head.

The following formula is used to determine the density of the casting material:

$$\text{Density (material)} = \frac{\text{Mass (grams)}}{\text{Vol (cm}^3)}$$

Measuring Combustion Chamber Size

1 *Mix a measuring solution of cleaning solvent and automatic transmission fluid (for color). Place the solution in a 50-mL graduated flask or syringe (it may come with the kit) calibrated in cubic centimeters (cc) or milliliters (mL). Place the cylinder head on a level surface. Use a carpenter's level to ensure that the cylinder head is level.*

2 *Seal the disc with some lithium grease or Vaseline around the plastic disk. Then, place it in the cylinder head's cylinder and combustion-chamber area.*

3 *Use the syringe to slowly draw in about 60 cc of the measuring solution. Typically, 52 to 53 cc's go into the combustion chamber through the hole in the disc.*

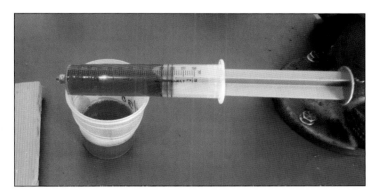

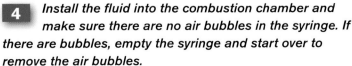

4 *Install the fluid into the combustion chamber and make sure there are no air bubbles in the syringe. If there are bubbles, empty the syringe and start over to remove the air bubbles.*

5 *Carefully fill the syringe to prevent any air from entering. The combustion chamber was completely filled with the solution when finished. A stock 1,600-cc cylinder head was used and should measure about 52 to 54 cubic centimeters. This is the size of the combustion chamber in cubic centimeters. This is the value for "V_3" in the compression-ratio formula. If you fly cut the combustion chamber, the chamber volume is reduced because you are making it smaller.*

For our example, mass (211.11) divided by volume (210.8) equals density (1.001).

Next, measure the volume of the cavity. Note that we have the casting material density:

$$\text{Vol (cavity)} = \frac{\text{Mass (cavity casting)}}{\text{Density (material)}}$$

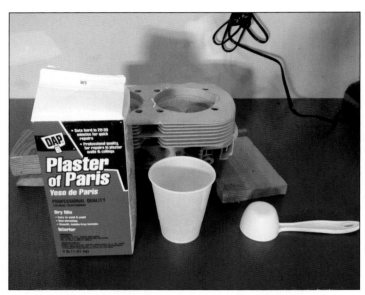

Mix about 2/3 cup of plaster with enough water to make a very thick but pourable mixture. Pour this mixture into a clean cup and let it harden. Tear the cup away from the casting. Measure the upper and lower diameters and the height of the casting. Calculate the volume of the casting. Weigh the casting to the nearest 0.1 gram. Then, calculate the density of the casting material to be used to calculate compression ratio.

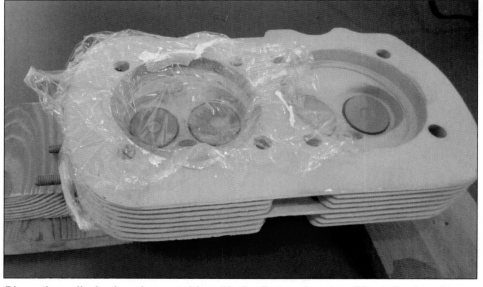

Place the cylinder head on a table with the flat surface up. Block the head to get the cylinder head level by using a carpenter's level. Line the cavity for each cylinder with plastic wrap.

For our example, mass (53.6) divided by density (1.001) equals 53 cc.

The volume of the cup casting was 210.8 cm³ (area = 62 cm x height of 3.4 cm = a volume of 210.8 cm³). Mass or weight of the casting material as measured on the scale was 211.11 grams, so 211.11 divided by a volume of 210.8 cm³ equals a mate-

rial density factor of 1.001. If I sand off 5 mm of that cavity casting material and it now weights 40 grams, the cavity volume would now calculate to 40 cc with an increase in compression ratio as calculated here.

$$\text{Displacement} = \text{Bore}^2 \text{ x Stroke x } \frac{0.0031416}{4}$$

$$V_1 \text{ Displacement} = 85.5^2 \text{ x 69 mm x } \frac{0.0031416}{4} =$$

$$396 \text{ cc x 4 cylinders} = 1,584 \text{ cc}$$

$$V_2 \text{ Deck height volume} = \text{Bore}^2 \text{ x Deck height x } \frac{0.0031416}{4}$$

$$V_2 \text{ Deck height volume} = 85.5^2 \text{ x 2 mm x } \frac{0.0031416}{4} = 11.48 \text{ cc}$$

Calculate the volume of the casting (cylinder cavity) by dividing the mass (weight) of the casting by the density of the casting material that was determined in Step 1.

Compute the compression ratio using this formula:

$$\text{Compression ratio} = \frac{V_1 + V_2 + V_3}{V_2 + V_3}$$

So:

$$\frac{396 + 11.7 + 40}{11.7 + 40} = 8.6:1$$

Compare the results with the engine specifications. Then, decide how much material needs to be removed to get to the desired compression ratio. If we calculated the compression ratio using our original combustion-chamber volume of 53 cc, the compression ratio would be near the factory level of 7.3:1.

Fly Cutting the Combustion Chamber

Fly cutting is used to raise the compression of an engine by grinding down the combustion chamber to make it smaller. It is a difficult alteration that changes several interactions in an engine. It is also a way to save the head where the combustion-area sealing surface has been damaged. Fly cutting the combustion chamber should be done by a machine shop that is experienced in working on VW heads. It is possible to purchase a cylinder head with the compression ratio needed for your engine build. When doing your own fly cut, buy a high-quality fly-cutter tool and use it in a drill press.

If you're a novice, get your heads professionally cut by a machine shop. Better yet, purchase high-quality heads from one of the several

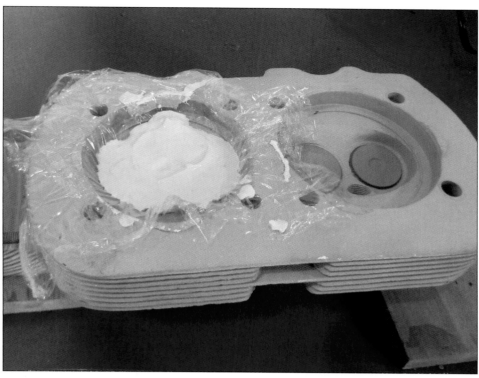

Mix enough plaster to fill one combustion chamber and pour enough plaster into the combustion chamber slightly above the full level. Allow the plaster to set and carefully pull the casting free from the head by pulling on the plastic wrap.

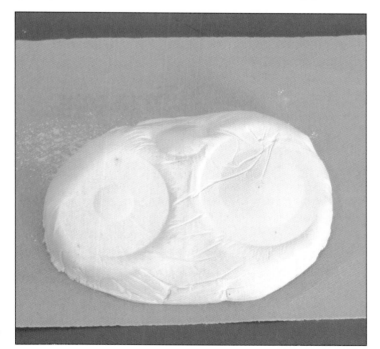

Remove the plastic wrap and place the casting flat side down on a piece of sandpaper on the table. Carefully rub the casting on the sandpaper until the overfill material is removed.

Place the casting back in the chamber to see if the top of the casting is level with the flat surface of the combustion chamber. If the casting surface is above the head, sand the casting a little more and check it again. If you sand off too much, you will have to start over.

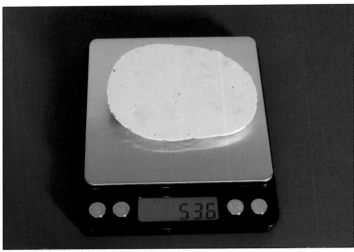
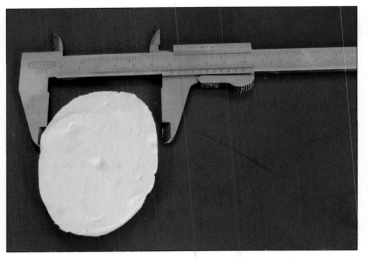

After an acceptable casting for the chamber is produced, weigh the casting and record the weight. Measure the thickness of the casting from the flat surface to the thickest point using a Vernier caliper or a surface plate and height gauge.

You can simulate fly cutting the head by sanding material from the casting. Measure the new thickness of the casting and subtract it from the previous value. The difference is the "simulated" amount milled from the head. Weigh the casting and recalculate the volume. Recalculate the compression ratio.

high-performance VW engine component companies, such as John Maher, EMPI, Air Cooled, Summit Racing, or JBugs. Examples of the various cylinder heads available with their sources and part numbers are in Chapter 4.

Changes That Occur When Fly Cutting

The combustion volume is decreased as the fly cut deepens. When the combustion-chamber volume (V_3) is reduced, the compression ratio increases. The measuring process described in this chapter may determine that you already have the compression ratio you need with the combination of crank and cylinders, so in some cases, fly cutting may not

be needed at all.

When the heads are fly cut, they move inward toward the crankshaft and camshaft. This is always true unless spacers are installed under the cylinders to accommodate longer strokes with pistons that do not have the correct compression height. The effects of moving a cylinder head through fly cutting are sometimes overlooked. The valve-adjustment screw moves down after the head position changes. The contact point moves toward the pushrods, which can cause clearance problems.

So, if you do this kind of fly cutting, it is necessary to build a mockup engine and make all the correct measurements to make sure that

no interference has resulted from the fly cut. It may be necessary to shim rocker-arm stands or rockers to accommodate dimensions after a fly cut.

The chart's engine size (page 33) is having a bore of 92 mm with a 0.060-inch deck height, which equals 10 cc. If you are increasing the displacement of your engine (V_1), this also increases the engine compression ratio, as you can see in the second column, where the compression ratio increases with no fly cut.

Dynomation Simulation Software

When designing your engine, simulation software is available to assist in your project before you turn a wrench or buy a component. Dynomation 6 software shows pressure waves and mass flow in cylinders and engine passages, the power an engine will produce and why it makes that power, and where you should make changes to optimize performance.

This software allows modeling of the compression ratio, ignition

Amount of Material Cut from Combustion Chamber						
	Standard No Cut	1.27 mm (0.050 inch)	2.03 mm (0.080 inch)	2.54 mm (0.100 inch)	3.05 mm (0.120 inch)	3.56 mm (0.140 inch)
Engine Size 1,701 cc (92 x 64 stroke)	7.7	9.5	10.0	10.4	10.9	11.4
1,835 cc (92 x 69 stroke)	8.5	9.2	10.6	10.0	10.3	10.7
1,969 cc (92 x 74 stroke)	9.1	9.8	10.3	10.6	11.0	11.5
2,047 cc (92 x 78 stroke)	9.5	10.3	10.8	11.2	11.6	12.0
2,180 cc (92 x 82 stroke)	9.9	10.7	11.3	11.7	12.1	12.6

system, camshaft, cylinder heads, and rocker arms. This software can be downloaded at motionsoftware.com/support.htm.

Dynomation 6 uses mathematical models to determine horsepower. This allows you to get information on what you need before spending a lot of time and money on expensive components that you may not need. It calculates engine conditions inside each cylinder throughout the 720 degrees of a four-stroke cycle. It helps you find the best VW air-cooled engine combination for your project. This allows you to determine the bore, stroke, valve sizes, fueling, induction, and ignition system using simulation without building anything.

You will find two engine simulation models:

1. The Filling-and-Emptying simulation provides a fill-in-the-blank scenario to improve better airflow through your engine along with common intake and exhaust manifold modeling.
2. The Full Wave-Action simulation can help you determine the best port sizes, port shape, intake-runner lengths, cam timing, and valve motion.

The short-block menu allows you to input the bore, stroke, number of cylinders, rod length, and pin offset.

Cylinder Head Category

For Volkswagen, select the cylinder heads and input the intake- and exhaust-valve diameters you want to use to see what difference they will make. The simulation software will allow a calculated guess of the valve diameters. Selecting a specific valve size fixes the valve size's theoretical peak flow for each port. Most cylinder heads flow only about 50 to 70 percent of this value. This percentage, called the discharge coefficient, can be an effective link between bench-flow data and predicted mass flow moving into and out of the cylinders.

Next, make the following induction category choices: intake

This is the final result of the fly cut. (Photo Courtesy ACE Performance Engines, Stephan Rossi)

manifold design, runner taper angle, average runner temperature, total induction airflow, and pressure drop.

Compression Ratio Calculator

Compression ratio is calculated by dividing the total volume within the cylinder when the piston is located at bottom dead center (BDC) by the volume that exists when the piston is positioned at top dead center (TDC). This software also includes a compression-ratio calculator.

Camshaft Selection

The camshaft component section in the software allows selection and modification of the camshaft. Camshaft grind and timing is a complex decision. There are many different camshaft measurement standards. The camshaft determines the breathing of the engine and the horsepower it can develop because it controls the beginning and ending of all four-stroke engine cycles. There are only two ways to determine the outcome of a modification: to run an actual test on an engine dynamometer or perform a computer simulation of the flow dynamics.

Dynomation 6 uses a lobe profile file in the simulation along with cam centerlines, cam advance and retard, rocker ratio, and lash. These can be altered to see what results are achieved when these specifications are modified directly from within the camshaft-component category. It also allows the input of specific valve lift values. The auto-calculation feature can be used to select valve-lift values. If the valve diameters are also being automatically calculated, cylinder-bore diameter and a cylinder head selection must be made before the program can complete the calculation of valve diameters and valve lifts.

The simulation component category determines the simulation model and RPM start, step, and finish values. All component categories are checked for completeness (based on the selected model). If all required components and specifications have been entered, the simulation will be performed, and the results will be displayed in graphs.

The free Dynomation 6 user's manual can be downloaded from the company's website.

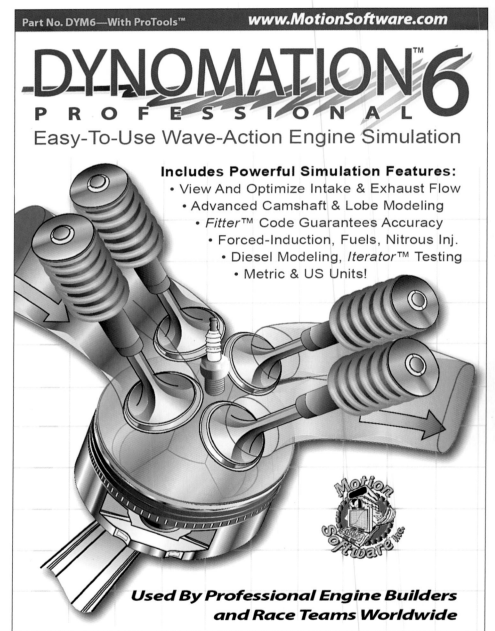

Dynomation 6 supports the following operating systems: Windows 7 SP1, Windows 8.1 SP1, Windows Server 2008 R2 SP1, Windows Server 2012 R2, Windows Server 2016, Windows Server 2019, Windows 10 IoT Enterprise 2019 LTSC, and Windows 10 Version 1903. (Photo Courtesy Dynomation)

ROTATING ASSEMBLY AND LUBRICATION SYSTEM UPGRADES

Engine displacement is a function of the piston bore and stroke. The more displacement, the more horsepower is produced. An engine with more displacement will generally last longer than supercharging it or using nitrous oxide. Past production engines from 1,130- to 1,600-cc were all oversquare (had a larger bore than stroke), which generated more torque and power at a higher RPM. An under-squared engine with a larger stroke than bore will develop more torque and power at a lower RPM. In an air-cooled VW engine, the only way to build an undersquared engine (not that you would want to) would be to use an older 75- or 77-mm piston set with a stroker crankshaft that had an 82- or 84-mm stroke. (See the bore and stroke tables in this chapter.) Generally, the larger the engine displacement, the more expensive the engine build.

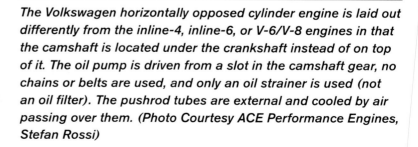

The Volkswagen horizontally opposed cylinder engine is laid out differently from the inline-4, inline-6, or V-6/V-8 engines in that the camshaft is located under the crankshaft instead of on top of it. The oil pump is driven from a slot in the camshaft gear, no chains or belts are used, and only an oil strainer is used (not an oil filter). The pushrod tubes are external and cooled by air passing over them. (Photo Courtesy ACE Performance Engines, Stefan Rossi)

Engine rotating assemblies include the crankshaft, connecting rods, pistons and wrist pins, and the cylinders and case that support them. (Photo Courtesy Shutterstock)

The VW engine first appeared in 1949 with 25 bhp. It was followed by a 36-bhp version, a 40-bhp version, and 50- to 66-bhp versions. The early engines are unsuitable cores for a high-performance Bug due to extensive case machining, crankshaft breakage, a lack of camshaft bearings, and a lack of case-saver 8-mm inserts. The 50-bhp 1966 Type 1 engine; 53-bhp 1,493-cc (1,500) engine; and 57-, 60-, and 65-bhp 1,584-cc (1,600) engines can all be used and modified for mild street use.

Engine Core Selection

The following engine options from 25 bhp to 65 bhp are listed.

25 bhp (1,131 cc)

The first VW Type 1 was brought to the United States in 1949. The displacement was 1,131 cc, or 69.0 ci (a 1.1L engine). It had 25 bhp at 3,000 rpm. The bore was 3.0 inches with a stroke of 2.5 inches. The compression ratio was 5.8:1. It was a basic, low-powered car. It was unsuitable for any horsepower-increasing upgrades. Aside from those in museums, very few of these engines remain.

36 bhp (1,200 cc)

The 36-bhp engine was used from 1954 to 1960. It can be identified by the generator bracket being part of the case (as opposed to it being a separate component on all later engines). This is unsuitable because extensive case machining would be needed. The crankshaft was prone to breakage from excess spark advance that would beat the number-1 and -2 main bearings so hard that the case bearing bores became oval shaped. Never use a 36-bhp core.

40 bhp (1,200 cc)

Next in line was the 40-bhp engine used from 1960 to 1963 in both the Type 1 and Type 2 vehicles. These are also unsuitable because they had poor cam follower and camshaft material. There were still no separate camshaft bearings. The cam was mounted directly in the case bores, so when the cam clearance increased from wear, there was no oil pressure, which would take out the rod bearings. The rocker-arm studs leaked oil into the combustion chamber and often broke. Valve-guide wear was a problem, and this engine also suffered from crankshaft breakage, as did the 36 bhp.

50-53-66 bhp (15,00 cc)

This engine was used in the mid-1963 to 1965 Type 2 and the 1962 to 1965 Type 3. It was basically a bored and stroked 40-bhp engine with all of the same problems that the 40-bhp engine had. This engine still did not have camshaft bearing inserts. It is also not a suitable high-performance core.

50-bhp 1966 Type 1 Only (1,300 cc)

This was a fairly decent engine, except it was still a 6-volt unit. It finally did had camshaft-bearing inserts with better head material. This core could be used for a mild street vehicle and can be easily converted to a 1,500- or 1,600-cc engine. The case does not have to be bored to fit the 1,500/1,600 pistons and cylinders, but the heads will need to be bored for the cylinder tops to fit. It also used 22-mm piston pins instead

The air-cooled VW engine uses cylinder sets that are removable. They are not cast into the block like water-cooled parent-bore engines. (Photo Courtesy ACE Performance Engines, Stephan Rossi)

Slip-in cylinder and piston sets do not require any machining because they use the stock case and cylinder head inner-diameter sizes and increase piston size by thinning the cylinder walls, which I do not recommend. (Photo Courtesy Scat Enterprises)

of the 20-mm pins found on earlier engines.

53-bhp 1,493 cc (1,500 cc)

This engine was used from 1967 to 1969 in both Type 1 and 2. "H" is the front serial number. This engine is good for mild street use and can be machined for high-performance use.

57-60-65-bhp 1,584 cc (1,600 cc)

This engine was used in the Type 1 from 1970 until the end of production in 1979. It was also used in the Type 2 from 1968 until the Type 2 went to a Type 4 flat motor and then the 1985 Waterboxer. This engine is very good for mild street use and can be machined for high-performance use.

Some older VW literature, in particular those printed in Germany, may show horsepower ratings in Deutsches Institut für Normung (DIN). This is the German Institute for Standardization in Germany, and it is the German equivalent of the Society of Automotive Engineers (SAE).

Stock Engine Setup

The VW engine is similar to an aircraft or some motorcycle engines in that the cylinders are easy to change. Rebuilders and book authors refer to these cylinders as either "machine-in" or "slip-in" cylinders. Machine-in pistons and cylinders require a special case or engine case and cylinder head machining before they can be used because they are larger than the original stock 1,600-cc diameter of 85.5 mm.

The early 36- to 40-hp engines before 1966 were 73- and 77-mm bore, and I don't recommend trying to build a sturdy engine from these units. The 1,300/1,500/1,600 engine should be the bottom engine for all high-performance modifications.

The cylinder hole within the case is the same for the 1,300/1,500/1,600 engine sizes. The 1,500- and 1,600-cc engine use the identical bore size in plate, but the 1,300-cc plate is smaller. The 1,500-cc engine is often upgraded to a 1,600-cc engine just by using the slip-in 1,600-cc cylinders and piston sets. If you are upgrading

a 1,300-cc engine to 1,600 cc, bore the 1,300-cc cylinder heads to the 1,600-cc size or replace them with 1,600-cc dual-port cylinder heads.

Most piston and cylinder sets are available in two versions: short stroke and long stroke (stroker). The short-stroke pistons are referred to as "A" pistons, and long-stroke pistons are "B" pistons. The A pistons are used on 69- to 76-mm-stroke engines, and B pistons are used on 78-mm-and-longer-stroke engines. The wrist pin location is the difference between the A and the B pistons. Make sure to use matching cylinder/piston sets for your crankshaft and connecting rod combination.

The 1970s-era 1,600-cc regular production VW engine had an 85.5-mm bore size. Slip-in piston and cylinder sets available in the 87- or 88-mm sizes can be installed without doing any case or head machining. Yet, most VW performance engine builders, including the author, do not recommend using these sets. The reason is these slip-in cylinder and piston sets are bored-out production sets with oversize pistons. The cylinder

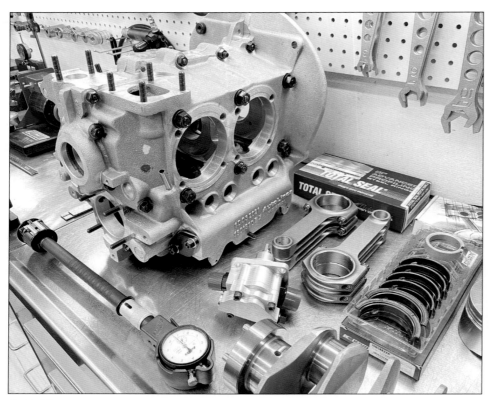

A 1,776-cc setup uses a 90.5-mm bore, 69-mm stroke counterbalanced crankshaft with cross drilled oil drillings, and an upgraded valvetrain. This provides a balanced engine for performance with good reliability and fuel economy for a daily street ride vehicle. Add a wider cooling fan inside a doghouse-style cooling fan shroud housing with an aluminum oil cooler. A dual carburetor setup with a performance exhaust system is used for good breathing. These cases come in 92- and 94-mm bores and have reliefs ground in the case for a stroker crankshaft. (Photo Courtesy ACE Performance Engines, Stefan Rossi)

walls are too thin to maintain good seal integrity, so as the engine heats up, the piston-to-cylinder compression ring seal breaks down and overheating and loss of power can occur.

There are now 88-mm cylinders with the same thickness as the 85.5-mm cylinders, but machining the head and case will be required. For example, EMPI piston and cylinder 88-mm-thick-wall machine-in sets are available (part number 98-1951-B).

The next bore size up from stock is 90.5 mm. They work well with the stock 69-mm stroke crankshaft with counterweights, so you can build the popular 1,776-cc engine. If you are having machine work done to use the 90.5-mm sets, go for a larger bore that will get more horsepower.

The larger Type 4 engine can be built with 96-mm bore x 71-mm stroke, with a FAT442 cam, ported 1,800 heads, and dual carburetors. Using the largest pistons available in tandem with a ported well-breathing cylinder head and the best camshaft makes it possible to produce significant and reliable horsepower from your engine.

The 90.5-mm-bore-size piston cylinder set is a common upgrade. This set has the same cylinder-wall thickness as a stock 85.5-mm 1,600-cc cylinder, and it is very reliable. They are generally a good choice and can last up to 100,000 miles. The 92-mm bore set was a slip-in set for the 90.5-mm bore with no additional machining, and it works well for low-mileage racing. They were prone to the same problems as the 87/88-mm slip-in combination of thinner cylinder walls. Yet, the 92-mm sets are now available in a new version with thicker walls with a 94-mm register at the top, and either a 94-mm register at the bottom or a 90.5/92-mm register at the bottom.

Mahle pistons come from the factory with a graphite coating that retains oil and reduces friction. Wiseco offers slipper-skirted, lightweight forged aluminum racing pistons for stroker engines. Wiseco and Mahle piston and cylinder sets are available from Scat, Gene Berg Enterprises, Air Cooled, JBugs, and Summit Racing. EMPI carries the Mahle kits and Grant Piston Rings. Scat carries the Deves VW piston ring line. These ring sets are designed for high heat transfer, high flexibility, and low wear rates.

An engine can most likely get about 50,000 miles before an overhaul is needed. I have seen some engines going more than 100,000 miles if the compression is set low and no turbocharging is done. The machining for 94 mm can be more expensive than the 90.5 mm because the case needs to be decked. Otherwise, the machine cost for the 94 mm is about the same as the 90.5 mm.

Once all of your engine components are selected, cylinder spacers and/or head gaskets will almost always need to be set to the engine's deck height. One of the best methods to find out which spacers are needed

Pistons, Cylinders, and Bore Size										
		Bore								
		83	85.5	87	88	90.5	92	94	96.5	101.6
Stroke	64	1,385	1,470	1,522	1,557	1,647	1,702	1,777	1,872	2,075
	69	1,493	1,585	1,641	1,679	1,776	1,835	1,914	2,019	2,237
	74	1,602	1,699	1,760	1,800	1,904	1,968	2,054	2,165	2,399
	78	1,688	1,791	1,855	1,897	2,007	2,074	2,165	2,282	2,529
	82	1,775	1,883	1,950	1,995	2,110	2,180	2,275	2,399	2,659
	84	1,818	1,929	1,997	2,044	2,161	2,234	2,332	2,457	2,724

Engine displacement is in cubic centimeters.

Stroker Crankshafts										
		Bore								
		83	85.5	87	88	90.5	92	94	96.5	101.6
Stroke	86	1,861	1,975	2,045	2,092	2,213	2,287	2,387	2,516	2,789
	88	1,905	2,021	2,093	2,141	2,264	2,340	2,442	2,574	2,854

Engine displacement is in cubic centimeters.

The 94-mm cylinders have the same cylinder-wall thickness as the stock 85.5-mm 1,600-cc engine set. However, because the fin area is the same and the engine has increased displacement, this configuration can run at a higher engine temperature than stock or 90.5-mm sets. (Photo Courtesy Ace Performance Engines, Stefan Rossi)

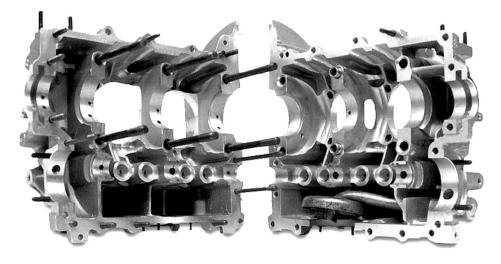

is to build a mock engine and then take measurements with a Vernier caliper.

Cases

If you are using an original aluminum/magnesium alloy case and it needs to be line bored, this can result in overheating and low-oil-pressure problems. It will need to be machined for a full-flow oil filter kit. The used ones may be worn out, and you will need to include the cost of machining against the purchase of a new case, which would include decking the case.

The engine case is extremely important because it is the foundation for all of the engine components. When using an older case for a high-performance application, machine it for cylinder and crankshaft space and drill it for a full-flow lubrication system. (Photos Courtesy Scat Enterprises)

Most aluminum and magnesium cases are labeled "AS41" or "AS21," which was stamped into the side of the case above the sump near the flywheel. There were also AS21 cases that were harder because the alloy contained more silicone. (Photo Courtesy Scat Enterprises)

An existing case can be machined, or one of several already machined cases can be purchased with all of the necessary high-performance features. (Photo Courtesy Shutterstock)

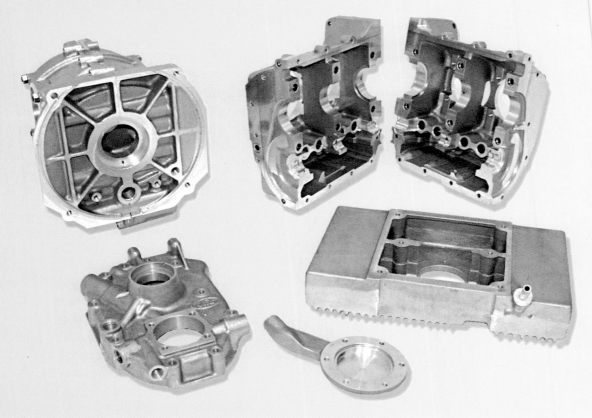

I recommend a new case such as the aluminum bubble case that is available from EMPI or the Scat Killer case that has received all of the needed machining for larger pistons, a stroker crankshaft, and a 4.5-inch quart removable oil pan with the external-sump oil pickup. (Photo Courtesy Scat Enterprises)

A case installation kit, which includes all the hardware for assembly, will also be needed. EMPI also offers a dual-relief AS41 magnesium alloy case that can be modified for high-performance and racing applications. Number 98-0431-B is a stock case. Big Bore AS41 case number 98-0438-B is bored for 90.5- and 92-mm cylinders with clearance for an 82-mm stroke crankshaft. Big Bore AS41 case number 98-0440-B is bored for 94-mm cylinders with clearance for the 82-mm stroke crankshaft. I do not recommend TIG welding the back of the case at the number-3 cylinder because it will weaken the case.

There are pros and cons for which case material is best for a high-performance air-cooled engine. The Type 1 and Type 2 cases were a magnesium aluminum alloy, which was selected because the tooling was less costly than using just aluminum. Weight was also a factor in fuel economy for a light vehicle, and it will be an issue to have a light engine in a race car. On the plus side, an aluminum case is quieter and stronger. When Volkswagen introduced its last air-cooled engine in the Type 4 and Vanagon, the case was all aluminum. Today, you have a choice between using all aluminum or a magnesium aluminum alloy case.

Scat Killer Case

The Scat Killer case has solid main webs. There are six hollow dowels that prevent the case halves from moving, which can distort the main bearing bores. It uses six chrome steel 7/16-inch-diameter main bearing studs (head bolts) to hold the case together.

This case is a three-piece design using an integral bellhousing with a

A heavy-duty bubble-top engine case is offered by EMPI. The roof is raised for clearance with a bubble top. This newly manufactured aluminum case is CNC machined with many high-performance features. Scat offers its Killer case with similar features. (Photo Courtesy ACE Performance Engines, Stefan Rossi)

removable front cover for cam timing adjustment. The oil galleries or rifle drillings are 1/2-inch diameter for positive lubrication under racing conditions.

It has been machined for a stroker crankshaft up to a 90-mm stroke. It can fit from 90.5- to 101.6-mm cylinder kits. It also uses a 4.5-inch wet sump with a removable oil pan and an external-sump oil pickup.

The Scat Killer case is used by some of the fastest VW racers, including Dave Perkins, Pro-Turbo; Mike Stewin, Pro-Stock; Jack Sacchettee, Super Street; and Damon Harmon, a Pro-Stock national champion.

EMPI Bubble Top Case

The EMPI Bubble Top case is offered in bore sizes 90.5 to 94 mm. The Scat Killer case has clearance for up to a 90-mm stroker crankshaft and 90.5- to 101.6-mm-bore kits.

This could build a 2,180- or 2,275-cc engine. These cases feature a medium oil-pickup tube.

The Bubble Top aluminum case has a raised-roof design, which is where the name Bubble Top came from. The top has a bubble in it, and it is a dual-relief-design case for Type 1, 2, or 3 applications with enough clearance for up to an 86-mm stroker crankshaft. It uses six shuffle pins for alignment on all main bearing saddles for a snug fit with a zero gap.

The number-3 cylinder area on the flywheel side has a solid-aluminum area for support. The oil gallery or rifle drillings have been drilled and tapped for full oil flow, and plugs are supplied. It has a larger oil pickup tube. It can be ordered with machining for a sand seal, using the EMPI Machine-In Sand Seal pulley seal. For cases that are not machined for a

The 8-mm studs kits are available to be used with 8 x 14.2-mm steel inserts. (Photo Courtesy Scat Enterprises)

If you are using an original case and going from a 10-mm stud to an 8-mm stud, get a kit to install case inserts in the older cases. The kits generally come with a drill and a tap. Just drill out the old case and install a steel insert for the 8-mm studs. (Photo Courtesy Scat Enterprises)

sand seal, use a steel hub pulley or a bolt-in sand seal pulley kit. The case is available in two bore sizes and for 8- or 10-mm main case studs. However, it will need to be modified for whatever fan housing is being used.

Gene Berg Cases

The Gene Berg case (part number CASBCL) is the same as VW part number B043-101-025, but the Gene Berg case has been machined for stroker crankshafts. If you are replacing an older single-oil-pressure-relief case, VW part number 113-198-033 is needed, which is a conversion kit for the relief valves. These parts are available from Gene Berg Enterprises.

VW part number B043-101-025 is a new magnesium Type 1 Brazilian-made case with the dual oil-pressure relief valves. It uses the 5/8-inch pickup tube. Sadly, this case uses the 10-mm case studs, so the 8-mm stud kit is needed with VW part number 043-198-035P for dual port or VW part number 043-198-035S for single port. These parts are available from Gene Berg Enterprises.

If you are machining an existing used case, a high-quality machine shop that is capable of doing the required machine work is needed to make a 94-mm bore x 82/84-mm stroke engine (2,275/2,332 cc). When a stroker crankshaft (stroke greater than 74 mm) is added (69 mm is stock), crankshaft throw and counterweight clearance becomes an issue. Preassemble the engine to make sure there is enough crankshaft clearance before final assembly.

I can understand the concern regarding longer strokes and clearance being an issue, but as long as you do not go to the extreme of 82 mm or longer, you should be okay. Also, if using one of the EMPI Bubble Top cases, they are machined for clearance up to 86 mm. Going beyond 86 mm requires additional machining, and you need to be careful from a reliability standpoint.

Back in 1970, when the 1,600 engine was introduced, the VW factory went from 10-mm main studs to 8-mm studs (head bolts). This might seem odd because the 10-mm studs are of course larger, but this is a light metal air-cooled engine with a lot of thermal expansion. The 8-mm studs expand and contract at the same ratio as engine temperature, keeping a uniform pressure on the heads and cylinders. The 8-mm studs screw into 14.2 x 8-mm (Scat part number 20133) steel inserts instead of the 10-mm studs into a threaded hole in the case that can pull out. It was also important not to overtorque the heads because if they were too tight, the thermal expansion could pull out the studs or inserts.

Lubrication System Modifications

Volkswagen kept buyers in the dark about any kind of heat condition or oil pressure in those Type 1 and Type 2 vehicles because there were no gauges except for the speedometer and later a fuel gauge. The lubrication system needs to be updated for performance applications and should include a full-flow oil filter, a larger oil sump, larger oil-pump gears, and an oil cooler (or adding an external cooler).

Oil temperature should be around 175°F to keep friction loss and pollution from fuel to the minimum. The oil temperature should not exceed 230°F for any continuous operation, but 230°F may be okay for those vehicles used for racing or short runs.

Engine Oil

Any high-performance engine depends on the qualities and properties of the engine oil that is used. There have been many achievements in the ability of high-technology engine oils to reduce engine wear, especially in high-performance engines.

One of the most important factors is that engine oil must be changed on a regular basis. The old rule used to be to change it every 3,000 miles. With the advent of synthetic oils and racing oils, some have increased that limit. In hot rodding, it is still a good idea to change the oil every 3,000 miles no matter what oil is used. The original VW design called for 30-weight straight oil with no multi-viscosity oils. Volkswagen required shorter oil change intervals because the cars had no traditional oil filter, only a strainer. The 1,600-cc engine had a larger oil pickup.

Some racing oils, such as Joe Gibbs Racing (JGR), contain a ZDDP additive. A zinc additive can be added to any engine oil. Mineral oils and non-synthetic oils work the best if the engine temperature is in the 170°F to 200°F range. When using a synthetic oil, an engine will deliver the same horsepower but at a lower oil temperature, which increases engine life. Most synthetic oils provide 0.5 to 1 percent more horsepower. Some high-performance racing oils to consider include JGR for racing applications, BND for street and racing, and Amsoil for street machines. You can also use Brad Penn high-performance engine oil with zinc, which is available from Scat or Royal Purple. For rebuilt engine break-in, use Pennzoil, GTX, or Valvoline along with an engine oil supplement (EOL).

SAE Oil Viscosity

Engine oils use an SAE number that indicates the viscosity (resistance to flow) range where the oil fits. Oils tested at 212°F have a number with no letter following it. SAE 30 indicates that the oil has been checked at 212°F. The viscosity falls within the SAE 30 grade number range when the

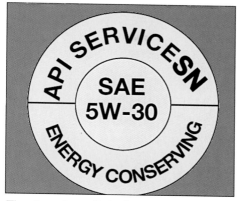

The American Petroleum Institute (API) developed an engine oil performance classification. This was done with the help of various manufacturers including Volkswagen. The oil is tested and rated in regular production automotive engines. The oil container is printed with the API classification. The API service classification and the SAE grade marking are available to help you determine what oil to use. The API oil doughnut with the API rating appears in the circle along with the SAE rating on the oil container. A rating with an "S" is for spark ignition engines, and a "C" is for diesel or compression-ignition engines. The latest rating is "SN Plus" for 2018-and-later engines.

oil is hot. Oils tested at low temperature, which varies with viscosity, are rated with a number and the letter W, which means winter, such as SAE 20W. Multigrade engine oils, such as SAE 5W-30 multigrade oil, meets the SAE 5W viscosity specification when cooled to 0°F and meets the SAE 30 viscosity specification when tested at 212°F.

Oils with a high viscosity have a higher resistance to flow and are thicker than lower viscosity oil. Thin oils provide improved cold-engine starting and better fuel economy. Thick oils provide improved protection at higher temperatures and are generally better for high-performance engines.

First, use synthetic oil that was designed for high-performance engines and make sure that the right oil filter is selected. This means that you cannot go with the good old VW strainer. Upgrade not only to a high-volume oil pump but also to a larger sump along with a high-quality spin-on oil filter.

Once upon a time, engine oil contained zinc dialkyldithiophosphate (ZDDP), which is an extreme pressure additive still used in some gear oils. However, it was removed from engine oils because it damaged the catalytic converter. Yet, we know that the VW air-cooled engine never used a catalytic converter and certainly none of our engine builds will be using one. ZDDP is a high-pressure lubricant that works really well to keep the flat cam followers (lifters) and cam in good shape, especially during break-in. Roller camshafts are not widely available for this application, but they do cure this problem for other applications.

Cylinder Head Temperature Gauge

When building a serious competition or high-performance engine, use a cylinder head temperature gauge and both an oil-temperature and oil-pressure gauge to know what is going on in the engine. I do not know of any published VW cylinder head temperatures. However, the Chevrolet Corvair did have published temperatures. A vintage Chevrolet technical service bulletin (TSB) listed cylinder head temperatures at 200°F to 300°F at idle, 350°F to 475°F at 30 to 60 mph, and up to 575°F from 3,000 to 5,000 rpm at wide-open throttle.

Oil-Temperature Gauge

EMPI, Scat, eBay, and other sources have various temperature and pressure gauges that can plug into an engine. These cylinder temperature gauge kits usually come with the gauge and a sender that install in the cylinder head between the fins. Some kits come with a burglary switch, where several temperature sensors can be put on each side of an engine, and they can switch back and forth to check to see if a cylinder head is overheating. They may not still be available, but Chevrolet offered a Corvair overheat switch that could be screwed into the fins or into a boss on the head.

The oil temperature can be measured with an electrical sending unit mounted in an oil passage or dipstick. The wire from the sending unit is connected to a dash temperature gauge. There is also the Gene Berg dipstick gauge (part number GB 227), which does not work with a gauge. It is connected to the standard VW oil-pressure switch. If the oil temperature goes over 225°F, the oil-pressure light will flicker until the temperature comes down. Scat and EMPI offer different adapters that will connect the oil pressure, temperature, and pressure gauges in a single assembly.

Oil-Pressure Gauge

Oil-pressure gauges can be either mechanical or electrical. The mechanical type requires oil lines to be installed between the engine's oil system and the gauge, which can be mounted wherever it's convenient in the vehicle. These gauges are not always accurate, and I've spent many hours trying to track down low oil pressure or pressure loss when the cause is a bad sender.

Type 1 and Type 2 engines came with an oil-pressure switch that turns on the dash light (an idiot light) if the oil pressure drops to between 2 to 6 psi. However, this may be too late because engine damage may have already occurred. For this reason, an oil-pressure gauge should be considered more important than cylinder-head or oil-temperature gauges. Keep the idiot light circuit in addition to the oil-pressure gauge. Also, use an electrically operated gauge for oil pressure. It will have a sender installed in a brass tee along with the standard VW engine oil-pressure switch. (Photo Courtesy iStock)

It is always a good idea to check oil pressure with a mechanical gauge when the gauge shows low oil pressure or the light is on. There are a number of manufacturers, including EMPI and Scat, that offer oil-pressure gauges. VDO was Volkswagen's supplier of gauges. They are available also from a number of specialty component firms.

The standard rule about oil pressure is for every 1,000 rpm, there needs to be 10 psi of pressure. So, an engine that turns at 5,000 rpm will need about 50 psi of oil pressure. If running a high-RPM engine, higher oil pressure will be needed. However, a word of caution: higher oil pressure blows standard oil cooler seals on engines that do not run at high RPM.

Remember that the stock Volkswagen does not use an oil filter. It only uses a strainer. Through testing, it has been discovered that when a full-flow oil filter is used instead of a bypass-type filter or no oil filter, there can be a 50-percent reduction of crankshaft wear, a 66-percent reduction in wrist-pin wear, a 19-percent reduction in cylinder-wall wear, and a 52-percent reduction in ring wear.

A full-flow filter kit can be added that includes a high-volume oil pump with full-flow oil filter. Oil pump assemblies with an attached filter in front of the cylinder head are not recommended because hot air blown directly over the filter will result in the oil overheating. The installation of high-volume oil pumps generally does not require any case machining. Some modification may be necessary when using an external oil cooler or turbocharger lubrication hookup with some oil line plumbing to the filter and back to the case. The Scat oil pump uses 32-mm-length oil-pump gears. (Photo Courtesy Scat Enterprises)

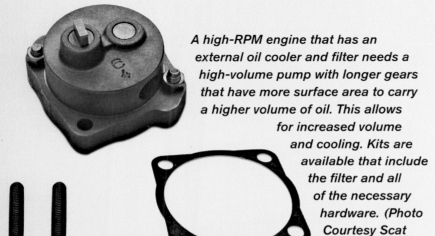

A high-RPM engine that has an external oil cooler and filter needs a high-volume pump with longer gears that have more surface area to carry a higher volume of oil. This allows for increased volume and cooling. Kits are available that include the filter and all of the necessary hardware. (Photo Courtesy Scat Enterprises)

The dual bypass case uses two oil-pressure-relief valves along the main oil gallery. One is in the front, and one is in the rear of the main gallery. Some aftermarket companies sell a higher-pressure-relief valve with a spool at the top that boosts pressure. I do not recommend this relief valve.

Oil Filters

When modifying an engine for competition or high-performance use, add a large full-flow oil filter using the various modification mounting kits available. This filter provides added oil capacity along with oil filtering. A popular filter that is commonly used is the Fram HP1 or the OC47 Filter from Scat (part number 50009). EMPI, Scat plus, and other air-cooled engine component suppliers offer full-flow oil filter kits (see the source guide). Be sure to install the external oil filter out of the path of hot air coming off the cylinder heads.

High-Volume Oil Pump

The original oil pump gears were 22 mm thick; the 1,600-cc engine had 26-mm-thick gears. Aftermarket high-volume pumps offer 26- to 32-mm-thick gears, larger bearings, can come with a remote spin-on filter, and have adapters for an external oil cooler and turbocharger hookup. These pump and filter assemblies bolt right in place of the stock oil pump so that no external hoses are necessary, unless you are using external cooler.

There are a number of kits with an adapter that bolts onto the front of the oil pump that uses external hoses to connect to a filter base where the full-flow oil filter screws on. It's important that you keep these hoses short and that they have an inside diameter of at least 1/2 inch. Use braided-steel-covered hoses and AN fittings for any external oil line

The best location for the remote oil filter is to the left of the engine. It can possibly be mounted on the engine, but it needs to be out of any hot-air path to avoid heating the oil. Also, consider using AN-type fittings to ensure a leak-free connection to the pump cover. (Photo Courtesy Scat Enterprises)

systems, such as an oil cooler or turbocharger lubrication.

High-Capacity Oil Sump

Oil takes a lot of abuse in an air-cooled engine. It has to provide both lubrication and cooling functions. Therefore, any type of performance upgrades or racing requires additional oil and pump capacity.

The oil sump is where engine oil is stored. In a VW engine, the oil is stored at the underside of the crankcase with no oil pan. The oil pump draws the oil from the underside of

The Scat billet full-flow cover (part number 6061) can be used as an external oil filter and as a possible oil cooler. First, block the pump's oil outlet with a threaded plug into the pump body. Run a braided-steel line from the outlet of this full-flow cover to an external oil filter with a built-in pressure relief. The oil goes through the filter and returns to the engine through another braided-steel line and into a fitting drilled into the main oil gallery on the left side of the case. An external cooler could also be plumbed. (Photo Courtesy Scat Enterprises)

Dual bypass cases are available from Scat, Air Cooled, and EMPI. The cases have all of the drillings necessary to use a full-flow oil-filter system. The dual bypass case has dual oil-pressure-relief valves along the main oil gallery. There is one in the front to the left of the pump and one in the rear of the main gallery at the flywheel end. (Photo Courtesy Scat Enterprises)

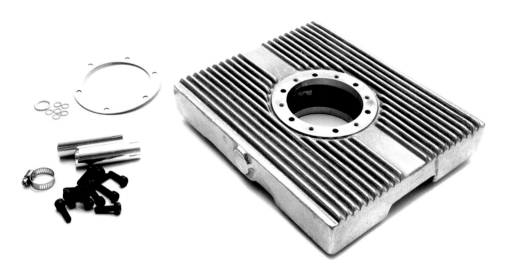

By using a thin bolt-on sump, oil capacity can be increased by 3.5 quarts without the loss of ground clearance. (Photo Courtesy Scat Enterprises)

A Killer case offered by Scat can also be used. It has a built-in high-capacity oil sump to increase oil capacity and keep the engine cooler when it is used with an external oil cooler. This sump is part of the actual case and offers ground clearance. (Photo Courtesy Scat Enterprises)

This billet two-stage dry-sump oil pump is for use with Scat Killer case installations. This pump is designed to provide a 2:1 scavenge-to-oil pressure ratio. (Photo Courtesy Scat Enterprises)

There are remote oil-filter brackets with built-in adjustable pressure relief with a bypass for sending excess oil back to the oil tank without entering the engine first. This helps prevent picking up excess heat in any high-performance engine with a dry-sump oil system. This kit includes a pressure-boosting relief valve for higher oil pressure. (Photo Courtesy Scat Enterprises)

the crankcase into the main galleries. This kind of system is termed a wet-sump oil system.

With a dry-sump system, the oil pan is very shallow. Therefore, the oil is pumped into a distant reservoir. The oil is cooled in the remote reservoir, and any trapped air is allowed to escape before being pumped back to the engine. The benefits of a dry-sump system are:

- Oil capacity is expanded because the scale of the reservoir isn't limited. A larger quantity of oil allows the oil temperature to be controlled.
- A dry-sump system allows the vehicle to corner and brake for long periods, which isn't possible with a wet-sump system because the oil is thrown to one side of the pan and far from the oil pickup.
- A dry-sump system also allows the engine to develop more power because the oil is kept away from the moving crankshaft.

The disadvantage of the dry-sump system is the expense, as it requires additional components and hoses. It is more complex than a wet-sump system due to the needed plumbing and connections, plus the additional components, which lead to more places where oil leaks can occur and alter the way routine maintenance is handled.

Windage Tray

The windage tray is designed to help control oil from sloshing from side to side. Where does the wind come from? Pistons push air down into the crankcase as they move from TDC to BDC. When the pistons move

A windage tray is a plate or baffle installed under the crankshaft. It is used to help prevent aeration of the oil. It helps to prevent turbulence in the oil sump. (Photo Courtesy Scat Enterprises)

from BDC to TDC at high speed, a lot of air goes into the crankcase and can aerate the oil.

A windage tray is used to help prevent this movement of air (wind) from affecting the oil in the pan. It is ideal for all competitive demands of high-speed cornering, quick acceleration, and hill climbing. It fits below the camshaft to a separate chamber,

helping to eliminate oil spray and froth that robs horsepower at high RPM.

Oil Cooler

The Porsche 912 oil coolers are considered to be more efficient than the standard 1,600-cc VW-engine oil cooler. The Porsche cooler will also take more pressure than the standard VW oil cooler. These coolers are less likely to fail if the pressure-relief valve was stuck closed or if an oil-pressure boosting relief valve is used.

However, companies such as EMPI, Scat, JBugs, Summit Racing, and Air Cooled offer a wide variety of internal and external oil coolers. For example, Scat offers an oil cooler (part number 113117021B) that fits VW engines if using the Scat doghouse oil cooler adapter (part number 50106). I also suggest the EMPI oil cooler (part number 021 117 021B 17-2806), which is a Type 2/4 or Porsche 914 1,700- to 2,000-cc, or oil cooler (part number 113 117 021 98-1161-B) for 1,300- to 1,600-cc using the doghouse shroud with

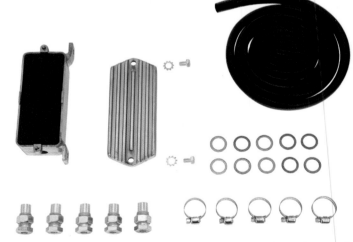

A universal oil breather box is a solid addition to relieve engine crankcase backpressure without the loss or spillage of oil. This breather allows the engine to breathe through a combination of vents from the air cleaner, valve covers, and crankcase. It uses internal baffles that separate the oil from the air and return oil back into the engine. The Scat kit contains the parts needed for the installation. (Photo Courtesy Scat Enterprises)

An internal doghouse oil-cooler adapter is used with a heavy-duty Porsche-style doghouse oil cooler (part number 113117021b). This adapter places a vertical oil cooler outside the original fan area in what is called a dog-house, which provides much better airflow to increase oil cooling. (Photo Courtesy Scat Enterprises)

The doghouse shroud is used with the internal engine oil-cooler adapter that places the oil cooler outside of the cooler fan area for better cooling. When it was along-side the fan, there was insufficient airflow over the cooler. This shroud is available from several suppliers in various paint colors, unpainted, and chrome plated. (Photo Courtesy Scat Enterprises)

A racing setup for an external oil cooler can be used in place of the standard oil cooler by using adapters from EMPI, Scat, JBugs, Summit Racing, or Air Cooled. If your build is a street vehicle and only uses an external cooler, the engine may run hot in traffic with only a remote oil-cooler setup. (Photo Courtesy Derale Performance)

If your engine build is for racing, install a large remote-mounted oil cooler connected to 1/2-inch-or-larger inside-diameter steel-braided hoses. The external oil cooler can be mounted on the left side of the vehicle in the left rear fender well to receive proper airflow. An electric cooling fan can also be installed to blow air across the external oil cooler. (Photo Courtesy Scat Enterprises)

A forged and counter-weighted crankshaft should be used and not a nodular cast-iron crankshaft. EMPI, Air Cooled, JBugs, Summit Racing, and Scat offer high-quality forged crankshafts. (Photo Courtesy Scat Enterprises)

Some companies, such as Scat, sell cast-iron crankshafts, but the original factory crankshaft was forged. The high-performance engine will most likely develop more horsepower than 50 bhp, and a cast-iron crankshaft will break and bend under pressure and pound out the case, main bearings, and/or wrist pins. (Photo Courtesy Scat Enterprises)

The Scat crankshaft Type 1 gear assembly kit is for use with all Type 1 crankshafts. It is likely that worn or faulty parts will need to be replaced with these components for the proper timing of the engine. The kit includes the timing gear, woodruff key timing gear, distributor drive gear, a crank lock ring, an oil slinger, a woodruff key crank pulley, and a crankshaft racer spacer. (Photo Courtesy ACE Performance Engines, Stefan Rossi)

the doghouse oil cooler kit to case adapter (part number 8894).

If you are not turbocharging or going for high horsepower, choose a smaller oil pump. If you are building a high-output engine, use a high-performance or competition engine oil cooler. These coolers are all fitted with 1/2-inch (NPT) female pipe thread fittings. Make sure to use 1/2-inch (NPT) male pipe thread fittings when mating a fitting to these coolers.

Crankshaft and Connecting Rods

The crankshaft and connecting rods should be used as a set and not individual components. The stock crankshaft stroke on the 1,300-/1,500-/1,600-cc engine was 69 mm. The earlier engines used a 64-mm stroke.

Crankshaft

The German VW engineers designed their air-cooled engine for low RPM, low power output, and high-mileage use. If your build is

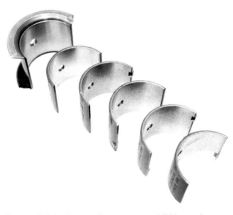

Installing new Type 1 VW engine main bearing sets is critical for all performance applications where reliability and longevity is essential. This minimizes case distortion under heavy loads, matching main bearings with the new crankshaft. (Photo Courtesy Scat Enterprises)

Install high-performance VW and Chevy 2.0-inch journal connecting-rod bearings with steel-backed special alloy bearings that are available in standard and oversize sets. (Photo Courtesy Scat Enterprises)

If you have the budget, use H-beam rods. They are very efficient on a high-performance VW engine for higher-RPM operation. They can withstand the higher RPM and the torque developed. (Photo Courtesy Scat Enterprises)

A bending force takes place because the two center rod journals are on the same side in a VW engine. This action puts all the force on one side of the crankshaft. This pounds out the case at the center main saddle and creates crank pulley and flywheel run-out. Also, this will destroy a case at the pulley end. Crankshaft bending can cause rod or crankshaft breakage along with flywheel failure. (Photo Courtesy ACE Performance Engines, Stefan Rossi)

designed for high-RPM operation for RPM developed power, it will develop more centripetal/centrifugal force that could bend the crankshaft at the center main.

If you are building a 1,776- or 1,914-cc engine that uses the stock 69-mm stroke, upgrade to a counterweighted standard-stroke crankshaft. If you are going for a larger-displacement engine (such as a 2,165 cc with a 94-mm bore and a 78-mm stroke or a 2,275 cc with a 94-mm bore and an 82-mm stroke), it is a stroker engine using a crankshaft with a longer stroke than the 69-mm stock unit. The drivability and torque of a stroker engine is exceptional and allows the engine to develop higher horsepower without higher RPM.

An engine that turns at high RPM will wear out faster. Street vehicles always see more usable power out of stroker engines than out of a small engine running at high RPM.

The engine you build depends on your budget and project goals. Forged and moly-treated 1,600-cc-series crankshafts range from $205 to $1,748.

Many Volkswagen engine builders in the field say that old connecting rods should never be resused or rebuilt. New 4340 I-beam rods can be purchased for about $150 a set. If the rods fail, you just wasted an expensive forged crankshaft and EMPI bubble or Scat Killer case.

Full-circle or roller crankshafts are not recommended. If a build is for drag racing, the sudden engagement of a high-performance clutch to a high-winding engine connected to slick tires will twist a full-circle crank out of alignment and destroy the engine. Also, if the compression ratio is higher than stock, any detonation will deform the aluminum roller cases.

The major suppliers sell forged crankshafts with counterweights in all of the popular strokes: 69, 74, 78, 82, 84, and even 88 mm. Street engines can use a stroker up to 84 mm with a properly machined old case or a cut new case with no loss in case integrity. For example, EMPI sells the Bugpack 4340 chromoly counterweighted stroker crankshafts. The right connecting rods must be used on all strokes of 82 mm and larger to achieve maximum reliability.

Connecting Rods

The H-beam design is lighter and has high strength by using a forged 4340 chrome molybdenum construction. The caps will generally use a fillet radius to reduce the amount of clearance required for stroker applications and are sleeved to the rod to eliminate cap shifting. Many of these have been magnafluxed to check for imperfections, and they are sold in matched sets of four. Use those that come with forged ARP 5/16-inch cap bolts.

If you are using a longer stroke than the stock 69 mm, a 78-mm-stroke crankshaft is a solid choice. The price is not much different from the 74- to 84-mm crank.

The 78-mm crankshaft is also the longest stroke that can be reliably

Estimate about $2,000 or more for a crankshaft with a long stroke plus the cost of special longer connecting rods. These crankshafts also need a set of long cylinders. A long-stroke crankshaft of this magnitude will tighten up things inside the case, so be careful and consult an engine builder with experience in this area. (Photo Courtesy Scat Enterprises)

Scat offers a flanged crankshaft for high-horsepower and high-torque engines to eliminate the separation of the flywheel from the crank during high RPM. (Photo Courtesy Scat Enterprises)

Longer crankshaft strokes require a longer connecting rod or a better-designed rod, such as the Bugpack H-beam (part number 4340). These H-beam connecting rods are available in lengths from 5.4 to 5.7 inches. (Photo Courtesy Scat Enterprises)

used with reworked stock connecting rods. A more reliable and lasting choice is to use an H-beam connecting rod. The 84-mm-stroke crankshaft needs the H-beam connecting rod.

The I-beam connecting rods are typically good up to 6,500 rpm. If running at a higher RPM, use the H-beam connecting rod that has been rated up to 9,000 rpm. The H-beam connecting rods are stronger and weigh less but are more costly

than I-beam connecting rods. If trying to control your budget, use the 82-mm crankshaft with I-beam connecting rods.

The top stroker crankshaft levels are 86- and 88-mm-stroke crankshafts, which are available from many suppliers, including Scat. If you are headed in that direction, use the Type 4 main bearings on a crankshaft with this long of a stroke. This job also requires special case machining, a Scat Killer case, or the EMPI

Bubble Case. The larger main bearings make the crankshaft stronger.

The rod ratio is the length of the connecting rod divided by the crankshaft stroke. The wrist pin or small end of a connecting rod is connected to the center of the piston bore, and the crankpin end is connected to the crankshaft. When the crankshaft stroke increases, increase the length of the connecting rod so that the rod angle is increased. A 78-mm stroke is the maximum that a stock connecting rod can handle without bolt failure. The stock connecting rod length will work as long as a strong rod is used, such as the EMPI stock rod (VW part number 311 105 401B or EMPI part number 98-0153-B).

The standard 69-mm-stroke crankshaft on up to an 82-mm-stroke crankshaft could use the standard Volkswagen 5.394-inch-length connecting rod if it is manufactured in chromoly. If going to a longer stroke, such as 84 mm, use the 5.5-inch or longer connecting rods.

Many VW high-performance engine builders recommend using a 5.7-inch or longer connecting rod for strokes longer than 88 mm. When the length of the connecting rod is increased, the piston is farther out from the crankshaft and could stick out of the cylinder. So, add cylinder spacers to adjust the piston travel. This should be done with an engine mock-up build to check all movement and clearances.

When the length of the connecting rods increases and longer cylinders or cylinder spacers are used, the engine will be wider. This is not an issue with a rail or a dune buggy. Yet, a Type 1 or 2 compartment is small, so take into consideration the engine width.

An 86-mm or longer stroker

engine with longer rods will not fit into a Type 1 engine compartment without a lot of sheet-metal reworking. If using standard connecting rods in an 86-mm-stroke engine, the engine life will be shortened with a low RPM range.

There is a lot of extra work with 86-, 88-, or even a 90-mm stroker engine stuffed into a small engine compartment. It may not be worth the time and expense for whatever performance gains. It will also require modifying the exhaust system or placing it outside of the engine compartment for a good fit.

Flywheel

If a counterweighted crankshaft is installed with all of the appropriate components, a lightweight flywheel can be installed. A light flywheel allows faster acceleration. A heavy stock flywheel weight takes more torque and horsepower to move the vehicle. The VW engineers made the flywheel heavy to smooth out firing pulses and stop vibration harmonics and torsional twist, because unlike big V-8 engines, it did not use a harmonic balancer or a torsional damper.

Be sure to lube the inside of any seal when installing it. Otherwise, it will burn when the engine is first cranked over (even by hand), causing small heat cracks in the seal lip. This usually is the cause of most premature flywheel seal leaks. Never put any sealer on the inside diameter (ID) or outside diameter (OD) of the seal or any oil on the OD when installing it. Gene Berg Enterprises sells a genuine VW graphited flywheel O-ring (part number GB 114). It is designed to let the flywheel slip over the end of the crankshaft.

Use a crankshaft with an eight-dowel-pin connection to eliminate the problem of the crank coming loose from the flywheel. In the past, the crank and flywheel would need to be drilled for an eight-dowel connection, but these are available from many suppliers today. (Photo Courtesy Scat Enterprises)

Never use a lightened flywheel with a stock crankshaft without counterweights. A light flywheel allows higher-RPM operation. Gene Berg's version of a big-engine harmonic balancer known as the "equalizer pulley" can be used. This pulley controls the twist and untwist of the crankshaft, controlling or dampening the harmonics. That is why it is called a harmonic balancer or a torsional damper.

When replacing or reusing the crankshaft or flywheel, always tighten the new gland nut and washer to 253 ft-lbs. (Photo Courtesy Scat Enterprises)

Install a flexible-lip silicone rear main seal that tightly seals against oil leaks and works up to 500°F. The Gene Berg flywheel seal (part number GB 113A) is a good seal choice. Be sure to lube the inside of any seal when installing it. Otherwise, it will burn when the engine is first cranked over (even by hand), causing small heat cracks in the seal lip. This usually is the cause of most premature flywheel seal leaks. Never put any sealer on the inside diameter or outside diameter of the seal, and never put any oil on the outside diameter when installing it. (Photo Courtesy Scat Enterprises)

CYLINDER HEADS AND CAMSHAFTS

When building a high-performance engine, the cylinder heads are a very important part of the performance equation. They are breathing apparatuses that feed fuel and air into the cylinders and allow the exhaust to escape, as controlled by the camshaft. So, valve size, porting, and valve cuts can make a large difference in a project engine's performance. With the right cylinder heads, a 1,776-cc engine (standard stroke with 90.5-mm cylinders) can easily develop more than 160 bhp.

Volkswagen redesigned its cylinder head many times. The original engine was a two-piece cast-aluminum medium alloy crankcase. It was a one-piece casting with a combustion chamber for two cylinders. A separate pressed steel valve cover is over the rocker arms, which were actuated by aluminum pushrods positioned below the cylinders.

Each cylinder had one inlet and one exhaust valve, and they were retained in the head by single-coil valve springs and forged steel retainers. The original stock-version springs fit directly against the cylinder head casting located in small machined pockets to prevent them from moving as the valves open and close.

The valve gear was very simple, consisting of four individual cast rocker arms that pivoted on hardened steel shafts and relocated by means of hairpin clips and spring

There are two basic types of cylinder heads that can be used on a 1,600-cc Type 1 engine: single port or dual port. Single-port heads have one intake port that serves two cylinders. Dual-port heads have an intake port for each cylinder. Single-port heads feed both intake valves and are restrictive, which limits power. The dual-port head is recommended for any performance build. If the engine overheats, a dual-port head is more likely to crack than a single-port head, so this is an engine-life factor for street vehicles. A dual-port head can last more than 100,000 miles without cracking when the engine is not over-revved and/or abused. (Photo Courtesy Shutterstock)

shims. The rocker-arm assemblies originally mounted directly onto the cylinder heads using cast-in pedestals designed to accept the rocker shaft, which was located with a machine clamp. Later designs of the rocker-arm assemblies were secured to the cylinder heads with steel blocks that were held in place with a pair of studs and nuts.

The first production heads were single-port units that used a siamesed inlet port that served the two adjacent cylinders. The single-port heads were used until 1968, although there were changes with the larger-displacement engines up to 1,500 cc.

In 1968, Volkswagen introduced a twin-port head on the Type 3 pancake engine. It finally made its way onto the Type 1 in 1970. This is now the universally used dual-port head. This new casting featured separate inlet ports for each cylinder, allowing the larger engines to breathe better. Older engines can be upgraded to these heads for bolt-on horsepower. For example, for bolt-on horsepower on an older 1966/1967 1,300 or 1,500 single-port engine, just use a set of dual-port heads with the larger carburetor and maybe a better-breathing exhaust to get a whole lot more performance.

VW Head Castings

Volkswagen used casting numbers 040, 041, and 043 for its factory stock dual-port cylinder heads. The 042, 044, and 050 are aftermarket castings used by Scat, CB, EMPI, and others to provide high-performance cylinder heads.

The 040 casting had the most fins and the best cooling. The 041 is not that good. The 044 is the best high-performance street head, but it needs to be ported for the best performance. The 040 casting can be used for stock engines and mild porting and the 043 for intermediate porting, but the 044 is the best for really large valves and ports.

The 044 head is cast for CB by the same company that makes the stock VW castings in Brazil. The 042 and 050 are cast by MoFoCo Enterprises Inc. in the United States. MoFoCo builds and sells VW competition heads and is located at 4170 N. Lydell Ave. in Milwaukee, Wisconsin.

Aftermarket high-performance heads will run hotter than heads based on the first VW 040 castings. Aircooled.net, for example, uses the 043 VW casting, which it considers to be better than the VW 040. The recent 044 heads are a solid basis for port sizes that might normally require welding on the plate.

Take care in selecting cylinder heads because many companies don't use quality components, such as retainers, guides, valves, and springs. Some heads with large valves may use stock-size ports, and these won't provide the performance that you will get by using larger valves. A number of these firms advertise flow numbers with their cylinder heads as a basis for comparison, but bigger flow numbers might not be better. Air speed through the port is much more important, but this measurement is difficult to quantify.

Any increase in engine displacement, such as going from 1,600 to 1,776 cc, requires an increase in head-valve size so that the engine will breathe properly. For example, a mild 1,776-cc engine with just a single carburetor will work well with the stock 35.5-mm intake valves and 32-mm exhaust valves. However, with a 94-mm bore with a 78-mm stroker crankshaft using dual Weber carburetors, the small stock valves will be a choke point that will suppress the engine.

For any engine with a displace-ment greater than 1,776 cc that uses dual carburetors or electronic fuel injection along with a high-lift, long-duration camshaft, it is vital that the valve size be increased. Install at least 40-mm intake valves and 35.5-mm exhaust valves.

The original VW factory dual-port head is a good starting point to build an efficient large-valve head for use on a fast street engine. It is probably better than some of the less-expensive aftermarket cylinder heads. The VW 041 dual-port head casting was made in South America and came with a 39-mm intake valve and a 32-mm exhaust valve. The intake valve is larger than stock and the actual intake port is a little different than the stock head, so the gas flow was better than if the original head had been used. An increase in intake valve size must be matched by an equivalent increase in the exhaust valve size to take full advantage of the improved airflow.

When using a stock head for any performance operation, it would benefit from a three-angle valve job and some minor porting, as is shown in this chapter. The inlet ports can be opened up by the careful use of the die grinder or Dremel tool.

Be careful not to remove the bump in the port directly below the valve-spring pocket. If it is removed, the head might be weakened in this vital area. If the sharp radius in the exhaust port is removed from just under the valve seat, this will provide some additional exhaust flow. However, be careful not to remove a lot of material so that the valve seat is undercut. If this happens, there is a possibility that the seat will move, especially if the valves flow from over-revving or using heavy-duty valve springs. It is better to concentrate on removing any obvious flow restrictions than to just grind a lot of material out.

Which cylinder heads are purchased is dependent on your project budget. If you have enough money, get heads with smooth ported passages along with larger valves. Large valves and smooth larger ports will deliver greater airflow. The better the engine breathes, the more air that flows in and exhaust out of your engine, which means more power.

In my opinion, if more radical port work is necessary, consider purchasing aftermarket heads from the companies listed in the source guide. Go with aftermarket cylinder heads that use the VW 044 castings that come equipped with larger valves and ports that have been straightened rather than having to do a lot of machining. They will also be cut to accept the larger 90.5-, 92-, or 94-mm cylinders. These heads will also use 3/4-inch long-reach spark plugs that will resist cracking between the plug boss and valve seats.

Some of the more radical heads may have been cut in areas that reduce the cooling fins, so they may not be appropriate for moderate street use. The high-RPM racing engines that these heads were designed for made short runs with a teardown afterward, so engine cooling was not a priority. If radical heads are to be used for a street vehicle or a dune buggy, cooling modifications may need to be made because cooling fins are important for street vehicles.

Many VW aftermarket parts suppliers offer complete dual-port cylinder heads with the three-angle valve job (30-degree, 45 degree, and 70 degree). Choose the bore and valve sizes for your project and these will

come assembled with stainless-steel valves; single or dual high-speed valve springs; high-performance retainers; hardened keepers; and rocker, exhaust, and intake studs. Scat, Aircooled.net Superflo, EMPI, and CB Competition Eliminator sell

high-performance cylinder heads for street application and competition use with large valves, ported passages, a three-angle valve job, 12-mm long-reach spark plugs, and full cooling fins to increase head cooling.

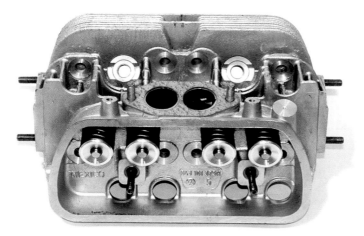

ACN stocker dual-port cylinder heads can be used to increase performance in the 90- to 100-hp range. This dual-port head uses 35x32-mm valves for street vehicles and comes with 14-mm x 3/4-inch long-reach plug threads, Hi Chrome valve seats, silicone bronze valve guides, heavy-duty valve springs, hardened keepers, and chromoly retainers. It uses a 59-cc combustion chamber in all bore sizes—from 85.5 to 94 mm. There is also a Level 7 head from Air Cooled that uses 44x37.5-mm valves, but it is more for off-road or racing applications. (Photo Courtesy Scat Industries)

High-flow heads do not work well below 3,000 rpm, but you will experience excellent performance and higher engine speeds. Large-valve high-flow heads can place the engine in the 220-hp range, provided that the crankshaft, rods, and cylinders can support it. These heads use 12-mm x 3/4-inch-reach spark plugs to prevent cracks at the threads. Use an exhaust in the 1¾ or 1⅞ size to use the flow capability of these heads to avoid tuning issues and overheating. The approximate combustion-chamber volume on these heads is between 66 and 68 cc, depending on bore size from 85.5 to 94 mm. (Photo Courtesy Scat Industries)

Scat

Scat manufactures Pro-Port Type 1 Wedge Port cylinder heads for high-RPM operation featuring stainless-steel valves, manganese guides, a three-angle valve job, unshrouded combustion chambers, and long-reach spark plug bosses, which are match-ported and polished. Part numbers vary for your specific application. The following are three options from Scat, although more are available.

For high-performance use, Scat offers the MINI-D-PORT, which features dual valve springs and chromoly retainers. It also has a smart port design for better performance at 2,000 to 6,000 rpm. The heads are swirl-polished with Venturi intake and exhaust runners, and they feature efficient combustion chambers for 1,915- to 2,275-cc engines with 90.5/92/94-mm bores.

The stock-port head features 37-mm intake valves and 32-mm exhaust valves for an 85.50-mm bore. It is a good option for replacing worn-out factory heads.

The Street Port Hi-Rev cylinder head features 40-mm intake x 35.5-mm exhaust valves, with single valve springs and 4140 retainers for a stock 85.5-mm bore. This head is an upgrade from the stock port heads.

EMPI or EMPIUS

These companies also represent Bugpack, JayCee, Race-Trim, and others. EMPI offers a variety of standard and high-performance cylinder heads. It offers far too many to list here, so go to its website (empius.com) to see what meets your needs. These cylinder heads use dual valve springs, chromoly retainers, hardened keepers, bronze valve guides, and stainless-steel valves with custom-fit gaskets included with each pair. They will also have the three-angle valve job.

I suggest using the EMPI GTV-2 CNC ported cylinder heads (part number 98-1560-B) with 44-mm intake and 37.5-mm valves for engines using 90.5/92-mm bores or part number 98-1561-B with the same valve sizes for 94-mm-bore engines.

Air Cooled Inc.

Air Cooled Inc. sells a variety of VW heads. I suggest the following two based on performance needs: ACN Stocker Plus Dual Port and Superflo S/F I.

ACN Stocker Plus Dual Port cylinder heads, which feature 35x32-mm valves, are made from brand-new castings that feature more flow than stock castings. The flow increase is in the 15- to 20-percent range. These are a good choice for enthusiasts who want a next-level-up-from-stock head, and users have reported dyno tests up to 130 hp with them.

Superflo (S/F I) cylinder heads use Cosworth oval intake ports, large valves, machined combustion chambers, and a reshaped exhaust port. Additional metal is placed under the valve seat to prevent sunken valves. A large rocker box area is built into the heads to allow the use of any size of rocker arm. This is a very high-performance head, and it is priced like it.

CB Performance Products Inc.

CB Performance Products Inc. offers a number of VW engine cylinder heads. I suggest the following depending on your needs:

The 044 Super Mag CNC Round Port cylinder heads feature a 40-mm intake and 35-mm exhaust valves available for 85.5-, 92-, and 94-mm bores. These heads are good for small-displacement engines and emphasize port velocity yet still flow well on higher-displacement engines.

The 044 Ultra Mag Plus CNC cylinder heads use 44-mm intake and 37.5-mm exhaust valves for 92- and 94-mm bores. These heads are similar to the previous head with the 044 casting, but they are optimized for 2,000-cc or larger engines. They also feature full CNC porting.

The 044 Super Pro cylinder heads with 45-mm intake and 37.5-mm exhaust valves are top of the heap from a performance standpoint and are only available in the 94-mm bore. These heads flow 224 cfm and are a good choice for a hot street or bracket racing application.

AA Performance Products

All XXB 501-series heads feature increased material at the intake surface, aiding in the flexibility to remove more material when porting. They also feature a modernized combustion chamber and a second full fin so that the heads can be fly cut to achieve the desired head CC volume. They have locked off rocker stud bosses for increased oil control and use long-reach 3/4-inch spark plugs to reduce the chance of cracking between the valve seat and plug. The AA Pistons website has a good listing of what heads work with what bore kits.

All 501-series heads are for the Type 1, 2, or 3 dual port. Within the 501 series, you have options based on valve sizes:

Part number 501 460 XXB X2 uses stainless-steel 44-mm intake valves and 37.5-mm exhaust valves.

Part number 501 440 XXB X2 has stainless-steel 42-mm intake and 37.5-mm exhaust valves.

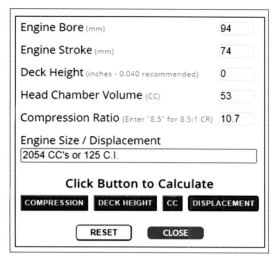

Engine Bore (mm)	94
Engine Stroke (mm)	74
Deck Height (inches - 0.040 recommended)	0
Head Chamber Volume (CC)	53
Compression Ratio (Enter "8.5" for 8.5:1 CR)	10.7
Engine Size / Displacement	
2054 CC's or 125 C.I.	

Click Button to Calculate

[COMPRESSION] [DECK HEIGHT] [CC] [DISPLACEMENT]

[RESET] [CLOSE]

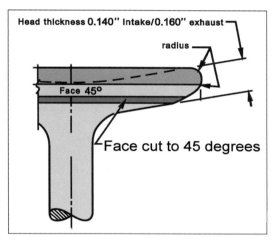

Head thickness 0.140" Intake/0.160" exhaust

radius

Face 45°

Face cut to 45 degrees

Air-cooled.net offers an engine calculator to assist in developing a 4-cylinder VW engine. Enter the bore, stroke, deck height, head chamber volume, compression ratio, and engine size to get any of the values left blank.

The edge thickness for the intake valve should be 0.050 inch for the intake valve and 0.070 inch for the exhaust valve with a slight radius. The exhaust valve should overhang the seat by 0.040 inch. The valve's head thickness should be 0.140 inch on the intake and 0.160 inch on the exhaust. The face angle is 45 degrees and narrowes to a 0.040- to 0.060-inch face width.

should've already replaced the valve guides. This is important because any play in the valve guides will affect the grinding of the valve seats.

It's important to pay attention to details. As much as 3 to 5 hp can be gained by doing this competition valve job (if it already is not part of the cylinder head). The seats must be moved outward to coincide with the intake valve edges. The seats are to be widened to 0.080 to 0.100 inch on the exhaust valves and 0.100 inch on the intake valves. Valve seats that are narrower than this will reduce the flow through the ports.

The valves also have to be undercut to reduce the actual width of the seat on the valve itself. This is done to improve the airflow. The repeated opening and closing of the valves causes an impact on the valve seat. The valve and seat should provide a gas-tight joint for compression of the fuel and air in the combustion chamber. The impact leads to wear of the valve and seat, causing poor sealing.

Part number 501 420 XXB X2 has stainless-steel 40-mm intake and 37.5-mm exhaust valves.

Valve Grind

I have recommended the three-angle valve job (30-degree, 45-degree, and 70-degree cuts). Many aftermarket competition cylinder heads have a three-angle valve job. If you are going to use the original dual-port heads, perform this three-angle valve job with new valves. If this is a process that you cannot do, then have it done by an automotive machine shop or purchase aftermarket cylinder heads.

Before cutting seats, you

Valve and Seat Cuts

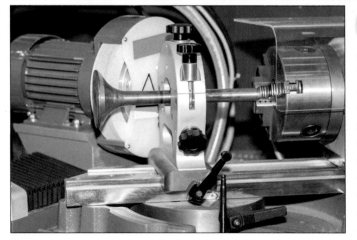

1 *To restore the sealing effect, rotate the valve in a valve-grinding machine with an abrasive stone and grind to the specified closing angle of 45 degrees. Then, undercut the 45-degree face angle to narrow the face width to 0.040 to 0.060 inch. Use the 45-degree stone to blend the valve angles into the face and underside of the valve. The valve grinder uses a rotating stone to restore the face surface and reduce the stem length to maintain proper assembled height. (Photo Courtesy Shutterstock)*

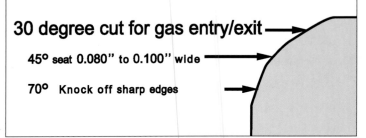

30 degree cut for gas entry/exit

45° seat 0.080" to 0.100" wide

70° Knock off sharp edges

3 Cut the valve seat to the VW specification of a 45-degree angle, and the seat will be narrowed to 0.080 to 0.100 inch using the 30- and 70-degree cutters. The top cut of 30 degrees allows for smoother gas entry and exit.

2 Mount the valve in the valve grinder and let the machine rotate it slowing while you rub 150-grit sandpaper just below the margin of the valve on the edge to create a slide radius. Then, polish it first with 400-grit sandpaper and then with crocus cloth. You want a hand-ground radius that is not too sharp.

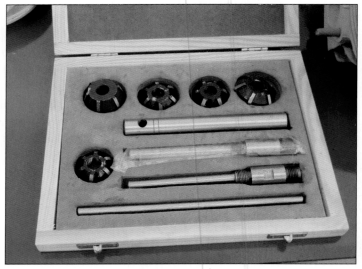

4 Use a valve-seat cutter instead of a valve-grinding stone.

5 In this valve-seat performance cut, first use a 45-degree valve-seat cutter to cut the existing valve seat to a clean 45-degree angle.

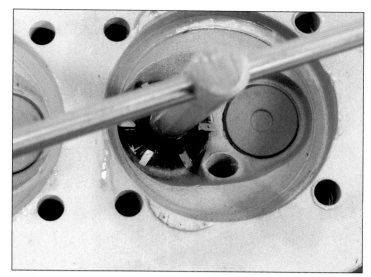

6 Cut the valve seat at the very top using a 30-degree cutter for a chamber entry and exit. You will be cutting above the 45-degree-angle seat. The goal is to get to a 0.080- to 0.100-inch-wide valve seat with the 30-degree cut, providing better airflow into the combustion chamber.

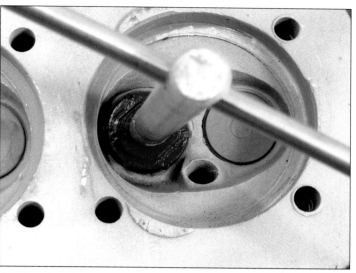

7 Use the 70-degree cutter to knock off any sharp edges on each side of the seat to narrow the seat if needed to get to 0.080 to 0.100 inch wide. Polish the completed seat area with emery paper to radius the seat edges to make it as smooth as possible.

To eliminate any sharp edges in the flow path, use emery cloth or crocus cloth to radius the seat edges both into the port and onto the combustion-chamber area. Sharp edges are not wanted in VW combustion chambers because they cause detonation. Valve edges need to be smooth, and chamber edges at the ceiling surface are also not wanted.

Plug threads that are exposed to combustion when the plug is fully torqued into place can also cause detonation and preignition. If the threads of the plug boss are exposed when the plug is installed, grind back the exposed thread so that the plug-in comes flush with the chamber when torqued in place or use additional spark plug sealing washers.

Valvetrain

The valvetrain is the system that operates the poppet valves, both intake and exhaust valves in the cyl-inder heads. The crankshaft turns the camshaft. The camshaft lobes push the lifter outward. The lifter pushes the pushrod outward. The pushrod pushes out on the rocker arm, which pivots as a first-class lever and opens the valves. The valve spring closes them as the cam lobe allows.

Camshaft

The cam lobes must open and close the valve at the proper time in relation to the position of the pistons, which is called valve timing. If the cam lobe pushes the valve open too fast and the force of lifting that mass at high RPM is high, the camshaft

Use a Vernier caliper (a dial or digital type) to measure the seat width and make sure it is within the specification.

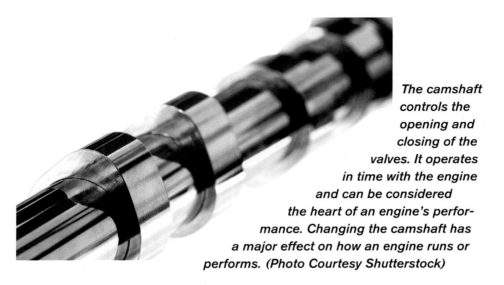

The camshaft controls the opening and closing of the valves. It operates in time with the engine and can be considered the heart of an engine's performance. Changing the camshaft has a major effect on how an engine runs or performs. (Photo Courtesy Shutterstock)

lobes will wear rapidly. To help prevent high wear, the valves must be opened slowly. If the valve is lifted too fast, the inertia of the valvetrain causes the valve to continue opening after the camshaft lobe has reached the full lift position, causing valve float. If the camshaft lobe does not allow the valve to close gradually, the lobe may drop out from under the lifter, leaving slack in the valvetrain.

Valve Timing

Camshafts are rated by their valve timing, which determines how much, how long, and when the valves open, which affects horsepower and torque. The valve timing determines the engine's operating range. Valve timing enhances airflow and cylinder pressure in a definite range. The optimal valve timing can be tested on an engine dynamometer. A few degrees' change one way or the other can have a huge effect on engine performance. No one camshaft works best at all engine speeds, so valve timing is a compromise. The important terms used to rate or measure valve-timing events are valve lift, duration, and overlap.

Valve Lift

Valve lift is the amount the valve is open, or the distance that it is lifted off of its seat. It is measured in thousandths of an inch or hundredths of a millimeter. Each cam lobe has a specific amount of lobe lift.

There are basically two types of lift to consider. The first is a "reliable" amount, which is the conservative level of mechanical lift that will affect the least wear and be better for long-term use. This is usually

the profile of the stock camshaft—nothing radical, nothing to accelerate wear.

There are also high-lift cam designs that give maximum power but with greater wear to the valvetrain. Normal high-performance camshafts have valve lifts in the 0.400 to 0.432 range and high-lift cams have greater lifts in the 0.450- to 0.600-inch range. High-lift camshafts do not necessarily have a long life, nor do the components in contact with them. Camshaft lift in the 0.478- to 0.624-inch range is mostly for off-road or drag-competition engines.

The most accurate way to measure the camshaft lobe lift is to rotate the camshaft between centers and measure the rise and fall with a dial indicator on a mockup of the engine. Valve lift is significant to the breathing of an engine because, up to a certain point, the valve head is a restriction to airflow. Once a valve in a street engine reaches about 0.300-inch lift, the port flows as if the valve was not there. However, it is helpful to lift the valve higher than

LOBE LIFT

BASE CIRCLE

Some cam lobes have measurable lift for more than 180 degrees of rotation. So, the smallest measurement is not the true base circle, and micrometer measurement will not give an accurate number. Lobe lift can be measured with a micrometer by subtracting the smallest measurement (across base circle) from the largest (from heel to nose) measurement. When trying to increase engine power, more lift is better because more valve lift increases airflow, which increases the power potential. To achieve more valve lift, change the camshaft or the rocker arms.

this point because the valve then spends more cam duration time at or above 0.300 inch.

To get the best airflow, it is important to keep the valves open as long as possible. High lift places greater loads on the valvetrain. This is especially true in VW pushrod engines because of the extreme changes in rocker-arm angle that high lift causes. High valve lifts can also cause valve-to-piston interference but generally not on VW air-cooled engines.

Duration

Duration is the number of crankshaft degrees that the valve is open during the crankshaft's rotation. At the end of each stroke, the piston is either at TDC or BDC. A stroke requires 1/2 of a crankshaft rotation, or 180 degrees.

Camshafts are rated by crankshaft duration. There are two slightly different standard measures for duration. First, there is the duration advertised by the camshaft manufacturer, which is the total amount the valve is open (shown in crankshaft degrees plus an additional 0.050 inch). The second measure of duration is called checking duration, which is the period that the valve is open after 0.050-inch (also measured in crankshaft degrees).

More airflow is obtained at higher engine speeds when the valve is open above 0.050-inch lift, but it is at the expense of low-end power. In camshaft selection, it is a tradeoff of low engine speed power for higher RPM power or vice versa.

Duration used to be measured from zero lift just before valve opening to zero lift just after valve closure. However, it is important to take up valvetrain slack along with closing the valve lightly so that the lobe

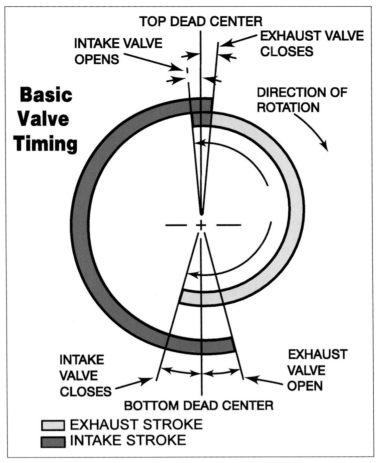

Basic Valve Timing

This valve timing diagram shows the periods in which the intake and exhaust valves are open and closed. If a valve is described as opening at TDC and closing at BDC, the total time it is open is 180 degrees of crankshaft rotation. Since intake valves always open before TDC and close after BDC, the additional degrees must be added to 180 degrees to determine the total duration. If an intake valve opens 6 degrees before TDC and closes 16 degrees after BDC, the duration of the valve opening is the total of 180 degrees + 6 degrees + 16 degrees = 202 degrees. The same is true of an exhaust valve that opens at 16 degrees before BDC and closes at 6 degrees after TDC: 16 + 180 + 6 = 202 degrees of duration.

moves the valve very slowly at the beginning and ending of its cycle. For this reason, it is difficult to determine or measure precisely when the valve begins to open or close.

To resolve this issue, camshaft manufacturers now measure duration at specific points in the valve lift. The most popular specific point is 0.050 inch. This measuring point provides an accurate point at which to start and stop measuring duration. The higher the lift at which the duration measurement begins and ends, the less rated duration a camshaft will have. The duration of a cam lobe measured between the 0.050-inch lift points can be more than 50 degrees less than that measured between the actual opening and closing points.

Early opening and late closing of the valves is required because the intake air and exhaust gas have inertia (change of motion). Neither air nor gas begins entering or leaving the cylinder as soon as the valve opens, so some valve opening time is wasted. All camshafts open the intake valve just before TDC, just before the piston begins its intake stroke, thus giving the intake charge some time to get moving into the cylinder.

Due to exhaust-gas inertia, all camshafts open the exhaust valve before BDC on the power stroke before the piston starts its rise on the exhaust stroke. This gives the exhaust gases more time to get out of the cylinder

Camshafts keep the intake valve open after the pistons reach BDC. As the piston starts up after passing BDC and begins the compression stroke, it takes time before compression pressure builds to the point that it would push a portion of the intake charge out of the cylinder. It is possible to keep the intake valve open after BDC to place more charge in the cylinder. Most camshafts keep the exhaust valve open after TDC at the beginning of the intake stroke. Inertia continues to move the exhaust out the exhaust valve despite the intake valve having opened.

A common mistake of engine builders is to install a camshaft with too much duration. This extended duration of valve opening can result in a rough idle and low manifold vacuum, which causes carburetor metering problems and a lack of low-speed power.

Longer camshaft durations help overcome the inertia of the incoming and outgoing air. A long-duration cam allows more time to fill the cylinder with air and fuel and also allows more time to exhaust more spent gases. The result is more horsepower at high RPM. Most street engines have camshafts with a moderate amount of duration to provide the best compromise between horsepower and fuel consumption.

Overlap

Overlap is when the intake valve opens before the exhaust valve has closed. Many four-stroke

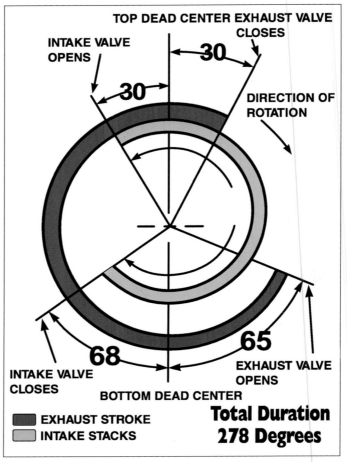

engines use a short overlap period. A long-duration camshaft usually extends the overlap period, which helps make large amounts of power available at high RPM.

The overlap period packs more air and fuel into the cylinder by opening the intake valve near the end of the exhaust stroke while the exhaust valve is still open. The exhaust gas rushes out of the cylinder and helps to pull in the intake mixture, even though the piston has not yet reached TDC. The exhaust valve will still be open when the piston starts down the intake stroke. This does not allow exhaust gases to be sucked back into the cylinder at high RPM because air velocity is high and the outward

movement of exhaust gases is still pulling the air-fuel mixture into the cylinder.

Selection

The camshaft choice is going to be affected by a number of factors. The most important factor is the intended engine build use. Some engine builders say they are building a combination vehicle with a high-lift camshaft that they want to drive on the street and occasionally take to the drag strip. Yet, an engine that was built for the drag strip will not be very drivable on the street. Engines with radical cams are not good in stop-and-go traffic. The following table shows some camshaft selections that can be used.

Camshaft duration has more of an effect on how an engine runs than any other single valve-timing specification. If the intake opens at 30 degrees BTDC and closes at 68 degrees ATDC, the duration is 30 degrees + 180 degrees + 68 degrees, for a total duration of 278 degrees. A camshaft with a lot of duration is an excellent performer at high RPM. A low-speed engine may have a valve duration of 236 degrees, but the same engine designed for high speed may have more than 278 degrees of duration (both measured at 0.050-inch lift).

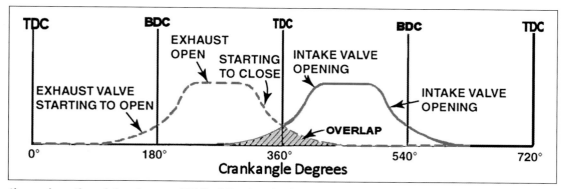

Valve overlap is the number of degrees of crankshaft rotation between the exhaust and intake strokes where both valves are off their seats or open at the same time. The intake and exhaust valves are usually designed to both be open for a short time when the piston is near TDC at the beginning of the intake stroke. If an intake valve opens 12 degrees before TDC and an exhaust valve closes 12 degrees after TDC, add the two figures to determine the overlap, which is 24 degrees.

Camshafts for Use with Standard 1:1 Rocker-Arm Ratio					
Common Use	Duration	Valve Lift	Cam Lift	Duration at 0.050 inch	Lobe Center
Street	276 degrees	0.420 inch	0.383 inch	236 degrees	108 degrees
Street and/or Off-Road	284 degrees	0.430 inch	0.392 inch	247 degrees	108 degrees
Street and/or Off-Road Competition	294 degrees	0.435 inch	0.397 inch	253 degrees	108 degrees
Drag Racing/Off-Road	301 degrees	0.460 inch	0.428 inch	262 degrees	108 degrees

Will the engine be used for street, dune buggy, sand rail, drag racing, or some other track professional competition? Choosing the correct camshaft for a fast street car is a delicate balancing act between getting the most power out of the engine combination and making sure that the end result is still drivable on the street. If you are installing a high-lift cam with radical duration into a 1,904-cc road engine with a 90.5-mm bore and 74-mm stroker, it may seem like it will get a lot of horsepower, but it may turn out to be difficult to drive with practically no fuel economy.

High-lift, long-duration camshafts tend to push the powerband up the RPM range, making the engine harder to drive on the street. In traffic at a low RPM, the engine will most likely hesitate, and there will probably be a significant increase in fuel consumption. Yet, if a large engine was built with large valve heads that

flow great and dual carburetors or fuel injection, the only way to extract the most power is to increase the cam duration and valve lift. Again, select the camshafts based on the vehicle's intended application.

There are camshafts that will work well for almost any build. If the plan is to drive the vehicle on the street, get a camshaft that matches the build with increased horsepower along with everyday drivability. A camshaft with a duration of 284 degrees and a 0.392-inch lift works pretty well for street engines in the 1,700-cc group, such as the 1,776-cc engines that use dual 40-mm carburetors. If the engine is larger with ported and polished high-flow heads, use a cam with 294 degrees of duration and a 0.0397-inch lift for street or off-road competition or one with 301 degrees of duration and a 0.460-inch lift for drag racing or off-roading. Camshafts like these are

available from many of the aftermarket VW components suppliers that are listed in the source guide.

The Dynomation 6 performance simulation software was introduced in Chapter 2. A computer simulation could help determine port sizes and shape along with camshaft timing values to achieve the desired horsepower. It also allows selection and modification of the camshaft grind.

There are many different camshaft measurement standards. The camshaft controls an engine's breathing and the horsepower that it will potentially develop because it controls the beginning and ending of all four-stroke engine cycles. Knowing the measurement will aid in component selection. It is possible to build the engine using your best guess and then run it on an engine dynamometer or do a computer simulation of the component selections before spending unnecessary dollars.

EMPI Camshafts with High-Lift Grinds For 1.4:1 to 1.5:1 Rocker-Arm Ratio							
Camshaft Use	Part Number	Valve Lift at 1.4	Duration	Cam Lift	Duration at 0.050 inch	Lobe Center
Off-Road Competition (Medium Displacement)	22-4007	0.500 inch	288 degrees	0.357 inch	244 degrees	108 degrees
Street/Strip (Large Displacement)	22-4008	0.534 inch	298 degrees	0.382 inch	258 degrees	108 degrees
Competition Drag/Off-Road	22-4010	0.539 inch	310 degrees	0.385 inch	266 degrees	108 degrees
Street/Strip (Large Displacement)	22-4013	0.536 inch	281 degrees	0.383 inch	250 degrees	108 degrees
Off-Road Competition (Medium Displacement)	22-4065	0.478 inch	280 degrees	0.342 inch	236 degrees	108 degrees
Competition Drag/Off-Road	22-4087	0.561 inch	320 degrees	0.401 inch	276 degrees	108 degrees
Competition Drag Only/ Off-Road	22-4089	0.582 inch	328 degrees	0.416 inch	282 degrees	108 degrees
Competition Drag Only/ Off-Road	22-4097	0.622 inch	328 degrees	0.443 inch	287 degrees	108 degrees
Competition Drag Only/ Off-Road	22-4098	0.624 inch	332 degrees	0.446 inch	291 degrees	108 degrees

The 0.050-inch number is what really tells how the camshaft will perform in an engine. This is because airflow through the heads is not significant until the valve is open about 0.050 inch. The longer the cam duration, the larger the engine displacement and RPM range needs to be to use that duration. The cylinder heads, induction system, and exhaust system should be decided at the same time with the intended camshaft.

Street-profile and race-proven-profile camshafts are available from Scat, EMPI, Air Cooled, JBugs, Summit Racing, and others. Select the appropriate camshaft for your application and install it using new cam lifters with assembly lube. It is possible to consult one of these aftermarket performance companies for the selection. Be sure to have your engine specifications, rocker-arm ratio, and compression ratio when contacting the experts.

Performance camshafts are also selected based on what rocker-arm ratio is being used. Consider going with a mild camshaft and a large-displacement combination. This can provide substantial power without having to run higher RPM ranges that will really wear out the engine. The sample table from EMPI on camshaft selection for large-displacement VW Type 1 engines using a high rocker-arm ratio shows many options. Always consult the component or parts manufacturer for all available camshafts.

Camshaft Gear, Cam Followers, and Pushrods

One option is to use the Scat C95 Type 1 camshaft with 1.25:1 or 1.4:1 rockers. It has a 0.416-inch camshaft lift, 0.520-inch valve lift (with 1.25 rockers), and 294 degrees of advertised duration along with 262 degrees of duration at 0.050 inch. This camshaft is similar to the Engle W125.

Pair it with a dual 2-barrel-carburetor setup along with good-breathing dual-port heads. This camshaft needs heavy-duty dual springs and will work with both 1.25:1 and 1.4:1 rocker sets. This camshaft works well with a compression ratio of 9.5:1 to 10.5:1 and has a power range from 4,000 to 6,500 rpm.

When selecting a new camshaft from any of the aftermarket suppliers, install new cam followers at the same time. Most of these aftermarket companies offer cam followers that match their camshaft in terms of the material compatibility. When using a relatively mild camshaft, there is no need to use anything other than the regular stock Volkswagen cam followers. However, if the engine is expected to see high RPM most of the time, select a lightweight lifter.

All aftermarket performance camshafts that run at high RPM will require the use of dual valve springs. Only the mildest of cam profiles allows you to

These high-lift and high-revolution performance camshafts require a bolt-on cam gear to replace the soft and fragile magnesium gear that is part of a stock camshaft. If you use a compatible camshaft with this gear, drilling is not required. Use a camshaft that is wedge-keyed for ultimate strength. (Photo Courtesy Scat Enterprises)

An adjustable cam gear kit can also be used that allows you to dial in the camshaft timing with the offset washers and a steel camshaft/crankshaft gearset with straight-cut teeth for less drag. This reduces thrust load on the cam bearings, preventing premature failure. New stock replacement camshafts are also available in both early flat-gear and late dished-gear designs. (Photo Courtesy Scat Enterprises)

If you are using high-performance camshafts, performance lightweight lifters are needed. Lightweight racing lifters provide a 10- to 15-percent increase in horsepower with a decrease in oil temperature. (Photo Courtesy Scat Enterprises)

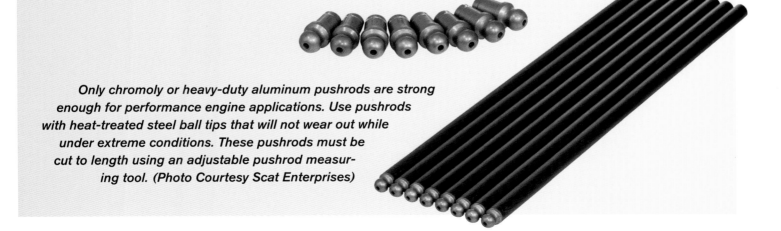

Only chromoly or heavy-duty aluminum pushrods are strong enough for performance engine applications. Use pushrods with heat-treated steel ball tips that will not wear out while under extreme conditions. These pushrods must be cut to length using an adjustable pushrod measuring tool. (Photo Courtesy Scat Enterprises)

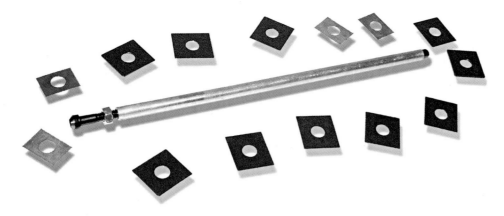

Cutting and assembling pushrods can be difficult. For this reason, use an adjustable pushrod for any hope of achieving optimal rocker geometry, such as the EMPI pushrod measuring tool (part number 16-9600). Adjust out, lock down, measure, and cut the pushrods. Use the adjustable pushrod tool to cut the pushrods to the desired length. Then, tap in the ends using a hammer and two old lifters. Sometimes, depending on the pushrod brand, they have to be drilled out to match the pushrod ends. (Photo Courtesy Scat Enterprises)

get away with just heavy-duty single springs. Dual valve springs are available from a number of sources, but the valve-guide boss on stock cylinder heads requires machining for the springs to fit. Most of the aftermarket high-performance heads listed here come assembled with stronger valve springs. When upgrading to these valve springs, also upgrade the pushrods and rocker arms.

Use aluminum pushrods because they are quieter when they get hot. Some firms sell mild steel pushrods and label them as chromoly, but they may not be, so check what you are buying. Pushrods must be the correct length because the pushrod length changes as the engine width changes. Using the proper-length pushrod ensures that the rocker arm is pushing the valve straight in at the half-lift point. If rocker geometry is off, the valve will be pushed up or down, resulting in excessive valve-guide wear.

If the compression ratio was changed by fly cutting or the camshaft and rocker-arm assemblies were changed, measure the camshaft lift and cut the pushrods to fit the new valvetrain geometry. The correct rocker-arm positioning is important to avoid wearing out the rocker's valves and springs.

If these values are not correct, there could be camshaft failure, especially if the valve springs are allowed to coil bind at maximum lift. This will require the use of an adjustable dummy pushrod that is available from either Scat (part number 20204) or EMPI (part number 16-9600). It is a good idea to build a mockup engine to ensure that everything is okay with the bottom then and now with the heads installed, checking for the correct valvetrain geometry.

Rocker Geometry Setting Procedure

1. Install hardened valve lash caps on the valve stems when using stainless-steel valves, which will spread the load between the valve stem and the rocker contact area.

2. Place the rocker assembly onto the two studs on the rocker-arm pedestal (use new studs) and see if the rocker assembly bosses bottom out on the pedestals without any rocking.

3. If they do not bottom out, remove the rocker and install a 0.015-inch shim on each pedestal. Then, reinstall the rocker assembly that will allow the rocker assembly to sit flat on the head.

4. Adjust the adjustable pushrod to a length that allows fit in between the lifter and rocker arm for cylinder number-1 intake valve, lubricated at both ends.

5. Rotate the engine to TDC for the number-1 cylinder, and the adjustable pushrod will drop.

6. Torque the rocker-arm assembly to 14 ft-lbs, back out the valve adjustment screw all the way, and then turn it back in a half turn and tighten the lock nut.

7. Adjust the pushrod to zero lash, which is when there is no end-play in the rocker arm.

8. Now, rotate the crankshaft clockwise until the number-1 intake valve is fully open. This is when the rocker moves as far as it will go.

9. Install a dial indicator so the button rests on the number-1 intake valve spring retainer with 1/2 inch preload and lock it in place.

10. Rotate the crankshaft counterclockwise until it reaches the maximum lift for the camshaft. We will use 0.420 inch for this example.

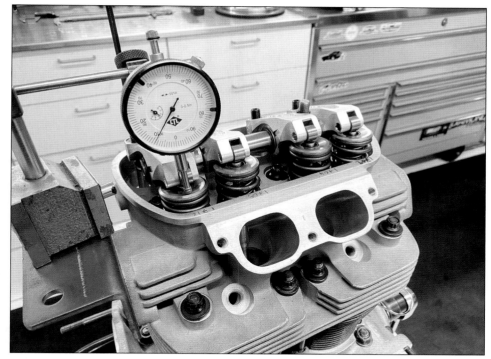

When mounting the dial indicator button on the valve-spring retainer, make sure the plunger will rotate the dial enough to measure over 0.450 inch. (Photo Courtesy ACE Performance Engines, Stefan Rossi)

design. The stock rocker ratio was 1:1 on early 40-bhp engines. Volkswagen changed the rocker-arm ratio to 1.1:1 on late 40-bhp engines and on the later 1,300-, 1,500-, and 1,600-cc engines.

The rocker-arm ratio is the relationship between pushrod and valve movement. A VW stock camshaft with 0.300-inch lift opens the valve 0.300 inch with 1:1 rockers and 0.330 inch with 1.1:1 rockers. If running at higher RPM (about 4,500 rpm) and using heavy-duty valve springs or a high-performance camshaft, the stock rocker assemblies will fail. The solution is to either strengthen the existing rocker assembly or install the better alternative.

To strengthen a stock rocker assembly, simply shim it by removing the wave washers and replacing them with solid washers. These washers come in varying thicknesses: 0.015, 0.030, and 0.060 inch. Try different ones until the combination that gives about 0.005 inch per rocker side clearance is found. A rocker shim kit costs about $10. If

11. If the valvetrain geometry is correct, the rocker ends will be parallel with the gasket surface of the cylinder head.

12. If this is not so, add shims, which are available in 0.015, 0.030, and 0.060 inch.

13. Each time the shim thickness increases, readjust the adjustable pushrod.

14. After the rocker ends are parallel with the cylinder head, remove the adjustable pushrod and measure it. Next, the pushrod sets can be cut to length using a plumber's tubing cutter.

15. Clean out the cut end using the tubing cutter's sharp end and blow out any debris with an air gun.

16. Install the hardened end into the cut pushrod using two discarded lifters.

17. Reassemble the rocker shafts and adjust the valves to 0.006 inch.

Rocker Arms

The original VW rocker arms are only good for street use. They are too weak for high-performance applications that exceed the stock

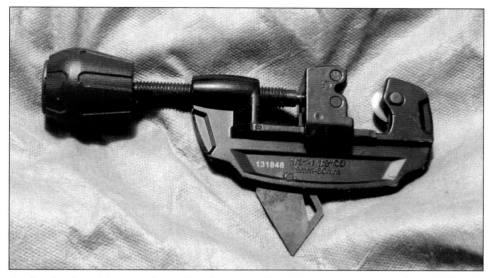

A plumber's tubing or pipe cutter is a good tool to get an even and parallel cut on each pushrod. It is much better than using a hacksaw. Most of these cutters have a triangular blade used to clean out the hole.

using dual valve springs, then solid rocker shafts with bolt-on ends are needed.

The alternative to stock rocker arms is to use a different ratio rocker, such as the EMPI kit (part number 17-2954). Rocker kits are bolt-on kits with all the modifications discussed previously. Rockers are available from 1.1:1 to 1.5:1 ratio that provide an increase in valve lift. It should also be noted that the camshaft has a limitation on how fast it can accelerate the lifter and the valvetrain. This means that the rocker arm can only open the valve so far before it has to start closing the valve again. A different-ratio rocker arm helps overcome this limitation because it multiplies the lift.

The stock camshaft will work well with ratio rocker upgrades as bolt-on horsepower. There are also specially designed camshafts that are used with ratio rockers. The benefit of a ratio rocker camshaft is that it can get more valve lift without losing engine life. However, a ratio rocker

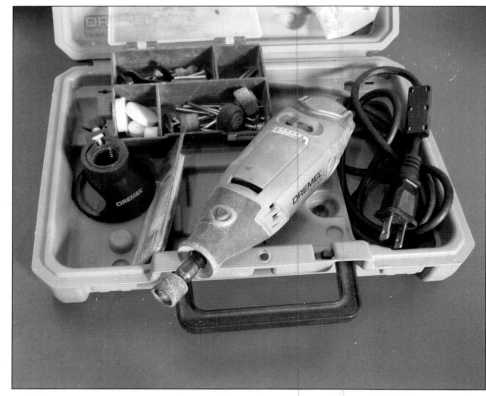

Cylinder head porting tools and accessories are used by engine builders to open up and smooth intake and exhaust ports for better breathing. They will port or smooth rough head castings around the intake and exhaust ports for smoother airflow. The engine can develop more power and efficiency. It can improve fuel efficiency, giving more miles to the gallon as you roar around a track or down the highway.

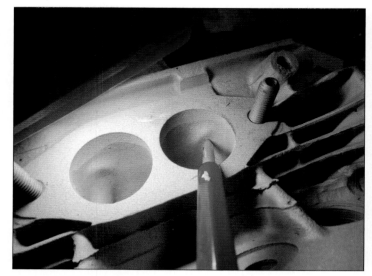

Resist the temptation to eliminate the tiny bump that protrudes into the port next to the manifold flange. That bump is the outer edge of the valve-spring seat, and it should not be ground away.

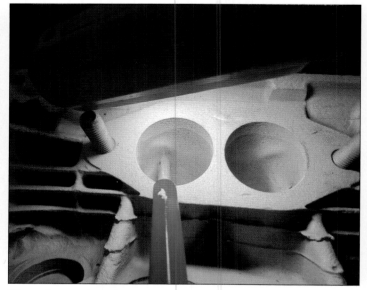

There is another tiny bump in the dual intake port. That bump is the outer edge of the other intake valve-spring seat. Do not grind this one either.

set is more expensive. A ratio rocker camshaft can still be used with a stock rocker assembly. The camshaft will last, but there will not be any performance gains.

Porting

Porting is a term that is used to refer to the modifications of the valve pockets behind the valves and ports connecting the valve pockets to the intake and exhaust manifold flanges. For many years, engine modifiers would hollow out the ports, but they could wind up making holes in the port walls. If the pocket behind the valve could be opened up to the inner dimension of the valve seating surface, many modifiers would not hesitate to do that. Not much attention was paid to the combustion chamber into which the valves open. In some instances, a ported head sometimes seems to detract from the low-RPM performance of the engine.

If you have access to a flowbench, you can test the head after it is ported. Heads can also be purchased from one of the VW high-performance component manufacturers, where they may provide some flowbench figures for their heads. The use of a flowbench has caused many engine builders to become more conscious of intake manifold design requirements, including the size of the carburetor or fuel system that is feeding the engine. Many ported heads can actually flow less air than the stock heads, so it's important to follow some guidelines if doing any head porting.

1,600 Dual-Port Heads

Valve shrouding takes place when the edge of the valve is too close to the combustion-chamber

Start working on straightening the port rudder to flow toward the valve with the stock guide in place.

Smoothing out the radius starts under the seat with a porting tool. The stock valve guide may need to be removed to perform this operation.

wall, which makes it hard for the air-fuel mixture to go around the valve. Some engine builders make this gap larger for greater airflow. Porting can increase the gap in this area so the valves work in and out of the combustion chamber to increase airflow.

In the intake port, the following modifications can be done without removing the guide from the port. First, grind the valves as described previously in this chapter and seat the valves with lapping compound. Radius the seats by taking emery paper and removing any sharp edges on the seats. Radius the inside corner. Leave the connection below the seat intact.

From the intake-manifold side, match the manifold and head flanges so that the flange does not project to the manifold runners. Radius the port at the side closest to the rocker-cover flange, blending the opening into the port rudder with a gentle radius. Smooth the port toward the valve from the manifold side. Do not remove the bump at the top side of the port closest to the rocker chamber. The port is very thin at this area.

If opening the port at the area closest to the rocker chamber, a hole

After the performance valve job, the valves should be sunk approximately 0.100 inch. This gives a broad entry angle to the chamber floor, which will help airflow.

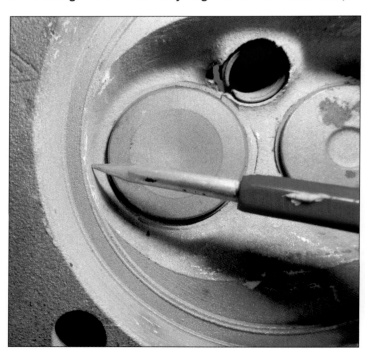

Use a porting tool radius (or round off the port runner) to straighten the mixture path to improve the air and fuel flow.

Smooth out this area on the non-plug side for slight flow improvement. Clay can be used to correct mistakes on a test head. This can be done after fly cutting to increase the compression ratio.

may be created. If this happens, the hole will have to be welded. You can use a 1/4-inch radius file for the width of the valve at the end of the chamber, taking the end of the chamber out of the bore diameter. The non-plug side of the chamber can be laid back slightly on dual-port heads only. The job is pretty much done, as any other chamber modifications will cause the port to flow less air.

I am covering the 1,600-series dual-port heads. The goal is to achieve the best flow through the stock intake valve, which is what we are dealing with in this section. The challenge is to leave the combustion-chamber shape alone with some minor exceptions.

Split-Port Cylinder Heads

Scat sells a high-performance ported split cylinder head for the Type 1 1,600-cc engines and 1,700/1,800-cc Type 4 engines in four different bore sizes from 90.5 to 105 mm. These heads can be used with fuel injection or Weber and Dellorto carburetors along with turbochargers.

For maximum performance, I suggest purchasing heads from EMPI or Scat that have been professionally ported. These heads also incorporate a swirl combustion chamber that improves the air and fuel mix and compresses the mixture better while speeding up the flame travel to increase horsepower and improve cooling. These heads have cooling fins for 360 degrees of head cooling. They use equal-length cylinder studs so that the head sealing is improved between the barrel and the head. (Photo Courtesy Scat Enterprises)

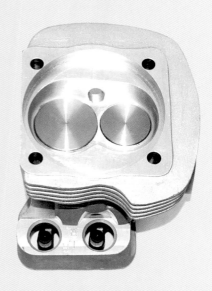

The split-port head valves open toward the center of the cylinder, which increases the intake and exhaust mixture flow by more than 20 percent over the best 1,600-type dual-port performance heads. They have a reduced valve angle of 6 degrees (compared to 9 degrees on a dual-port head), so the valves become unshrouded. (Photo Courtesy Scat Enterprises)

IGNITION SYSTEM AND UPGRADES

For combustion to be controlled and occur properly, several tuning parameters and engine parts must perform within suitable parameters. The air-fuel mixture must not be too lean. The cooling system must remove heat efficiently. High-octane fuel is needed if the compression ratio is high. Over-advanced timing can raise combustion-chamber pressures drastically and raise combustion-chamber temperatures.

Detonation

Detonation takes place when an expanding combustion flame front compresses and heats a portion of the air-fuel mixture in a corner of the combustion chamber that is already at a very high temperature. A portion of the air-fuel mixture explodes before the flame front can get to it. This explosion creates a second pressure wave in the combustion chamber that causes the cylinder pressures to rise at an uncontrolled rate, raising cylinder temperatures above acceptable limits.

This second pressure wave in the combustion chamber collides with the cylinder wall and the piston top. This collision causes the cylinder walls to vibrate and sound like a bell ringing with the distinctive pinging sound. Note that diesel engine knock takes place at the beginning of the combustion cycle as opposed to gasoline engine spark-knock (detonation) that takes place at the end of the combustion cycle.

Mild detonation causes a loss of power and efficiency because part of the thermal energy in the gasoline is wasted and produces no useable power. It can also increase the rate of engine wear with these high cylinder pressures increasing the loads on the pistons, rings, connecting rods, crankshaft, and bearings. Uncontrolled detonation can create enough pressure to break pistons.

Detonation is a secondary ignition of the air-fuel mixture that is caused by high cylinder temperatures. It is commonly called "pinging" or "knocking."

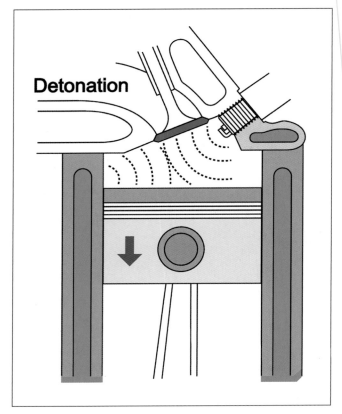

Detonation

The most common cause of detonation is advanced ignition timing, full throttle acceleration, a compression ratio that is too high, high operating temperatures, spark plugs that are too hot, or lean mixtures. Detonation in VW air-cooled engines can be a problem. The cylinder pressures of severe detonation can blow a head gasket or crack the main bearing caps, the cylinder head, or the engine block. This level of damage can occur in a racing engine but seldom occurs in a street vehicle unless left uncontrolled.

Preignition

There is another important difference between detonation and preignition. Unlike detonation, which makes a characteristic noise, preignition is silent, despite what is often written in some automotive texts.

The confusion developed because preignition and detonation often take place at the same time.

Preignition can raise pressure and heat in the cylinder to the point of causing detonation. If the point of preignition occurs at a place in the combustion chamber far from the spark plug, two flame fronts consume the intake charge. The unburned portion of the air-fuel mixture that is trapped between the two advancing flame fronts is compressed and superheated, which causes it to detonate.

Preignition Causes
- Hot spots inside the combustion chamber, such as spark plug threads, can protrude into the combustion chamber or sharp edges on a piston top can become hot enough to ignite the charge.
- Carbon deposits in the combustion chamber can ignite the charge.

- Spark plugs can have too hot of a heat range, which means the electrode does not dissipate heat fast enough and may get hot enough to ignite the charge without a spark.
- Cross-firing occurs where electrical induction between spark plug wires takes place because the plug wires are cracked and the spark can jump from wire to wire.
- Prolonged preignition can create enough heat to melt spark plug electrodes, valve heads, and combustion chamber surfaces or burn holes in piston crowns.

Ignition System

The automotive ignition system includes components and wiring necessary to create and distribute a voltage up to 40,000 volts or greater. Ignition systems apply battery voltage to the ignition coil positive side and pulse the negative side to ground. When the coil negative lead is grounded, the primary (low-voltage) circuit of the coil is complete and a magnetic field is created by the coil windings.

When the circuit is opened, the magnetic field collapses and induces high voltage in the secondary winding of the ignition coil. This is used to generate a voltage great enough to bridge a gap across the spark plug electrodes, creating a spark. The early ignition systems used a set of contact points to make and break the electrical connection to ground. Electronic ignition uses a sensor, such as a pickup coil or a hall-effect switch, to signal an electronic module to make and break the ignition coil primary side ground.

When the ignition switch is turned on, voltage should be available at both the positive terminal and

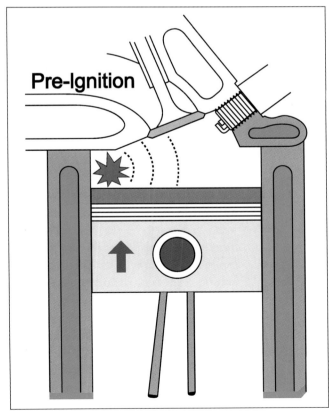

Pre-Ignition

Another form of abnormal combustion is called preignition, which is the result of the air-fuel mixture being ignited too early, before the spark plug fires. This is the main difference between detonation and preignition. Detonation always occurs after the spark plug fires, and preignition takes place before the spark.

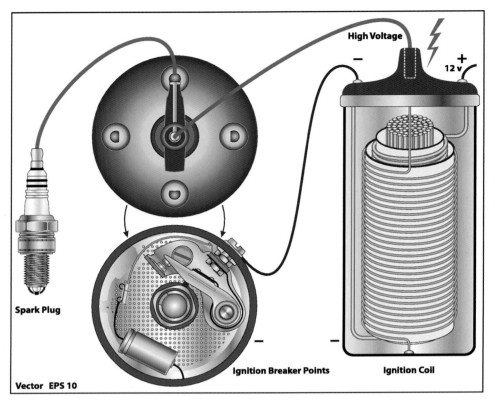

Spark Plug

High Voltage

12 v

Ignition Breaker Points

Ignition Coil

Vector EPS 10

The primary windings of the coil extend through the case of the coil and are labeled as positive and negative. The positive terminal of the coil attaches to the ignition, which supplies current from the positive battery terminal at battery voltage. The negative terminal is attached to contact points or the ignition control module (ICM) or igniter, which opens and closes the primary ignition circuit by opening or closing the circuit ground. (Graphic Courtesy Shutterstock)

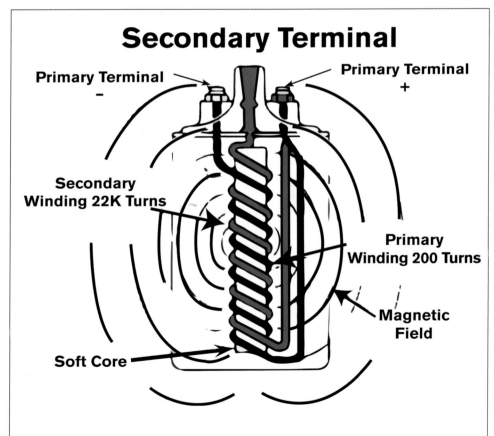

Secondary Terminal

Primary Terminal –

Primary Terminal +

Secondary Winding 22K Turns

Primary Winding 200 Turns

Magnetic Field

Soft Core

The center of an ignition coil has a core of laminated soft iron. This core increases the magnetic strength of the coil. Surrounding the laminated core are approximately 20,000 turns of fine wire. These windings are the secondary coil windings. Surrounding the secondary windings are approximately 150 turns of heavy wire, which is the primary coil winding. The secondary winding has approximately 100 times the number of turns of the primary winding, which is referred to as the turn ratio (100:1). The primary and secondary windings produce heat because of the electrical resistance in the turns of wire, so some early coils contained oil to help cool the ignition coil.

the negative terminal of the coil. The labeling of positive (+) and negative (-) of the coil indicates that the positive terminal is more positive (closer to the battery positive terminal) than the negative terminal of the coil. This is referred to as coil polarity.

Coil polarity positive or negative is established by the direction of the coil: to the left or to the right. The correct polarity is then indicated on the primary terminals of the coil. If the coil primary leads were reversed, the voltage required to fire the spark plugs is increased by 40 percent. The coil output voltage is directly proportional to the ratio of primary to secondary turns of wire used in the coil.

Ignition Coils

The ignition coil creates a high-voltage spark by electromagnetic induction (EMI). The principle of EMI states that when a magnetic field crosses or cuts across a conductor, a voltage is induced in that conductor. Some automotive ignition coils are true step-up transformers in which the primary and secondary windings are not electrically connected.

Self-Induction

When current begins to flow into a coil, an opposing current is created in the windings of the coil. This opposing current generation is caused by self-induction and is called inductive reactance. Inductive reactance is equivalent to resistance because it opposes any increase in current flow in a coil.

When an ignition coil is first energized, there is a slight delay of approximately 0.01 second before the induction (ignition) coil

reaches its maximum magnetic field strength. The point at which a coil's maximum magnetic field strength is reached is termed saturation. If it is switched to a capacitor-discharge ignition (CDI) system, it has very little self-induction because the discharge of capacitors saturates the ignition coil.

Mutual Induction

An induction (ignition) coil uses two windings: a primary and a secondary. When a change occurs within the magnetic flux of the primary winding, it'll induce a current within the other secondary winding. So, if the current is stopped from flowing (circuit open), the collapsing flux cuts across the turns of the secondary winding and creates a high voltage in the secondary winding.

When two coils are brought in close proximity to each other, the magnetic field in one coil tends to link with the other coil. This generates voltage within the second coil. This magnetic property of a coil affecting or changing the voltage in another coil is called mutual induction. The collapsing magnetic flux also creates a voltage of up to 250 volts within the coil.

Creating 40,000 Volts Under the Hood

All ignition systems use electromagnetic induction (EMI) to produce a high-voltage spark from the ignition coil based on the work of Michael Faraday. EMI means that a current can be created in a conductor (coil winding) by a moving magnetic field across a conductor.

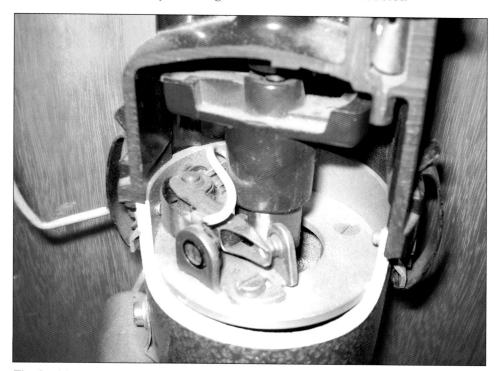

The ignition components that control the current in the coil primary winding by turning it on and off are known as the primary ignition circuit. The components necessary to create and distribute the high voltage produced in the secondary windings of the coil are called the secondary ignition circuit.

When the primary circuit is closed, a current of 2 to 6 amperes can flow through the primary coil windings, which creates a strong magnetic field inside the coil. When the primary coil winding ground return path connection is opened, the magnetic field collapses and induces a voltage from 250 to 400 volts in the primary windings of the coil and a high-voltage (20,000 to 40,000 volts) low-amperage (20 to 80 mA) current in the secondary coil windings.

This high-voltage pulse flows through the coil wire to the distributor cap, rotor, and spark plug wires to the spark plugs. For each spark that occurs, the coil must be charged with a magnetic field and then discharged.

Ignition System Selection

The stock VW ignition system can be used if it is a mild build or street vehicle with a stronger coil. It is possible to upgrade to a distributor-based or crankshaft position (CKP) sensor–based electronic or capacitive discharge ignition (CDI) system if the engine is for racing/off-road or uses electronic fuel injection and a turbocharger.

The MSD 6AL CDI system can be triggered by an electronic trigger or breaker points. The CDI system will fire plugs that are even worn out. Detonation and preignition should figure into the ignition system operation with regard to ignition timing.

The ignition system does not increase acceleration and top speed or horsepower. Electronic ignition systems will reduce ignition point maintenance and are generally more reliable than breaker point ignition systems. An electronic ignition upgrade kit can be purchased for about $50, where new points and a condenser is about $25 on a reoccurring basis. Another reason to consider electronic ignition is that the standard VW breaker points can float or bounce at high speeds unless using a heavy-duty spring.

Distributors

In the past, Volkswagen used a number of different distributors that are no longer available. However, there are aftermarket companies that offer different distributors and ignition systems to meet the needs of a build. EMPI, Scat, JBugs, Air Cooled, and Gene Berg Enterprises have a large assortment of replacement ignition distributors and also offer a PerTronix Ignitor electronic ignition for use on Bosch 009 or 010 Distributors.

Basically, there are three types of spark advance identifiable by how the spark was advanced from its base setting from 7.5 to 10 degrees before TDC. There is an all-mechanical or centrifugal advance distributor, a combination vacuum and centrifugal advance distributor, and an all-vacuum advance distributor. All of the different Bosch distributors out there fall into one of these three categories, except for electronic capacitor discharge. The distributor ignition system must have an advance system so the engine will produce sufficient power.

Some engine builders choose a bus or transporter distributor (part number 211-905-205F). Look for a spark advance of 28 to 34 degrees before TDC at 2,500 rpm. EMPI offers a point-type single-vacuum advance distributor and a centrifugal advance distributor that has the same advance curve as the Bosch 0-231-178-009 distributor. This distributor will give the 28 degrees before TCC at 2,500 rpm. EMPI (part number 9441-B) is a centrifugal advance distributor with electronic ignition, eliminating the points and condenser. It also has the same advance curve as the Bosch 009 distributor.

Typical timing advance is completed by 3,500 rpm. The Bosch distributors of the past are well made. If you can get one of the 0-231-178-009 units with the centrifugal advance, this would be a good

---

Primary Ignition Circuit

1. Battery
2. Ignition switch
3. Primary windings of coil
4. Ignition points or other solid-state triggering switches
5. Solid-state ignition module or igniter
6. CDI unit

Secondary Ignition Circuit

1. Secondary windings of coil
2. Distributor cap and rotor unless distributorless unit
3. Spark plug wires
4. Spark plugs

Distributors

EMPI Stock Distributors and Upgrade Kits

Two models of centrifugal advance distributors are available with the same advance curve and the same tune-up components as the Bosch 0-231-178-009: EMPI Centrifugal Advance Distributor with standard curve (part number 9431-B) and EMPI Chrome Centrifugal Advance Distributor with standard curve (part number 9428-B).

A Chrome Vacuum Advance Distributor (part number 9440-B) is available with the same advance curve as the Bosch 0-231-178-009009 distributor with points, cap, rotor, condenser, and O-ring.

A Cast Steel Distributor (painted black) (part number 9471-B) is available with the same advance curve as the Bosch 0-231-178-009 distributor.

Scat Stock Distributors

Scat offers Flame-Thrower and Point-Type Bosch Centrifugal Advance VW Distributors (part number 0-231-178-009) for all Type 1–3 applications. They use 22 degrees total advance at 2,600 rpm. The distributor is retarded 3 degrees on number-3 cylinder to reduce cylinder head temperature.

JBugs Stock Distributors

JBugs sells the Bosch Style 009 Centrifugal Advance VW Distributor (Code: 0231178009) as well as the Kuhltek Vintage Cast Iron Mechanical Advance VW Distributor (Code: 0231178010).

Air Cooled

Air Cooled offers replacement parts for stock distributors, such as points and condenser along with electronic ignition upgrade kits.

Gene Berg Enterprises

Gene Berg offers replacement parts for stock distributors such as points and condenser along with electronic ignition upgrade kits. They offer a points set with a heavy-duty spring (part number GB 622A) for high-RPM operation in a street machine. ■

One of the most popular distributors was the Bosch distributor (part number 231-178-009). The distributors were made by both Volkswagen and Robert Bosch. When Volkswagen built these engines, there were many different Bosch distributors. (Photo Courtesy Shutterstock)

pick. Then, add the EMPI number 9432 kit to upgrade the distributor to electronic ignition.

Remember that a coil with an internal resistance or a separate external ballast resistor must be used. The Bosch points distributor (part number 0-231-178-009) was designed to run at a maximum of 5,500 rpm, but it can go above this RPM until points float or bounce. If the points float, this changes ignition timing with possible misfires and engine damage.

Advance Curves

Increased advance in the lower RPM range is generally used in vehicles that will be engaged in an acceleration contest, such as drag racing. This is because the engine passes through the low RPM range very quickly or is not used at all. Also, long overlap cams pump part of the

The stock ignition can be improved by upgrading the 009 distributor to an electronic ignition using the PerTronix kit or others available from Scat, EMPI, Gene Berg, or Air Cooled. Test the advance curve prior to installation in the engine by placing the distributor in an older Sun distributor machine. (Photo Courtesy James Halderman)

fuel charge back into the manifolds at low speeds even at full throttle, which will reduce the density of the charge and allow more advanced to be used. Mechanical advanced changes can provide significant full throttle acceleration.

When the distributor advance curves change, the initial setting can be increased by the number of crankshaft degrees. Experiment with initial timing settings to determine the optimum position just short of any detonation. Make sure that the checks are done with the exhaust system installed so you can listen to the engine. If using an older distributor, make sure that the shaft cannot be wiggled sideways in the housing and the plate that holds the ignition module is secure. If the plate wobbles, get another distributor.

In the engineering world, it has been stated that there is an optimum spark timing for any combination of engine running conditions that result in maximum mean effective pressure and thermal efficiency. This timing is termed as minimum advance for best torque (MBT).

Setting Ignition Timing on a Dynamometer

If the ignition timing is set on the chassis dynamometer, it may be too advanced, causing detonation that typically results in engine damage. This takes place because the dynamometer operator will move the distributor for the best timing light flash reading, and it may be too advanced because timing is typically not set under load.

The engine is unloaded during all factory timing light settings. This may not apply with digital timing lights. Detonation can occur when the engine is not allowed to take advantage of combustion-chamber turbulence because spark plug temperature is increased by advancing the timing. Air-cooled engines usually cannot tolerate excessive spark advance because there are already enough issues with regard to keeping it from overheating. If close to 32 degrees of total advance, you're probably going to hear some detonation. Try increasing the size of the main jet, as running slightly richer may help.

Coil

Replace the stock coil with the Bosch Blue Coil, which is also available from EMPI (part number 9409-B), if you are still using ignition

Scat sells the MSD 8202 Blaster 2 with a 45,000-volt maximum output.

The MSD Pro Power performance coil (part number 8201) and Chrome Blaster 2 (part number 8200) have 45,000 volts (resister included). (Photo Courtesy Holley)

In 1975, the high-energy-ignition (HEI) distributor system was developed by General Motors and has been copied by many racing and high-performance ignition system manufacturers, including Holley MSD (formerly Mallory). The PerTronix Flame-Thrower is used on VW air-cooled engines in many street and track racing engines. The HEI coil was shaped like an "E" and was called an E-Coil. (Photo Courtesy iStock)

points. Scat, EMPI, Gene Berg, and Air Cooled also offer the Compu-fire High Output Coil (part number 17-2959), which can be used with either breaker points or an electronic ignition setup. This coil is epoxy filled and produces 40,000 volts of power. The primary resistance in this coil is 3 ohms, and no ballast resistor is needed when using this coil.

Electronic Ignition

With the old points–type ignitions, the points were the ground control switch for the coil to turn the primary coil circuit on and off. In an electronic system the primary circuit current is controlled by a power transistor (switching device) inside the ignition module or igniter, which is controlled by one of the following triggering devices.

Pickup Coil (Pulse Generator)

The rotation of the distributor shaft is used to time voltage pulses. The pickup coil, which is a magnetic pulse generator, is installed in the distributor housing. This magnetic generator uses a trigger wheel (reluctor) and a pickup coil.

The pickup coil is composed of an iron core surrounded by wire coil at one end and a permanent magnet at the other end. The coil center is called a pole piece. The pickup coil signal turns on a transistor inside an ignition module or controller that is used by the engine control module for piston position information and engine speed. Mechanical ignition points used in the past would just mechanically open and close the coil primary ground.

Hall-Effect Switch

The Hall-Effect switch requires a small input voltage to generate an output or signal voltage. The Hall-Effect is a voltage, which is dependent upon a magnetic field. The Hall-Effect switch generates a voltage signal in semiconductor material by passing current through it in one direction and applying a magnetic field to it at a right angle. If the input current is constant and the magnetic field fluctuates, an output voltage is generated that changes in relation to the strength of the magnetic field.

Most Hall-Effect switches have a Hall element, a permanent magnet, and a rotating ring of metal trigger wheel. When the trigger wheel blade crosses the gap between the magnet and the Hall element, it creates a magnetic shunt or bypass that alters the magnetic field strength through the Hall element and creates a voltage signal. The transistor transmits a digital square waveform at varying frequency to the ignition module or controlling computer. Hall-Effect switches are used as the switching device on most of the VW electronic ignition upgrade kits.

Electronic Ignition

Electronic ignition is the way I would go in a high-performance VW engine that runs at high RPM. A centrifugal advance distributor such as the Bosch distributor 009 or 010 is needed as a base. You then upgrade it to electronic switching control from points by using one of the following kits:

Gene Berg Enterprises sells an igniter ignition for high RPM (up to 6,000 rpm). It also sells the Compufire electronic ignition under part number GB 624C.

The EMPI electronic ignition upgrade kit (part number 9432) fits all distributors that used Bosch 044 ignition points. This kit must be used with a coil that has an internal resistor or add an external resistor.

The EMPI Accu-Fire electronic ignition kit for 0-231-178-009 Bosch distributors uses Bosch 044 points. This kit also works with EMPI distributors (part numbers 9431-B, 9428-B, and 9441-B). Coil specifications are Primary 3.4 ohms, Secondary 7.8 ohms.

The PerTronix Ignitor electronic ignition upgrade kit is an easily installed upgrade kit for a points distributor of the Bosch 0-231-178-009 design. The ignitor, which is the control module that replaces the points, will deliver twice the voltage to the spark plugs and feature an adaptive dwell (time for coil build up).

The Scat Compufire electronic ignition kit (part number CF11100) delivers 60,000-plus volts for the Bosch-type 009/010 distributor. This is another upgrade kit

that converts the existing standard points-and-condenser ignition system into an electronic ignition. There is no points float, and it is more weather resistant and provides better ignition timing and a more consistent spark. It uses the existing distributor to house the trigger sensor.

Electronic Distributor

EMPI's centrifugal advance distributor with electronic ignition (part number 9441-B) eliminates the points and condenser. Use a coil with an internal resistor or a separate external ballast resistor standard curve similar to Bosch 231-178-009.

EMPI part number 9437B is an electronic single-vacuum advance distributor with a magnetic pickup and amplifier attached to the distributor, and it is also an option. The advance curve begins at 1,000 rpm with a total of 18-degree centrifugal advance at 2,400 rpm with 10-degree vacuum advance. It will require a Bosch Blue or other high-energy coil (3.4 ohms primary/12k ohms secondary) with a built-in resistor. You can use an external ballast resistor between the power source and distributor if the coil does not have a built-in resistor.

Scat Ignitor II Plug N Play VW distributor and coil (part number D180810) is an electronic ignition distributor direct replacement unit with a hardened shaft for extreme durability. It has an extra spring set included for custom curving. It should be used with the Chrome Flame-Thrower II Coil (part number 45001) at 45,000 volts.

Distributorless Ignition System

The distributorless ignition system (DIS) is also called an electronic

ignition (EI) or a waste-spark ignition. This system uses a computer or a controller to operate the ignition coils. A four-cylinder engine, like a VW, uses two ignition coils, each coil operating two spark plugs. Each coil is a step-up real transformer, where the primary winding and secondary coil winding are not electrically connected as in most coils.

Each end of the secondary winding is connected to a cylinder exactly opposite the other cylinder in firing order, which is called a companion or paired cylinder. What this means is that both spark plugs fire at the same time. When cylinder number 1 is on the compression stroke, its companion cylinder number 4 is on the exhaust stroke or what is called TDC overlap.

The spark that occurs on the exhaust stroke at number 4, for example, is called the waste spark because it does no useful work and is used as the ground path for the secondary ignition coil winding. The voltage required to jump the spark plug gap on cylinder 4 on the exhaust stroke is only 2 to 3 kilovolts and provides the ground circuit for the secondary coil circuit.

The remaining coil energy is used by the cylinder on the compression stroke of number-1 cylinder. One spark plug of each pair always fires straight polarity and the other cylinder always fires reverse polarity.

The Dub Shop offers a distributorless system in conjunction with its electronic fuel-injection system. It requires the installation of a crankshaft position reluctor type of crankshaft pulley with 36 points and a crankshaft position (CKP) sensor behind the pulley.

The Compufire DIS ignition system called for Volkswagen to stop using a distributor altogether. It eliminates the points, rotor, condenser, and even the distributor cap. The high-energy coil fires direct to the plugs, having received the signal from an electronic sensor. It's totally waterproof, dustproof, and dirtproof, and it fires alternate cylinders simultaneously for cleaner, more efficient fuel burn. It requires a centrifugal advance distributor (EMPI part number 9431B or an equivalent) to obtain an engine RPM and triggering signal. (Photo Courtesy Scat Enterprises)

The MSD Pro CDI ignition uses an optical sensor that uses light from a light-emitting diode (LED) and a phototransistor to signal the engine controller or computer to turn off the primary current. An interrupter disc between the LED and the phototransistor has slits that allow the light from the LED to trigger the phototransistor on the other side of the disc. Most optical sensors located inside the distributor use two rows of slits to provide individual cylinder recognition (low-resolution) and precise distributor angle recognition (high-resolution) signals.

Magneto Ignition

A magneto is like an alternator that generates a spark without the use of outside voltage from a battery. It produces pulses of high current to the spark plugs. Manufacturers may use the term tension instead of voltage or high tension, which is high voltage.

In a magneto, the engine rotates a magnet inside a stationary primary coil between the poles of a magnet. This coil is like the stator of an alternator. During each revolution, a cam opens the contact breaker points one or more times, which interrupts the primary current and causes the electromagnetic field in the primary coil to collapse. Due to the collapse of the magnetic field, voltage is induced across the first coil. Due to the opening of the breaker points, an arc goes across the breaker points. A capacitor

The MSD Digital 6AL is rated at 10,000 rpm and 45,000 volts. It is specifically designed for high-performance street or bracket racing and contains rev-control to protect the engine from over-revving.

Some engine builders still use a magneto ignition system. It was used in the past by many drag and circle track racers. Many of these race vehicles are pushed into gear to get them started, so a battery and starter are not needed. A magneto ignition could be used if this is the intended use for the engine.

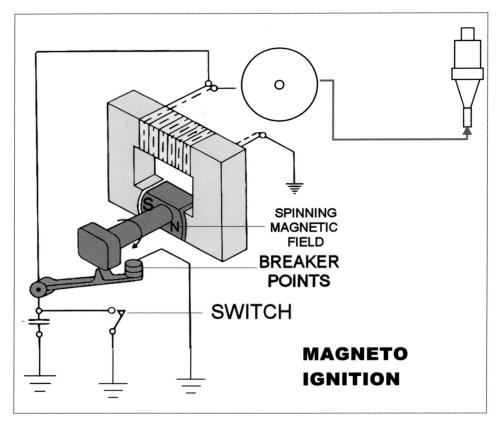

is placed across the points to suppress the arc.

A secondary coil, with more than 100 times as many turns as the primary coil, is located next to the primary coil. So, if the primary coil had 200 turns, the secondary coil would have 20,000 turns (100 x 200). When the primary current is opened by the breaker points, a voltage is induced across the secondary coil.

The amount of voltage developed by the collapse of the magnetic field across the secondary ignition coil is determined by the turns ratio in a magneto. This voltage will be large enough to arc across the spark plug gap burning any fuel.

Capacitive Discharge Ignition

Multiple spark discharge (MSD) will produce a series of sparks every firing of the spark plugs. This is due to capacitor discharge into the ignition coil. Capacitive discharge ignition (CDI) systems are a solid-state version of the magneto ignition system.

In CDI systems, the breaker points are replaced by an analog or a solid-state transformer. It is found in some racing vehicles, such as NASCAR. The CDI system does not have the long charging times found

A magneto is a self-contained ignition device that was used in alcohol-fueled internal-combustion engines to produce a very high current to ignite the alcohol fuel. This type of ignition system is primarily found on lawn mowers, small tractors, chain saws, alcohol-fueled drag racers, and small aircraft engines. Magnetos have used the term tension *in place of the term* voltage *in the past, and the term* high tension *is used to mean* high voltage.

in high-inductance ignition coils. So, it was more suitable for small engines and racing engines.

CDI systems use the discharge current output from a high-voltage capacitor to jump the electrodes in a spark plug. A charging circuit charges a high-voltage capacitor, and when ignition points open or the electronic triggering device operates, the system then stops charging the capacitor. This allows it to discharge its voltage to an induction coil before going to the spark plug.

The standard VW points-type ignition system is an inductive ignition system. It relies on the mutual inductance of a primary and a secondary coil to collapse the magnetic field and dump high voltage through a core to jump the spark plug gap. This takes place because the mag-

netic field breaks down when the current to the primary coil winding is opened, which is called a disruptive discharge.

A CDI system incorporates a short charging cycle with a fast voltage rise as compared to the induction-type ignition coil. However, the spark line is short and isn't sensitive to shunt (bypass) resistance thanks to the fast voltage rise. The limited spark duration can be too short to provide reliable street vehicle ignition. The fix for a short spark duration was a CDI module that fires the spark plug multiple times when the spark is below 3,000 to 3,500 rpm, such as module MSD 6AL.

Above this RPM, even a multi-spark ignition only has enough time to fire once. The question is whether it is more important to have

a medium-intensity, long-duration spark or a very high-intensity, short-duration spark. I find that in racing applications, the multi-spark CDI approach has become the leading-edge system.

Ignition spark energy is measured in millijoules (mJ). A standard VW induction-type ignition system will deliver about 25 mJ. An average CDI system delivers 50 mJ, and the MSD 6AL has 135mJ of spark energy with an output of 530 volts from the capacitor discharge and 40,000/45,000 volts to the spark plug.

Ignition Timing

Combustion burn time takes about 3 ms (0.003 or 3/1,000 of a second). This burning time is comparatively constant throughout the entire engine speed range. To get optimum efficiency from the expanding gases inside the combustion chamber, the burning of the air-fuel mixture should end by about 10 degrees ATDC.

If the burning of the mixture remains after that point, the expanding gases don't exert much force on the piston because it's moving away from the gases. To accomplish the goal of burning the air-fuel mixture completely by the time the piston reaches 10 degrees ATDC, the spark must be advanced as engine speed increases.

Initial Timing

Most VW air-cooled engines are equipped with a distributor, unless they are using an electronic direct ignition system used with fuel injection. It may be possible to adjust the base or the initial timing. The initial timing is usually set to fire the spark plug between zero degrees (TDC) or

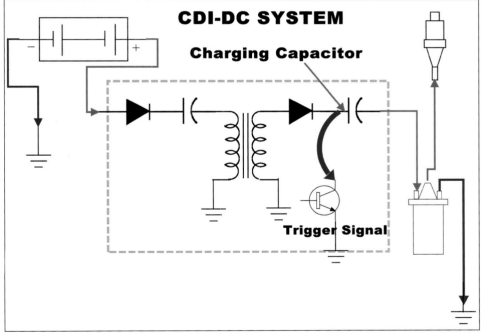

The CDI system contains a special induction coil, transistorized pulse amplifier, and magnetic pulse distributor. It can be triggered by a crankshaft position sensor, breaker points, igniters, or transistorized amplifier. CDI features a high-voltage condenser connected across the first windings of the coil. The input to the coil is constant and ensures complete saturation of the coil, which ends within the desired secondary voltage output at high engine speeds.

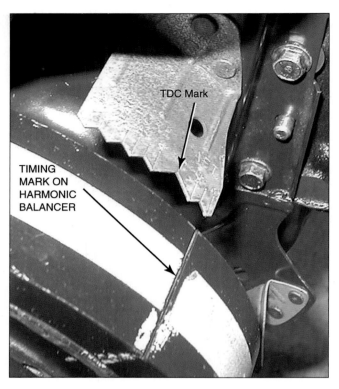

TIMING MARK ON HARMONIC BALANCER

TDC Mark

Ignition timing refers to when the spark plug fires in relation to the position of the piston. The time when the spark occurs depends on engine speed and therefore must be advanced as the engine rotates faster. (Photo Coutesy James Halderman)

slightly BTDC. Ignition timing can change as the timing gear wears, and readjustment is often necessary on high-mileage engines.

Detonation Control with Forced Induction

The main detonation issue when using a turbocharger or supercharger is that detonation needs to be managed. To do that, a device that retards timing during boost is needed. This device will allow running of normal timing settings to allow easy starting under normal driving conditions.

There are a number of aftermarket companies that offer a boost retard device to retard the ignition timing during turbocharger or supercharger boost. Some of these will retard timing 1 degree for each pound of boost. MSD offers such devices. Follow the instructions supplied for installation at holley.com/support/ for:

- MSD Boost Retard Control (part

number 7762)
- MSD Ignition Retard Module Selectors (part number 8676)
- MSD Ignition Three-Stage Retard Controls (part number 8970)

Ignition Timing with Forced Induction

Most turbocharged or supercharged VW engines operate best on 28 to 34 degrees of total advance. Having more total advance will not give any horsepower or performance gains. The distributor, whether breaker point or solid-state, should have a centrifugal advance system. Measure the timing marks on the crankshaft pulley or install one with timing marks.

To measure, employ a measuring instrument, calculate where 34 degrees would be located. Often, 34 degrees is a very safe figure and may provide near optimum performance. After marking off 34 degrees, start the engine and increase the speed to where the complete distributor's mechanical advance is in its original place. This could be somewhere over 2,500 rpm. Then, read the new 34-degree mark that very same because the original TDC mark at idle speed.

Adjust the distributor so the new mark on the damper lines up with

Crankshaft pulleys are available that are already marked with ignition timing degrees. Some of these also have 36 reluctor spaced tabs on the back side of the pulley for a crankshaft position sensor. (Photo Courtesy the Dub Shop)

the zero on the timing pointer. This action could provide 34 degrees of total timing. If the goal is 32 degrees of total timing, line up the mark on the crankshaft pulley with the 2-degree ATDC mark on the timing tab rather than zero.

Spark Plugs

Spark plug life can be an issue with high-performance VW engines. Generally, it is not possible to get normal spark plug life when an engine is modified to gain more horsepower. Some enthusiasts' magazines state that capacitor discharge ignition (CDI) systems increases spark plug life up to five times from the standard breaker point ignition. Stock range plugs were recommended in the VW service manual with slightly colder ones used.

When modifying the engine for more horsepower, colder plugs are needed for best performance, but they do not necessarily work for street or highway driving. Spark plug failure can cause backfire if the correct ones for the application are not used, and they can wear out quickly. A plug that is too hot will last only a few miles and can cause preignition and detonation.

Many VW owners and engine builders prefer NGK or Bosch spark plugs. Most aftermarket suppliers sell these plugs along with DENSO and Champion. Scat only sells DENSO plugs, and EMPI only sells Bosch and NGK. The older Bosch plugs are no longer available.

The Bosch W8AC superseded the WR8AC and was the preferred 14-mm thread plug. The R in the plug designation stands for resistor plug. The WR8AC is a hotter plug and best for most normal driving along with cold climate operation and stop-and-go traffic. The W8CC is the same plug without the resistor. The WR7AC is a colder plug used for turbocharged engines.

Many of the big-valve high-flow heads recommended in Chapter 4 come with long-reach 12-mm x 3/4-inch spark plug bosses. These provide strength to reduce the chance of cracks between the valve seat and plug. These applications will need 12-mm threaded plugs.

The old guys like me remember the older Champion UL-82Y, which has been superseded by the Champion L82YC. It was designed for the VW engine. It uses a projected nose that acts as a warm plug at low speeds and cools off to act as a cold plug as engine speed increases. This L82YC plug uses an auxiliary gap that increases plug life between replacements.

When the spark has jumped the auxiliary gap, it will have enough voltage so that the electrode path is used instead of leaking away fouling deposits that can build up on the shell. The stock spark plug gap of 0.028 works pretty well for modified engines. The reach or length of the older VW plugs was 1/2 inch measured from the outside of the washer to the tip of the threads.

It's important to check the plug thread length when the stock cylinder heads are off because any exposed threads in the combustion chamber can get hot and cause detonation or preignition. If building a street engine and using a 14-mm threaded spark plug with a longer reach, a thicker plug washer or multiple washers may be needed. They should be crimped copper or crimped aluminum that will not conduct heat out of the plug. Washers are available in 0.060, 0.080, and 0.100 inch sizes. However, many high-performance cylinder heads use long-reach 12-mm x 3/4-inch spark plug bosses for strength to prevent seat cracking.

Resistor Spark Plugs

When a spark jumps the electrode gap, there is a large amount of electro-motive force (EMF) that results in electro-motive interference (EMI) or radio frequency interference (RFI). RFI causes radio static and can interfere with an electronic fuel-injection computer. Resistor spark plugs are used to stop this interference. A resistor is

Spark plugs are manufactured from ceramic insulators inside a steel shell. The threads of the shell are rolled, and a seat is formed to create a gas-tight seal with the cylinder head. The reach is the length of the threaded part of the plug. The heat range of the spark plug refers to how rapidly the heat created at the tip is transferred to the cylinder head. A plug with a long ceramic insulator path will run hotter at the tip than a spark plug that has a shorter path. (Photo Courtesy iStock)

Current Spark Plug Heat Range Equivalents			
NGK	Bosch	Denso	Champion
2	10	9	18
4	9	14	16–14
5	8	16	12–11
6	7–6	20	10–9
7	5	22	8, 7
8	4	24	6-61-61
9	3	27	4, 59
9.5	–	29	57
10	2	31	55
10.5	–	32	53
11	–	34	–
11.5	–	35	–

placed within the plug to suppress the RFI from the plug.

Mallory, MSD, Crane, and ACCEL sell a high-output ignition CDI system for VW engines. Some high-output systems require use of resistor plugs, while some will use an internal resistor. Make sure to use the CDI manufacturer's recommendations for spark plugs, coils, and plug wires.

CDI ignition systems require a special inductive-type resistor spark plug such as the Champion Q-type or NGK Z-type. This is because inductive resistor plugs require less voltage than a regular resistor plug to work. Non-inductive resistor–type plugs on these systems can create an open circuit or bad plug.

Heat Range

A spark plug with a good heat range operates between preignition and fouling temperatures to provide the best performance. The spark plug recommended by the engine maker is designed to function in the proper heat range for most operating conditions. The length and configuration of the insulator tip, along with the conductivity of the center electrode determine the spark plug heat range.

Spark plugs can house different heat ranges. The thinking was to accommodate different engine builds with different applications. The reason for a built-in heat range is that the spark plug tip must operate at a high enough temperature to prevent fouling and yet remain cold enough to avoid preignition.

Heat range is a measure of spark plug capability to transfer heat received from the engine combustion chamber to the cylinder head. It is the range in which the plug works best thermally and is based on how a spark plug absorbs and dissipates the heat. Many spark plug original equipment manufacturers such as Bosch and NGK use different heat range scales. It is not possible to compare plugs from different manufacturers without a conversion table.

The Robert Bosch heat range decreases as the number decreases. Cold plugs have a low number and hot plugs have a high number. For

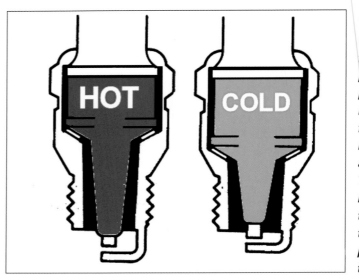

The rate of heat transfer, whether fast or slow, is a product of spark plug design and identifies the difference between a hot spark plug and a cold spark plug. The length of the lower insulator and the conductivity of the center electrode primarily determine the heat range.

example, a Bosch W8AC is hotter than a W7AC plug.

NGK and DENSO heat range is the opposite of Bosch because a lower number NGK heat range is hotter than a higher numerical heat range (as shown on page 88). Hot plugs have a low number and cold plugs have a high number. For example, an NGK DP7EA9 is hotter than a DP9EA9 plug.

A "hot" plug transfers heat more slowly and operates at a higher temperature than a "cold" plug. The cold plug has a faster rate of heat transfer and operates at a cooler temperature when installed in the same engine and operated under the same conditions. Therefore, a colder plug may be best suited for a full load or continuous high-speed racing. A hotter spark plug may be better for a street vehicle at prolonged idling or stop-and-go city traffic. A spark plug's heat range is determined by:

- Ceramic insulator nose surface area
- Insulator tip: long versus short nose
- Thermal conductivity (absorb/transfer combustion heat) of insulator and center electrode
- Insulator material
- Center electrode material of copper, platinum, or iridium

Range with Forced Induction

Run spark plugs that are one to two ranges colder than the normal spark plug on an engine using a turbocharger or a supercharger. The bigger boost pressure, the colder the plug needed. On street applications, cold plugs will foul more easily than hot plugs, so I recommend the standard plug for a street build.

The MSD Heli-Core 8-mm ignition wire set is high performance with low resistance for maximum voltage. This set is designed to prevent inductive crossfire. (Photo Courtesy Scat)

Spark Plug Wires

Most ignition wires used in racing today are 8 mm. A 300-ohm resistance spiral core wire is need for most racing vehicles using a high-performance ignition system. The ignition wire must a deliver high energy output for maximum spark at the plug.

Radio frequency interference (RFI) suppression is needed to meet the demands of on-board electronics, such as electronic ignition, sound systems, and computer controls. Ozone-resistant silicone jackets are needed to repel water, oil, grease, and fuel, and they should be designed to withstand temperatures up to 500 degrees. Here are some suggestions:

Scat

Scat offers three color options for PerTronix Flame-Thrower low-resistance, high-performance plug wires, all for male cap applications. They are red (part number 45-804404), black (part number 45-804202), or blue (part number 45-804303).

EMPI

EMPI offers stock ignition wire sets in black (part number 9314) and grey (part number 9313).

EMPI also offers 7-mm wire sets that use a double-jacket cover to protect against heat and feature deluxe spark plug boots that seal at the cylinder tin. They use a 22-inch coil wire that allows the coil to be mounted in various locations. These wires are copper core non-suppressed. Colors available are yellow (part number 9400), blue (part number 9407), red (part number 9411), and grey (part number 9402).

A third option from EMPI is 90-degree, 8-mm suppressed ignition wire sets with 90-degree end caps. A 32-inch unassembled coil wire is used to allow for various coil mounting locations. These sets are for Type 1, 2, and 3 engine configurations. They are available in yellow (part number 9389), blue (part number 9390), and red (part number 9391).

Another offering from EMPI is 90-degree Megavolt ignition wire sets that feature 90-degree end caps. Included is a 32-inch unassembled coil wire used to allow various mounting locations. These are also copper core non-suppressed that are designed for all Type 1, 2, and 3 engine configurations. They are available in yellow (part number B352020), blue (art number B352022), red (part number B352023), and grey (part number B352026).

Taylor also makes great wires, available from EMPI. Taylor Spiro Pro "409" Race wire sets are 10.4-mm diameter suppressed wires. They have a silicone ignition wire core, woven fiberglass over-braids, and silicone jackets. The set comes with a 32-inch unassembled coil wire that can be cut to length. Available in red (part number 9397), blue (part number 9396), black (part number 9395), grey (part number 9393), or yellow (part number 9394).

EMPI also has premium ignition wire sets. They are 7-mm ignition wire sets similar to the factory Bosch wire set (part number 09-001) that Bosch discontinued. They use 1K ohm resistance for each Bakelite connector end. The coil wire is suppressed, and the other four wires use copper core and the wires are grey in color. Part number 98-9925 fits Type 1 50-79, Ghia 56-74, and Type 2 50-71 models, while part number 98-9925-0 fits Type 1 50-79, Ghia 56-74, and Type 2 50-71 models.

Robert Bosch ignition wire sets have the black Bakelite ends ignition wire set (part number 98-9986-B) for the Type 1 50-79, Ghia 56-74, and Type 2 50-71.

JBugs also sells the EMPI wire sets.

Gene Berg

Popular supplier Gene Berg also offers wire sets. Part number GB 625 wire sets are a premium copper core replacement for Type 1 and 2 with original VW ends and air seals. It has a radio noise resistor type of coil wire and plug ends.

Part number GB 625-311 is a Bosch silicone replacement for Type 3 with 90 degree ends at cap end, and radio noise resistor ends. Finally, part number GB 625D is an aftermarket wire set for Type 1 and 2 applications.

Air Cooled

Aircooled.net offers a variety of wire sets. It supplies Megavolt plug wire sets with a 2x silicone jacket and copper core. Also available is Bosch plug wire sets (part number 09-003) for 1967 Type 3 engines (part number 311-998-031). Also available are Taylor Spiro Pro 8-mm silicone plug wire sets, and Bosch (of Mexico) plug wire sets (part number 111-998-031A).

POWERTRAIN UPGRADES

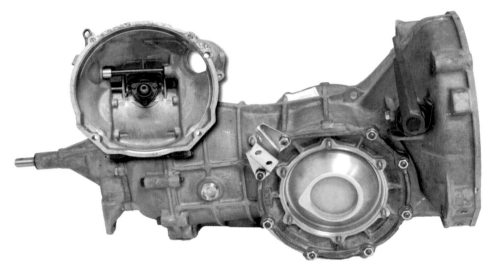

Scat and EMPI offer replacement transaxles with or without axles in standard or close-ratio gearing. The PRO models contain the four-spider-gear differential, which is needed for high-horsepower engines. (Photo Courtesy Scat Enterprises)

If you're building a slightly tuned engine for your Type 1 and not building a 200-plus-hp vehicle, I suggest not doing many transmission modifications. Sadly, there are no aftermarket heavy-duty transaxles for these vehicles. It might be a good idea to use a transaxle that has a lower final-drive ratio, such as 3.78:1 (as opposed to the 4.37:1), which will provide better fuel economy. If you are building in the high horsepower range, beef up the clutch pressure plate, release bearing, and clutch disc. In the transaxle, beef up the differential with extra side or spider

If your build is more than 230 hp and is used for drag racing or sand use, get a lightened flywheel and use a Scat flanged crankshaft with eight dowel holes. If this type of crankshaft is not used, it needs to be wedge mated. Wedge mating is marrying the flywheel to the crankshaft end. First, remove the dowels. Drill the flywheel and crankshaft together to make sure they are in line. Check the crankshaft for trueness and perpendicularity to the axis. If this is good, measure the diameters of the crank end and the flywheel bore to a 0.0005 interference fit. If this will not work, either have the flywheel bore or crank end diameter chromed and ground to achieve the proper press fit. (Photo Courtesy Scat Enterprises)

A chromoly forged-steel flywheel for Type 1 and Type 4 that is drilled for an offset pattern with eight dowel pins can be used. It has a 130-tooth (12-volt) ring gear, and it fits all Scat crankshafts and eight-dowel-pin Type 1 through 3 cranks. (Photo Courtesy Scat Enterprises)

gears and make sure your engine and transaxle are adequately supported.

Flywheel

If you are building a street or track high-performance application, use a lightweight flywheel because it allows faster acceleration. The heavy stock flywheel weight takes more torque and horsepower to move the vehicle. The heavy flywheel smooths out firing pulses and stops vibration harmonics and torsional twist. This is the reason for using a counterweighted crankshaft, especially when using a light flywheel.

Clutch Pressure Plate

If an engine build is over 90 bhp, use the Kennedy (K.E.P.) Performance Stage 1 pressure plate. This Kennedy pressure plate is good up to about 220 hp. If horsepower is higher than that, use the Kennedy Stage 2 pressure plate.

Drag and sand race applications must use the Stage 2 so that the clutch doesn't slip. All of these pressure plates are 200 mm in diameter. Kennedy clutches are used in drag racing, off-road and sand competition, as well as performance street applications. All are supplied with a metal center ring. You can remove the center ring for late-model applications. I recommend using the 200-mm clutch size, since it has much more grip. However, for applications with more than 50 hp, and up to about 120 hp, use the Kennedy pressure plate. It is a 180-mm pressure plate with a stock 180-mm clutch disc.

EMPI offers Kennedy pressure plates for drag racing, off-road, sand competition, and high-performance applications. They all come with a metal ring. The center ring is removable for all late model–style release bearings:

- Kennedy Stage 1: 1,700-pound pressure plate (part number 4090)
- Kennedy Stage 2: 2,100-pound pressure plate (part number 4092)
- Kennedy Stage 3: 2,600-pound pressure plate (part number 4093)

The Kennedy (K.E.P.) multi-finger diaphragm spring racing pressure plate for high-performance builds is available in 1,700-, 2,100-, and 2,500-pound versions. It has been load tested and jig assembled to ensure proper pressure. (Photo Courtesy Scat Enterprises)

A less-expensive pressure plate is available for use with lower-horsepower engines for street use with an apply pressure of 1,200 pounds. (Photo Courtesy Scat Enterprises)

The Quicksilver 4-puck Feramic competition clutch discs have special Feramic pads that are bonded and riveted to a stainless-steel drive plate. They are not affected by oil, grease, or heat. The slip rate is controlled by the pressure plate. It grabs hard at 2,500 pounds. Its pressure or slips into engagement is equal to 1,700 pounds. (Photo Courtesy Scat Enterprises)

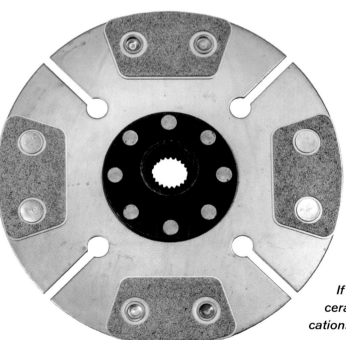

If building a mild street application, use a 180-mm 4-puck ceramic clutch disc that is designed for lower-horsepower applications. (Photo Courtesy Scat Enterprises)

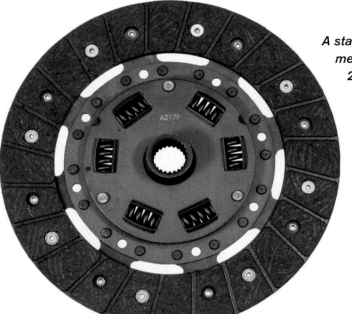

A standard Sachs clutch disc using a wear-resistant metal-woven-lined face is available for standard 180- or 200-mm sizes with rigid- or spring-type hubs. It replaces original equipment. (Photo Courtesy Scat Enterprises)

If you are building an engine for drag racing or off-road racing, use the Kush clutch disc with a solid center and no damper springs in a 200-mm size for a high output. (Photo Courtesy Scat Enterprises)

Use German-made heavy-duty roller throw-out bearings that have a ball bearing that replaces the stock carbon-type bearing. They are offered by most VW parts suppliers. (Photo Courtesy Scat Enterprises)

- Kennedy Stage 4: 3,000-pound pressure plate (boxed) (part number 4094)

Scat also offers the Kennedy pressure plates under these part numbers:

- 1,700-pound multi-finger racing clutch E&L – Stage 1 (part number KEP1700)
- 2,100-pound multi-finger racing clutch E&L – Stage 2 (part number KEP2100)
- 2,500-pound multi-finger racing clutch E&L – Stage 3 (part number KEP2500)

EMPI also offers a Sachs heavy-duty, high-performance pressure plate for performance applications. These pressure plates provide a strong clutch operation with good spring pressure over stock pressure plates. They are available in 180 mm for the older Type 1, 2, and 3 1,200/1,300-cc engines and in 200 mm for the newer 1,500/1,600-cc engines. EMPI also offers a specific

200-mm Sachs pressure plate for the 1600-cc engine. This 200-mm pressure plate is rated at 1,700 and 2,100 pounds and it is balanced with the removable center ring to work with early- or late-model transaxles. The 1,700-pound plate is EMPI part number 4080 and EMPI part number 4082 for the 2,100-pound plate.

Clutch Disc

The stock disc can be used for all applications up to 120 hp. From 120 hp and up, there is a choice of employing a dual-material clutch disc. This disc uses metal-woven pucks on one side and organic material on the opposite for a smooth engagement.

Another excellent disc is the Daikin clutch disc that engages smoothly and grips exceptionally well. A Stage 1 Kennedy pressure plate and a dual friction disc is about as adequate as a Stage 2 Kennedy pressure plate and a Daikin disc. It is possible to use the Daikin

disc and a Stage 2 Kennedy on a 230-hp engine.

Transaxle

The original transaxle used in the Type 1 was designed for a 50- to 60-bhp engine. The first transaxle was not synchronized, and the housing was a two-piece unit that was split lengthwise and called the Split Case. It was used up until 1953, when it was replaced by another split case unit that had second, third, and fourth synchronized with first gear still not synchronized.

This split case transaxle was in production until 1960, when it was replaced by what is known as the tunnel transaxle. The tunnel transaxle was an all-synchronized gearbox and basically the same transaxle Volkswagen used with the swing axle. A later version was introduced in 1969 with independent rear suspension and constant velocity joints.

The early Type 1 tunnel transaxles prior to 1969 were swing axle because the inner joint was a swinging device and did not use the CV or U-joints.

The biggest advantage of the tunnel-type transaxle was that it could handle more horsepower. The swing axle casting was pretty weak and was prone to breakage and leaks, so it is not recommended for any high-performance engines. The later independent rear suspension differential casting was stronger, but the splined output shafts are prone to breakage with extensive or hard use.

Most of the aftermarket suppliers offer heavy-duty axle driveshafts as a complete replacement. The engines built based on this book will definitely need the later

For a heavy-duty clutch system, install a heavy-duty cross shaft with the heavy-steel bearing fingers and shaft. It is welded 360 degrees around the bearing fingers. EMPI sells a heavy-duty cross shaft with a bronze bushing kit. In the industry, is known as the heavy-duty cross shaft Type 1 73-79 (part number 18-1055). (Photo Courtesy Scat Enterprises)

Strengthen your independent rear suspension differential assemblies with a heavy-duty differential for use with all VW sedan transaxles. This design doubles the strength of your stock spider gear section with the addition of two spider gears for a total of four spider gears without changing differential action. This is needed for any drag racing or rugged off-road driving. Use the Bugpack independent rear suspension differential without spider gears (part number B507210). (Photo Courtesy Scat Enterprises)

Close-ratio 8620 competition transaxle gearsets are available for all performance drag racing, off-road, slalom, and competition racing. This lowers the final-drive ratio of third and fourth gears. (Photo Courtesy Scat Enterprises)

tunnel-type transaxle. If a build is strictly a street unit, use a swing axle tunnel transaxle with a stronger mount kit.

If running a Super Beetle suspension with independent rear suspension and an engine in the 100- to 120-hp range, buy a heavy-duty differential housing with an extra set of spider gears. This heavy-duty four-spider differential side gears will accept the stock CV-joint output shafts. This setup offers the advantage of good handling, and the rear wheels will not suffer the same radical camber changes as on the swing-axle design.

The stock differential unit is more than adequate for most uses, but it has only two spider gears to carry the load, so there is a tendency for them to break. This usually happens when the clutch is dropped, causing one wheel to spin because there isn't a limited-slip differential to control the power. To fix this, there are a number of beefed-up differential kits on the market that can add an extra pair of spider gears to an otherwise stock differential unit. The correct solution is to use a heavy-duty differential casing that contains four spider gears. Each pair is properly located on a hard shaft, which will probably solve

any differential problems.

The typical stock Volkswagen transmission can survive the stress of 120-plus hp. Although it is not recommended to use the stock transmission, it will work okay when running a 65-hp 1641 engine. If doing any drag racing, it is possible that something in the transmission will break if it has not been beefed up for that type of use.

For the most part, as long as the transmission mountings are in good shape and some of the reinforcement components that are available from Gene Berg, Scat, or EMPI are installed, you should be okay. When

Volkswagen designed these transmissions way back in the 1960s and 1970s, they were pretty strong, but there are some things that can be done to improve a transmission.

Aftermarket close-ratio gears have teeth that are deeper and cut at less of a helix can be used. This makes the gear stronger, but they will be noisier. Volkswagen used two types of pinion shafts in their transaxles: a splined design and a keyed design. They are interchangeable, but many builders feel that the keyed design, which uses a larger nut in place of the snap ring, is the better design.

For heavy-duty modifications, weld the blocker ring on the third and fourth gear rather than relying on the factory interference fit. If left alone, the hubs can spin under power, losing drive. After welding them, they should be ground down flush on a belt sander.

Competition Aluminum T6 Aircraft Quality Aluminum Spool does not use differential gears. It is ready to bolt into any swing axle with an eight-bolt pattern. This final-drive spool is designed to give even traction to both rear wheels for drag racing applications.

Transaxle Mounting

When mounting the transaxle in a performance-based vehicle, limit the engine and transaxle movement as much as possible. There are some options available to mounting the transaxle. For example, fabricate or buy a rear engine hanger.

This hanger is a strong square section of steel to hold the transaxle supports that will fasten to it. The bar passes under the rear of the crankcase and prevents the engine from dropping as the vehicle accelerates.

The stock motor mounts can be replaced with a set of urethane mounts that are more rigid than the original rubber pieces. The urethane mountings provide a much more rigid placement but at the expense of a slightly increased noise inside the vehicle. However, the urethane mountings have been known to crack and split, so check them regularly.

Scat and Bugpack offer red urethane transaxle mounts that are injection-molded for rigidity and strength to allow the engine and transaxle to flex and reduce vibration. For example, Scat's Urethane Trans Mount Kit (part number 70169) and EMPI Urethane Trans Mounts 61-72 Type 1 (part number 9540) are urethane mount kits sold with hardware.

Many suppliers also offer solid thick-gauge steel transaxle mount kits that reduce wheel hop during hard acceleration, which is typically caused by a high-horsepower engine. It adds strength and mounts directly to the transaxle case on 61-72 Type 1 vehicle.

For a street vehicle that develops only 100 to 200 bhp and only sees casual track use and the radial tires do not slip, the best all-around solution is to install new factory mountings and maybe a traction bar. This will be a good combination that offers the best of both worlds: firm transaxle location and little noise.

Gene Berg Enterprises offers a rubber-mounted transaxle support to limit engine and transaxle movement. Scat sells padded transaxle saddle and strap mounts (part number 70169), OEM mounts not included. EMPI offers a Type 2 independent rear suspension conversion kit for a Type 1 for added strength and reliability as well as a Bus to Bug Trans Mount Kit with Hardware (part number 3195).

INDUCTION SYSTEM

In this chapter, various types of inductions systems are discussed to help you determine what is best for your build. Let's start with the basics of carburetion.

Carburetion

The carburetor is a fuel-metering device that uses the Venturi principle. The carburetor has gone from a simple design to the more complex Weber IDA/IDF or Dellorto DLRA carburetors that are used in high-performance and racing vehicles.

The carburetor mixes the right quantity of gasoline with air. If there is not enough fuel mixed with the air, the engine runs lean and hot, and engine damage could occur. If there is too much fuel mixed with the air, the engine runs rich and will either not run at all or flood, producing black smoke, which is fuel burned without air. This causes stalling, fouled plugs, increased cylinder-wall wear, and wasted fuel.

Two functions to consider when improving air-cooled engine performance are: 1) consuming the maximum amount of air-fuel mixture, and 2) removing the maximum amount of energy from the air-fuel mixture.

Venturi

The difference between vacuum or low pressure and atmospheric pressure at 14.7 psi allows a carburetor to work. A Venturi is a tube or a passage with a tapered or narrow area in the middle, in our case, the carburetor throat. It causes an increase in the speed of the air flowing through that makes suction or negative pressure from the pistons to suck the air/fuel into a carburetor.

When the air molecules move through the narrow passage of the boost or auxiliary Venturi, they must separate. The stream of air gets thinner

The carburetor is a fuel-metering device that operates under the Venturi principle. It has evolved from a basic design to the more complex models used in racing vehicles, such as NHRA racing. There should be no vacuum leaks (air pressure getting in), and the carburetor floats should be properly set. Carburetors mix the right amount of gasoline with air. If there is not enough fuel mixed with the air, the engine runs lean and will either not run at all or damage may occur when the engine is running. If there is too much fuel mixed with the air, the engine runs rich and may not run due to flooding. (Photo Courtesy Shutterstock)

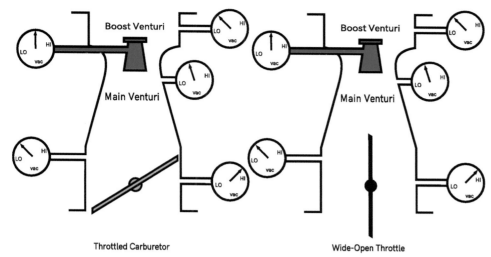

Boost Venturi

Main Venturi

Boost Venturi

Main Venturi

Throttled Carburetor

Wide-Open Throttle

Carburetors use more than one Venturi; there is a boost Venturi inside the main Venturi. The boost Venturi has a much lower pressure or vacuum than the main Venturi and is attached to the nozzle that injects the fuel. The boost Venturi has the most vacuum in the carburetor. When the throttle is closed, there is high vacuum. When the throttle is open, there is low vacuum or high pressure. EMPI, Scat, and others sell various-size Venturi for the IDF carburetors.

with fewer molecules. This causes the pressure in the smaller hole or boost (auxiliary) Venturi to be less than the pressure above it. These designs are also called a multi-Venturi carburetor. To keep it simple, I will refer to the boost or auxiliary Venturi as the boost Venturi.

The boost Venturi is a restriction in the air inlet path, which measures air and creates a low-pressure area. Do not confuse the boost Venturi with the main Venturi, which in some case can be removed and a larger Venturi installed.

A discharge nozzle in the boost Venturi connects to a fuel bowl, which is vented to the atmosphere. The nozzle is located higher than the gasoline level in the float bowl. Any decrease in pressure at the nozzle causes fuel to flow through it. As air is sucked through the carburetor by the engine intake strokes, fuel from the nozzle is added to the airstream in relation to the speed of the air or the velocity.

The association between the main Venturi diameter and throttle diameter needs to be balanced. I saw a Weber graph in one of my engineering textbooks that included RPM, engine displacement, and main Venturi diameter. This graph was based on the following formulas and dynamometer testing. For example, a 1,776-cc engine should use a 28-mm main Venturi, and a 2.0L build should use a main Venturi within the 30- to 35-mm range.

EMPI did a recent comparison between its new HPMX IDA–type carburetor and a Weber IDA on identical 1,776-cc engines using a 28-mm main Venturi with the following components:

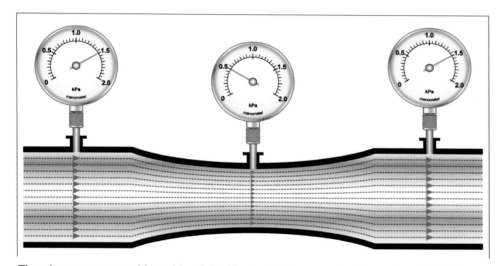

The air pressure on either side of the Venturi is the same in the center, but at the Venturi, the pressure is much lower. This causes suction that pulls air and fuel into the intake manifold depending on the throttle opening. Atmospheric pressure is available outside the engine air intake, and vacuum or low pressure is located inside the intake manifold below the throttle plate. (Graphic Courtesy Shutterstock)

This is the removable Venturi for IDA, IDF, and Dellorto carburetors. (Photo Courtesy Scat Enterprises)

- Mahle pistons
- 8-dowel crankshaft

Weber 48 IDF carburetor kits are drag-race certified and offer increased horse-power from a bolt-on carburetor with reliability and performance. Complete kits are sold with a new IDF carburetor, high-flow manifolds, and linkage. Complete bolt-on kits include carburetors, offset aluminum manifolds, the hex bar link-age, air cleaners, some fuel line, and mounting hardware. (Photo Courtesy Scat Enterprises)

- Eagle 120 camshaft
- Stock rebuilt dual-port heads
- Offset manifolds
- Solid cam followers
- 30-mm oil pump with mini sump and external filter
- Bosch 009 distributor
- Stock fuel pump
- 5/8-inch exhaust

The main Venturi on both carburetors was 28 mm. The results showed that these engines performed quite well with the 28-mm main Venturi using 0.135 main jets. Roger Crawford ran the dyno test and had the following results: 101.07 ft-lbs of torque at 4,500 rpm and 90.35 bhp at 4,900 rpm.

For most builds, it's better to pick a smaller main Venturi diameter than a big one, that you think will provide maximum horsepower. A large main Venturi and throttle bore will provide high-RPM power, given that a build has the camshaft, compression, exhaust, inlet port diameter, and valve diameter designed for high RPM. However, this may happen at the expense of lower-RPM manageability.

Smaller main Venturis will move the horsepower curve, so it is developed at a lower RPM. This provides the advantage of more usable power throughout the RPM range, with more total available power than a high-RPM engine of comparable displacement. In other words, bigger is not always better.

I recommend sizing the carburetor main Venturi about 3 to 5 mm smaller than the throttle valve opening on mild builds and use the same-size main Venturi as the throttle valve opening on high-performance racing engines. For example, the Gene Berg website recommends larger main Venturis only on builds used for drag racing and off-road applications. These applications will most likely be using the 40/44/48 IDA/IDF or Dellorto carburetors.

The maximum airflow past the throttle butterfly is about 70 percent of the intake valve diameter for normal camshafts and around 85 percent for a racing camshafts. This suggests that an inlet port diameter should not be bigger than 80 to 85 percent of the valve diameter. This is often how the formulas below were derived:

- Throttle bore diameter formula: $D = (0.8 - 0.9) \times (V \times n)$
- Main Venturi diameter formula: $d = (0.7 - 0.9) \times D$

D = Throttle bore diameter (mm)
d = Main Venturi diameter (mm)
V = Cylinder displacement (liters)
n = Engine speed (RPM)
d = 0.7 x 44-mm throttle valve opening
d = 28-mm Main Venturi

To have good midrange and better-than-average top speed using a carburetor, there should be a minimum pressure drop not greater than 3 inches of mercury at wide-open throttle. Some racing setups will have 1 inch of mercury at wide-open throttle as previously stated. However, there may be performance problems at the midrange RPM.

Fuel and air do not mix well at low air velocity, so the engine can be over fueled and run rich. It will also

The 4-barrel carburetor solved the midrange performance problem on large V-8 engines by having primary and secondary dual barrels. The primaries (the front half of the 4-barrels) provide idling and midrange, and the secondaries aid in performance for the high end. A 4-barrel carburetor does not provide good all-around performance on a VW air-cooled engine. However, a Holley 850-cfm carburetor with four booster Venturi used on a Landy Industries supercharger VW setup for drag racing has had marginal success. Landy Industries offered supercharger kits for 1,835- to 3,535-cc VW Type 1s with the 144 blower and without the doghouse, which could be used with either a Holley 4-barrel or a Dellorto carburetor. Ron Lummis Industries still sells a VW turbo kit that includes a Holly 850-cfm carburetor, which costs about $4,800. (Photo Courtesy James Halderman)

have low power at the RPM where the poor mixing takes place. The result is poor low-speed torque and weak midrange power. Your top end will have more power once the engine speed is increased to the point where the increased air velocity causes the fuel and air to meter properly.

Generally, the larger the main Venturi area, the greater the top end capability will be but with a resultant loss in low-end performance because it can be too large to provide adequate depression over the jets at low speed. VW carburetors that use a large main Venturi area can have poor low-end performance for street applications. This is the reason that fuel system engineers went to multi-Venturi carburetors with a boost and main Venturi.

Adding a larger main Venturi can cause flat spots at low speeds and reduced engine flexibility on street builds. A large main Venturi area will slow down the mixing and divert from good vaporization for street application and mild builds. I do not think that this would bother a drag racer, but it would create problems for a normal driving street vehicle.

A long-duration camshaft may further complicate a project by pumping back a part of the intake charge, further reducing the average air velocity through the main Venturi. If the engine is equipped with a carburetor with a large main Venturi area, the engine can momentarily misfire or even die when the throttle is quickly opened. This happens because the manifold pressure rises almost to atmospheric pressure, air velocity drops, and the fuel will dump onto the cylinder walls.

Carburetor Components

Compensation devices such as special jets, air bleeds, and emulsion tubes are built into the carburetor. These devices improve fuel atomization because they mix air with the fuel before it gets to the carburetor main jet. Thus, fuel flowing into the boost Venturi area has already been partially mixed as an air-fuel emulsion so that it will be more readily atomize by the fast-moving air.

At all speeds above idle, air passing through the boost Venturi determines the vacuum present at the nozzle, which is the pressure drop needed to drawl fuel into the airstream. If the air speed is too slow, the atomization will not be complete and fuel will deposit on the intake manifold instead of going into the cylinders.

The main Venturi (if removable, as we previously discussed) must be carefully sized so that the airflow through the carburetors will always be sufficient for adequate fuel and air mixing even at lower speeds. The result of this is smooth idling, good low-speed acceleration, and fairly decent midrange and top-end performance.

The major carburetor companies have been looking at these issues for years. The ideal racing combination should have a pressure drop not exceeding 1.0 inches of mercury at full throttle under load. The pressure in the intake manifold should approach atmospheric pressure at 14.7 psi under those conditions. Typical racing engines generally have a pretty rough idle along with fairly low-end torque. This issue connected to poor engine flexibility will mean quite a bit of gear shifting to keep the engine operating at a decent speed range so the air velocity is enough for good air fuel mixing and distribution to the cylinders.

Carburetor Modifications

The stock VW 1,600 engine was built with a Solex 34 PICT-3, which is a 1-barrel carburetor mounted on a center manifold mount with tubes connected to the cylinder heads by hoses. The main Venturi is 26 mm. They worked great for regular economic driving but not well for high performance. Remember, these were 50-bhp engines. With some simple changes to this carburetor, they can get some decent performance. Yet, if the mixture is richened with larger jets for high-end performance, the low end will suffer with holes in performance. A compromise solution is needed.

If aiming to keep the vehicle in the stock classes at the drag strip or autocross, you may want all of the performance you can get out of a stock engine. Stock carburetion is good for economy and low-end performance. The Solex 34 PICT 3 carburetor provides good low-speed torque but with restricted power output at higher engine RPM.

Changes can be made to the stock carburetor system to provide some performance improvements; however, there will be disadvantages. For example, if the mixture is richened for top performance, fuel economy will be lower, plus the engine will experience holes in its performance curve. Careful tuning of the stock carburetor can usually add horsepower, but it's hard to find this horsepower unless using a dynamometer to measure the changes.

Throttle Opening

Remove the air-cleaner temporarily and make sure that the throttle is fully open and not slightly angled when the accelerator pedal is all the way to the floor. The goal is a true wide-open throttle (WOT), so check and make sure the linkage provides for it. If the throttle is not fully open, find the reason.

If replacing the carburetor, make sure that the throttle fully opens to WOT. Many issues with the throttle failing to go WOT come from the design and location of the accelerator pedal. Dirt gets under both the front and back stops, so grind these off. The 1956–1957 roller-type accelerator pedal is good or use a complete 1967 pedal assembly. The 1958–1966 models had problems related to the throttle cable because it could bend and then the accelerator pedal would go sideways instead of straight down. When starting from a completely closed position, this reduced tip-in flat spots because the throttle was not situated in the right position to the progression ports. If the Beetle is moved from a closed throttle position and the throttle is not in the right position, you will have flat spots.

Air Cleaner

Reinstall the air cleaner, and never run without an air cleaner on a street machine. Leaving the stock air cleaner off on a street build can make the engine run lean. This is because the air cleaner holds the fuel fog or stand-off above the carburetor inlet at high speeds that allows this fog to mix with the incoming air.

Never run an engine without an air cleaner because it can destroy the engine very quickly. There are many performance air cleaners available on the market. (Photo Courtesy Scat Enterprises)

If switching to a flat filter on top of the carburetor, install a length of thin rubber hose that is the same size as the carburetor air inlet and then mount the flat air cleaner on the hose. This will fix the fuel fog issue, and it is the way the 4-inch velocity stacks work on the Weber IDA carburetors.

Main Jets

The Solex 34 PICT-3 jets are too small for maximum performance in a stock unit. The carburetor was originally jetted lean to pass federal and California emissions rules. When I worked for VW at Volkswagen Atlantic, one of the instructors, Fred Heiler, showed me how to take an ordinary thumb tack and open the jet up with it for better drivability. If using this carburetor and not going for one of the more elaborate carburetor systems or fuel injection, resize the main jet from 1.30 to a 1.40 along with going from a 1.75 to a 1.80 air-correction jet.

- Scat main jet 1.40 (part number 11075/140)
- Scat air correction jet 1.80 (part number 11076/80)
- EMPI main jet 1.40 (part number 43-5328)
- EMPI air correction jet 1.80 (part number 43-5441)

The Solex 34 PICT-3 carburetor also gives more control of the vacuum for the distributor vacuum advance if using one. Take crocus cloth and carefully smooth the surface of the main Venturi and inside the carburetor air horn, especially at the trailing edges. The throttle valve or butterfly leading edges can also be smoothed with crocus cloth or 1,200-grit sandpaper.

Volkswagen Intake Manifold

Manifold size is also very important. The small stock manifold is a performance limiter because it does not provide the airflow to make horsepower at higher RPM. It is necessary to increase the manifold size for more airflow and more power.

Volkswagen manifold outer diameter size increased with engine displacement. The 40 bhp was 0.940 inch outer diameter, the 1,300 used a 1.125-inch diameter, the 1,500 was 1.230 inches, and the 1,600 was 1.4 inches. The stock manifold tubing size ranges from 1¼ to 1½ inches.

Do not add more carburetion on the stock manifold because the flow path will be too small from the carburetor through the intake manifold. Also, don't just place a bigger carburetor flange on the stock manifold to fit a bigger carburetor. Use an intake manifold with a large enough inlet diameter to match the size of the throttle valve.

If not going with the large manifold and want to use a larger carburetor, one of the least expensive performance improvements is to install an open plenum manifold, plenum means plain old hole. This replaces the primary and secondary holes with one large opening or plenum. This will provide decent performance without spending a lot of money.

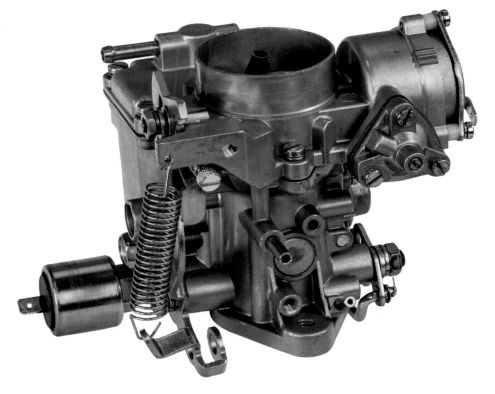

This Solex 34 PCIT-3 carburetor used a 26-mm Venturi to get a 50-bhp rating. It used a built-in idle-control solenoid that allowed the throttle to be completely closed at idle. The Solex 32 PDSIT carburetor used in the Type 3 dual-carburetor setup had a removable main Venturi, which can be used to experiment with larger main Venturi for top-end performance. (Photo Courtesy Scat Enterprises)

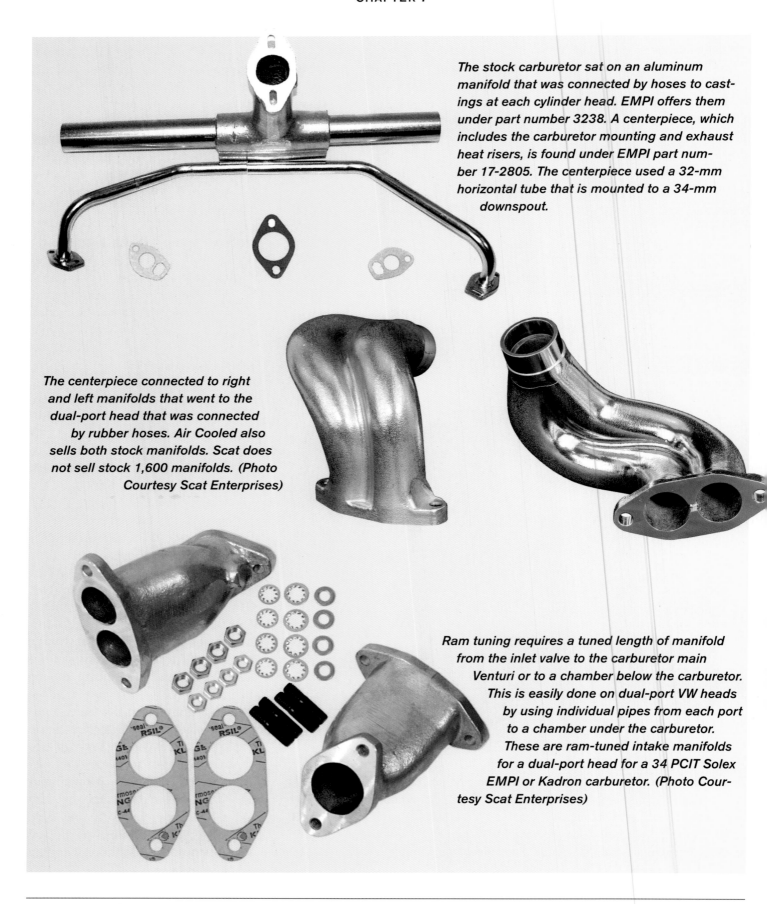

The stock carburetor sat on an aluminum manifold that was connected by hoses to castings at each cylinder head. EMPI offers them under part number 3238. A centerpiece, which includes the carburetor mounting and exhaust heat risers, is found under EMPI part number 17-2805. The centerpiece used a 32-mm horizontal tube that is mounted to a 34-mm downspout.

The centerpiece connected to right and left manifolds that went to the dual-port head that was connected by rubber hoses. Air Cooled also sells both stock manifolds. Scat does not sell stock 1,600 manifolds. (Photo Courtesy Scat Enterprises)

Ram tuning requires a tuned length of manifold from the inlet valve to the carburetor main Venturi or to a chamber below the carburetor. This is easily done on dual-port VW heads by using individual pipes from each port to a chamber under the carburetor. These are ram-tuned intake manifolds for a dual-port head for a 34 PCIT Solex EMPI or Kadron carburetor. (Photo Courtesy Scat Enterprises)

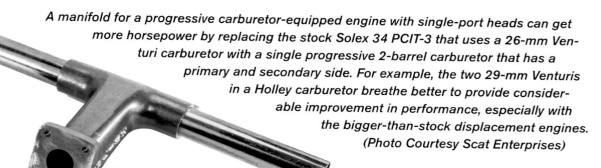

A manifold for a progressive carburetor-equipped engine with single-port heads can get more horsepower by replacing the stock Solex 34 PCIT-3 that uses a 26-mm Venturi carburetor with a single progressive 2-barrel carburetor that has a primary and secondary side. For example, the two 29-mm Venturis in a Holley carburetor breathe better to provide considerable improvement in performance, especially with the bigger-than-stock displacement engines. (Photo Courtesy Scat Enterprises)

Center-mounted carburetors for street use will need heat during cold weather so make sure that you have some type of heat riser device to get that heat. Center-mounted carburetors are not usually RAM tuned. Ram tuning is when you use a long tube from the carburetor throttle valve to the intake valve. This long tube gives the air-fuel mixture velocity that rams down the charge.

Intake manifolds generally come as part of a dual carburetor kit. Always use an aluminum manifold rather than steel. Aluminum manifolds have a better fit and conduct heat to the carburetors and eliminate icing problems. This means that dual carburetors with aluminum intake manifolds do not need intake manifold heat like the center-mount carbs.

Two-barrel carburetors can be a progressive design in that they use a mechanical- or vacuum-operated secondary throttle. The secondary throttle opens in relation to throttle position based on engine vacuum, which is a measure of engine load. This design uses a small primary Venturi for drivability with a larger secondary Venturi for additional power when the throttle opening is wider. The EMPI Progressive carburetor with an electric choke (for VW) is part number 44-1018-1. (Photo Courtesy Scat Enterprises)

The space available in the engine bay determines the manifold since the linkage needs to clear the alternator. This is different for off-road and race cars that most likely have a larger engine compartment. Due to air velocity, short manifolds produce more power at high speeds, and long manifolds produce more power at low speeds.

Carburetor Make and Model

There are quite a number of carburetor choices for VW air-cooled engines from a number of suppliers. Some are mentioned in the text but all that I know of are listed in this book's source guide. Some of these firms like Gene Berg offer carburetor throttle valve machining services as well.

Dual/Single One-Barrel Carburetor Systems

The Kadron Brosol Solex are Brazilian-manufactured Solex carburetors and work well, but the stock linkage is a problem. The linkage ball-joints can break or pop off. The Kadron Brosol (Solex) is the largest of the dual 1-barrel carburetors and produce the most power for a 1-barrel carburetor. EMPI makes pretty good linkage kits that solve this problem.

Dual EMPI 35-mm Solex-type carburetor kits are only for upright engines and are only available for dual-port heads. These carburetors work well for semi-stock and mild street vehicles.

The Solex 34 PCIT-3 was the original stock carburetor used on the Type 1. This carburetor works well on a mild street build with the modifications I listed under 1,600-cc stock modifications in a single- or dual-carb setup. EMPI offers stock replacements as well that can be modified.

Weber and Dellorto Carburetors

Some history on the famous Weber carburetor. Eduardo Weber worked for Fiat at the Turin plant

The Solex Kadron Brosol carburetor is offered in 40- and 44-mm throttle openings by EMPI. EMPI calls them the 40K series. This carburetor is a good choice for semi-stock or mild street vehicles. It uses a 28-mm main Venturi. Center-mount applications will need intake manifold heat to work well in cold climates. The original VW carburetion relied on it because center-mount setups can ice up without manifold heat. Manifold heat makes center mounts more drivable because fuel is more likely to be atomized and not condense on the way to the combustion chamber. (Photo Courtesy Scat Enterprises)

When absolute performance is the main objective and drivability is not as important, use the Weber 48IDA. This carburetor has been the choice of hot street Volkswagens and drag racing cars for almost 40 years. For engines greater than 2.3L, bore out the 48-mm Venturi up to 58 mm. Kits are available from Gene Berg Enterprises. (Photo Courtesy Scat Enterprises)

and later at one of their dealers. The name FIAT means Fabricating Italian Automobiles in Turin. Weber's company was named FIC or Fabricating Italian Carburetors, which was later taken over by FIAT.

Weber made carburetors as part of a conversion kit for Fiats. He developed the two-stage twin-barrel carburetors, which used two barrels of the same size. They could be set up so that each engine cylinder had its own carburetor barrel. The Shelby 289 Cobra V-8 used four IDA carburetors, with one barrel for each of the eight cylinders. In the name IDF/IDA, the "ID" stands for *Invertito-Doppio* or Inverted Double, and I believe the F was for FIAT and the A for Abarth. The IDA/IDF carburetors were used in Maserati and Alfa Romeo racing cars.

Dellorto FRDs and Weber ICTs are two brands and models that are pretty much equivalent. The Dellorto FRDs are no longer available. The Weber ICT is a good carburetor, but it is only recommended for single-port Type 1, Type 3, and Type 4 engines.

Weber IDA/IDF and Dellorto Carburetor Systems

The Weber 48IDA was designed for racing applications but will work well on the mild street applications as long as a 28-mm main Venturi is used. They do not have much of a progression circuit. The IDA uses two progression holes where the IDF uses four. So, it is either off idle or in full throttle.

The Weber IDF is the most widely used high-performance carburetor for Volkswagen air-cooled engines. The IDFs come in 40-, 44-, and 48-mm sizes, and work well for racing vehicle. These are also the carburetor of choice for off-road vehicles due to a better progression circuit and a better fuel control. These do not have flooding problems and have many advantages over the other carburetor setups such as:

- They are still being manufactured (parts are available).
- They work on a wide range of engines.
- They fit in the engine compartment with most air filters.
- There are four progression holes for smooth drivability.
- They use a vacuum advance port for distributors still using vacuum advance.

The Dellorto DRLA is the same carburetor as the Weber IDF but made by Dellorto, and it even looks like a Weber. It comes in 36-, 40-, 45-, and 48-mm main Venturi sizes. It's important to note that the DRLA carb sizing is larger than a Weber IDF. A 36-mm Dellorto is the same as a 40-mm Weber; a 45-mm Dellorto is equal to a 48-mm Weber.

The Solex 40P11 carburetor was used on older Porsche 911 and 914-6

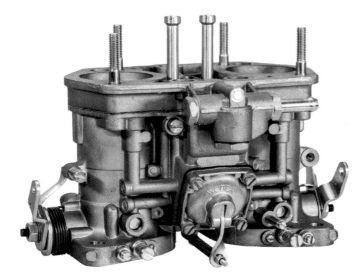

The Weber IDF series are interchangeable with 36-, 40-, 45-, and 48-mm Dellorto DRLA carburetors. The IDF and DRLA share the same intake manifold bolt pattern and air-cleaner pattern. In most cases, linkage can be interchanged. They are sold with factory jetting, which in most cases is too lean, so re-jetting is necessary. (Photo Courtesy Scat Enterprises)

Dellorto mostly makes motorcycle carburetors. The DRLA is the same as a Weber IDF, and all available service kits for Dellorto carburetors are available at dellortoshop.com. (Photo Courtesy Scat Enterprises)

vehicles. It is similar to the Weber IDF and Dellorto DRLA, except it used three barels instead of two and will not work on a VW 4-cylinder.

Carburetor Selection

The air-fuel quantity coming out of the carburetor must match the needs of the engine in the speed range for the best engine cooling. Decent engine air cooling comes from good carburetor metering so it does not go too lean, which leads to heat. The carburetor selection should be selected based on the build's piston size, valve size, port condition, and exhaust.

Remember that the build's purpose determines the carburetor choice; is it for street and a little drag racing or is it a high-performance racing or off-road vehicle? For any type of racing or off-road applications, use a Weber sized from 44- to 58-mm throttle opening IDA or Dellortos DRLA carburetors. Dellorto carburetors are available from dellorto.co.uk/product-category/complete-carburetors. Gene Berg Enterprises bores out the Weber IDA up to a 58-mm opening. EMPI, Scat, JBugs, Gene Berg, Air Cooled, and many others listed in the source guide sell Weber carbs.

These high-end carburetors may need modifications to the progression circuit for a street vehicle, but they are best for racing or off-road. The progression circuit provides fuel delivery for engine speeds from idle to more than 3,000 rpm under part-throttle openings and continues to provide fuel delivery up through 4,500 rpm. When at WOT, the fuel delivery is supplied from the main circuit with a continuance of fuel delivery from the progression circuit.

Center-mount applications need intake manifold heat to work well in cold climates. The original VW carburetion relied on it because center-mount setups can ice up without manifold heat. Manifold heat makes center mounts more drivable because fuel is more likely to be atomized and not condense on the way to the combustion chamber. (Photo Courtesy Scat Enterprises)

The progression circuit is the idle jet, idle air bleed jet, and idle mixture adjusting screw. The fuel supplied to it comes from the main jet via fuel delivery passageways. The Weber 44 IDF carb and Dellortos were designed for the Fiat Abarth engine. If these carburetors are used for street use and not modified, there will be a rough idle and flat spots.

Daily driven street vehicles should be equipped with a modified stock Solex 34 PCIT-3, progressive Weber 2-barrel, or a dual-tuned 2-barrel Weber or a Dual Solex 40 Kadron carburetor if the engine develops at least 70 hp. If using carburetors over electronic fuel injection, there are several carburetor systems to choose from.

Center-Mount 1-Barrel Carburetor Systems

Center-mount 1-barrel carburetor systems include the stock Solex 31 PCIT and 34 PCIT and a stock replacement, such as the Kadron or EMPI 40- to 44-mm throttle.

A Volkswagen stock carburetor may not be rebuildable because it may be worn out. The throttle shaft to bore area may have too much wear and will suck air. It is better to just replace it. EMPI and Scat offer a 34 PICT stock carburetor, which is not actually factory because Solex went out of business a long time ago. Yet, they are called stock because they are very similar to the original equipment. The Solex 30/31 is a good example, and this unit is jetted very lean. The main jet can be upgraded for better overall drivability.

EMPI offers its version of a stock replacement carburetor for PICT series. The EMPI 30 PICT-1 is a new carburetor that has been made to mirror the original Solex round-bowl 30 PICT-1 carburetor in operation and appearance. This carburetor is now approved for classes 1-2/1600, 5/1600, 9, 11. (SCORE International

Off-Road racing Class 1/2-1600 is an Open Wheel restricted suspension, limited Volkswagen motor class that competes within the SCORE off-road race series including the Baja 1000, Baja 500, Baja Sur 500, San Felipe 250 and therefore the SCORE Desert Challenge. No production vehicles are allowed during this class.)

EMPI also offers a version of the Solex 34 PICT-3 carburetor that is engineered to be just like the original and will work on all 1,600-cc dual-port engines. EMPI carburetors include gasket and studs.

Dual-Mount Dual 1-Barrel Carburetor System

The VW factory dual 32-mm Solex carburetor kit is a dual-mount 1-barrel system.

Center-Mount 2-Barrel Carburetor Systems

Center-Mount 2-barrel carburetor systems include the Weber IDF, Weber IDA, Weber DCNF, Dellorto DRLA, Solex 40P11, and Progressive Weber Carburetor. Just take out the stock center section with the 1-barrel mounting and install a 2-barrel mounting that connects to each side casting. It may need a brace to keep it steady when the throttle pulls on. This simple modification with the stock distributor timed at 7½ degrees BTDC will reduce any flat spots and add additional horsepower.

Do not use the Holley Bug Spray carburetor because it has not been in production or use since around 1978. Most VW engine builders use single or dual Weber, dual ICT, single or double Weber/EMPI IDA, or Dellorto carburetors. The Bug Spray was a performer back in the 1970s and 1980s but is outmoded due to age and wear.

The center-mount progressive 2-barrel works well when properly jetted, such as the Holley Weber progressive 2-barrel for a Ford Pinto. Later model units come with an electric choke, making it easier to start and drive a cold engine. Many stock carburetors came with electric chokes, and they definitely made life easier for the driver of a vehicle with a center-mount setup. It does, however, take time to set up. You can also use a Dellorto DRLA or Weber IDF or DCNF 2BBL carburetor for a non-progressive setup. These carburetors will provide performance in place of drivability.

Off-Road Dune Buggy Center-Mount Applications

Use a middle- or center-mount system for most sand dune and off-road applications due to their simplicity. Off-road and sand dune operation generates a lot of road debris and the dual carb setup, which is mounted on the engine skin, will be exposed to this dirt and sand. The center-mount system moves less than a dual mount because the dual carbs are set high and will move in the wind so to speak. There is little difference in the power produced by either system, so I recommend the center mount for any off-road use.

Dual Carburetor Systems Linkage

When choosing a dual carburetor system, choose the type of linkage to operate them in unison. Dual linkage comes in two forms: center pull or cross-bar (also called a hex-bar).

Center pull linkages do not generally compensate for thermal expansion. With the cross-bar (or hex-bar) linkage, throttle position is almost never affected by engine temperature with the associated growth and contraction.

Center-pull linkage uses a pivot system toward the center of the engine. When the gas pedal is pushed down, the linkage pulls and/or pushes the carburetor throttles open. (Photo Courtesy Shutterstock)

Thermal Expansion

The concepts behind thermal expansion are the dimensional changes exhibited by solids, liquids, and gases from changes in temperature while pressure is held constant.

The solid engine block is constantly dealing with different types of liquids and gases. Liquids expand and contract based on temperature differences. All through the expanding and contracting events, the liquids have to be able to withstand the pressures that are created in an engine and not lose their integrity.

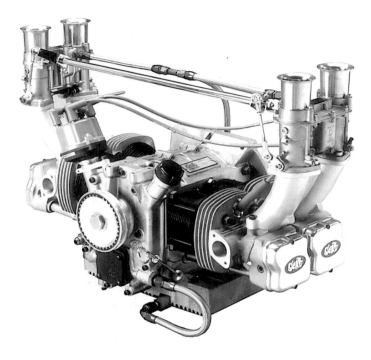

Cross-bar, or hex-bar, linkage pushes the throttles open from above the carburetors. Due to thermal expansion, an air-cooled engine will grow wider. This is important for the dual-carburetor linkage. When the linkage is above the carburetors, it is not as subject to engine heat. (Photo Courtesy Scat Enterprises)

There are a variety of hex-bar-linkage kits available for dual-carb setups. You are pretty safe with a cross-bar, or hex-bar, linkage for all dual-carburetor applications. Steel linkage is always better than aluminum. Aluminum is soft and expands faster and can cause the dual-linkage seizures.

Fuel Pumps

The purpose of the fuel pump is to deliver fuel to the carburetor or fuel-injection system using a pressure differential, which is done by creating low pressure in the tank and having atmospheric pressure push the fuel the length of the vehicle.

The VW mechanical fuel pump consists of a mechanical arm that contacts a pushrod driven by the camshaft lobe. Mechanical fuel pumps are suction units because they create low pressure in the tank and then atmospheric pressure pushes the fuel.

The standard VW mechanical pump works quite well for just about all applications. I recommend the Type 2 mechanical fuel pump because it puts out a steady 5 psi. The Type 1 will deliver between 3 and 5 psi. However, you must test the fuel pressure at idle using a T fitting to make sure it is not too high.

Electric Fuel Pump

Electric fuel pumps are generally pusher units, and the entire fuel

The VW mechanical fuel pump is mounted on the engine and operated by a pushrod from a lobe on the camshaft to an arm on the pump, which is half the engine or crank-shaft speed. (Photo Courtesy Scat Enterprises)

It is a really good idea to use a fuel-pressure regulator to prevent carburetors from flooding at low speeds. Some regulators have a dial to adjust the pressure, which makes on-the-spot adjustments easy. (Photo Courtesy Scat Enterprises)

A 12-volt solenoid-type electric fuel pump that produces 5.0 to 5.5 psi is available from EMPI (part number 41-2602). The pump comes with mounting hardware and instructions. Scat offers a solid-state 12-volt, lightweight, compact-design electric fuel pump that is rated to pump 30 gallons per hour at 3 pounds of pressure. It is highly recommended that a fuel-pressure regulator be used with these electric fuel pumps. (Photo Courtesy EMPI)

Fuel Injection

In 1967 (for the 1968 model year), Volkswagen introduced the first production electronic fuel-injection system on the Type 3. It was developed in conjunction with the Robert Bosch Corporation, and they called it the D-Jetronic System. This system replaced the dual Solex 30 carburetors.

It was a simultaneous fuel-injection system, meaning the injectors opened two at a time simultaneously for each turn of the crankshaft. So, one of the fuel charges sat there until it was ignited in firing order. The injection pulse takes place just before the valve opens, and the opposite cylinder gets the injection pulse about 180 degrees before the valve opens. All current electronic fuel-injection systems are sequential, and

the injectors open in sequence with the spark. The engine load sensing device was a manifold absolute pressure (MAP) sensor that measured intake manifold pressure.

There was another set of points in the base of the distributor that provided an RPM signal to the management computer called an engine control unit (ECU). These distributor points determined the timing of the injection pulses. This system was based on a Bendix patent licensed to Bosch. Different versions of D-Jetronic were used by General Motors, Ford, Toyota, etc. I do not recommend using the old Bosch D-Jetronic system from an old Type 3 for modern builds. They were prone to problems and use an antiquated injection system. ■

supply line can be pressurized to the engine. When pressurized, fuel will have a higher boiling point, so it is unlikely that vapor will form to interfere with fuel flow.

Most electrical pumps are driven by a small electric motor; some use a solenoid-operated piston. The solenoid-style pump has been around for many years, and I have had good success with them on electronic fuel-injected diesels. Unless your build uses electronic fuel injection, I see no reason to use an electric fuel pump. However, if the mechanical pump is being replaced with an electric, the solenoid unit works well with a pressure regulator. Do not exceed 5 psi pressure.

The relationship of pressure to volume is inversely proportional. That is, as pressure increases, the volume will decrease, everything else being equal. A certain amount of fuel pressure is always required to maintain engine performance by ensuring that fuel is available on demand. At the same time, however, an adequate fuel volume is needed to ensure that the proper amount of fuel can always flow to the engine, especially during peak demand situations.

High-Performance Engine Electric Fuel Pumps

For a 12-second power street and drag-strip vehicle, use the Holley RED pump with the RED regulator. Set the regulator for the correct pressure as outlined in the carburetion instructions. Do not use the Holley BLUE pump on a carburetor-equipped engine because the pressures are too high for a VW air-cooled engine. It can be used with a high-performance electronic fuel-injected engine. Use a "T" in the fuel line to provide fuel to each carburetor with the same length

of line to each carburetor. These fuel pumps are noisy, even when shock mounted.

You can use a Facet electric fuel pump in conjunction with (after) the stock pump. The size, a small 3 psi or large 4 psi, will be determined by the engine's demands. In more severe cases, the stock pump can be removed and one 4-psi large Facet pump can be used as the pusher at the tank and another one (small or large dependent upon needs) at the engine.

Electronic Fuel Injection

One way to fix any carburetion issue is to consider using an electronic fuel-injection system. This was how the original equipment manufacturers (OEM) (such as Volkswagen, General Motors, Ford, Fiat, etc.) solved their fuel economy and emissions control with high-performance issues.

Electronic fuel injection (EFI) uses a precise engine management computer to control the operation of fuel injectors and other functions based on a number of input sensors feeding information sent to it. This computer receives input from the input sensors for engine temperature, intake air temperature, manifold absolute pressure, and throttle position, all to determine the opening or pulse width of the fuel injectors.

The lower the engine temperature, the longer the pulse width, which is the injector "on-time," so more fuel is injected. As temperature increases,

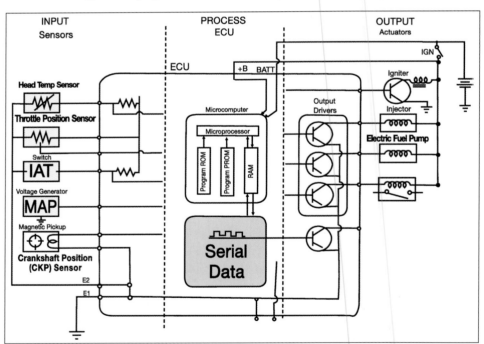

The electronic control unit (ECU) manages the entire fuel-injection system. It uses resistors, capacitors, integrated circuits, and other components. The largest chip is the microprocessor unit, which is called the central processing unit (CPU). Based on the input sensors, such as throttle position and MAP sensor load, the output is the pulse width of the fuel injector. An engine temperature sensor mounted in the cylinder head provides the ECU with the engine temperature to modify the injector pulse width.

ECUs are available from several companies. Due to the array of different fuel-injection products, buy a complete system with installation instructions from a company such as the Dub Shop or Gene Berg Enterprises. The MegaSquirt is an ECU used for VW electronic fuel injection. (Photo Courtesy the Dub Shop)

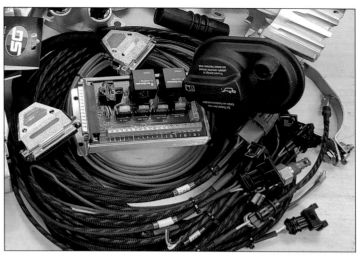

A complete wiring harness and relay board available from the Dub Shop is recommended for use with its MS2 or MS3 ECU, but it is not compatible with the MicroSquirt ECU. (Photo Courtesy the Dub Shop)

the pulse width becomes shorter and less fuel is injected. Let's look at some of the components of a modern electronic fuel-injection system.

Head Temperature Thermistor Sensor

A modified GM-type thermistor calibration sensor is used to measure surface temperature of the cylinder head as an input to the ECU. A thermistor is different than a resistor. It has a negative temperature coefficient (NTC), and the hotter it gets, the lower the resistance. It is different than the head temperature sensor placed under a spark plug, which is not a thermistor.

Relay Board

Some aftermarket suppliers, such as the Dub Shop, offer a relay board

A specific fuel-injection intake manifold is needed along with a throttle body where the throttle position sensor will be mounted. The correct injectors and fuel rails to feed those injectors are also needed. (Photo Courtesy the Dub Shop)

and a complete wiring harness, so you do not have to make your own harness. When all the input sensors are plugged in, just run the wire connections to this relay board, trim the wires to length, and screw them into the labeled terminal strip.

Gene Berg Enterprises sells the programmable Haltech fuel-injection system. I have not seen any other off-the-shelf systems, but you should check with some of the aftermarket suppliers listed in the source guide, as more product is introduced over time.

Intake Air Temperature Sensor

The intake air temperature (IAT) sensor is also a thermistor and used to measure the air coming into the intake manifold. The IAT is a thermistor in a circuit and is a variable ground, which uses a voltage divider network where the voltage is divided between the sensor input and a sensor ground inside the computer.

The ECU provides a 5-volt reference signal to the IAT sensor. When cold, the sensor provides high resistance, which the computer reads as high signal voltage. As the engine warms up, the thermistor sensor resistance becomes lower and the signal voltage drops, so that is the difference. Where the IAT is placed in the system is important.

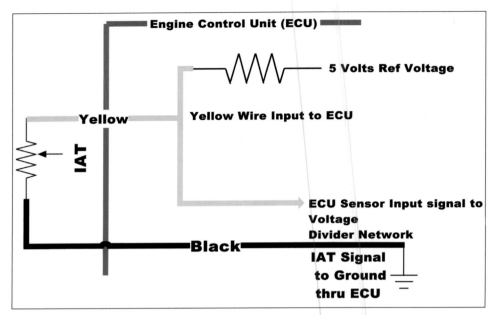

When you check voltage on the yellow wire when the engine is cold, it should read high voltage (3 to 5 volts). At normal operating temperature, the signal voltage should be low (0.47 to 1.45 volts).

Manifold Pressure Sensor

The manifold absolute pressure (MAP) sensor is the engine load sensor. It has a solid-state silicon wafer on one side, and the other side is connected to the intake manifold. As intake manifold pressure changes, the pressure pushing on the silicon wafer changes the output voltage to the ECU, indicating engine load.

This type of fuel-injection control method is known as a speed density system. It measures intake airflow by sensing changes in intake manifold

pressures resulting from engine load and speed changes. The ECU uses the MAP sensor to read these pressures. The ECU combines MAP along with temperature, RPM, and throttle position to calculate the injector opening time. If using a Dub Shop EFI, an external MAP sensor is needed.

The manifold absolute pressure (MAP) sensor requires a vacuum reference from a port after the throttle plates to measure engine vacuum or low pressure. (Photo Courtesy the Dub Shop)

In a naturally aspirated engine, the IAT sensor is located before the throttle body or in the air filter housing. In single-throttle-body applications, the IAT is placed after the throttle body. In a turbocharged or supercharged application, it needs to be placed after the turbocharger or supercharger. This is because the intercooler modifies the temperature, and the ECU needs to know the air temperature going into the intake manifold after being modified by a boosting system. (Photo Courtesy the Dub Shop)

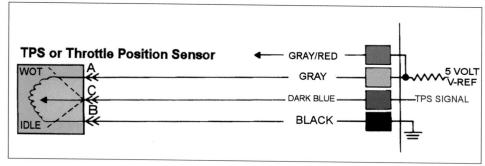

The throttle position sensor (TPS) provides throttle-angle data to the ECU. It is a good example of a three-wire sensor that uses a reference voltage wire, a ground circuit back to the computer, and a signal voltage wire.

Since the polarities of the ignition primary and secondary windings are fixed, one plug always fires in a forward direction, while the other always fires in reverse. This arrangement requires more energy than conventional systems. Coil design, saturation time, and the primary current flow on DIS systems are able to produce the necessary energy to accomplish this. These systems are also called waste spark systems. (Photo Courtesy the Dub Shop)

Throttle Position Sensor

The ECU monitors the throttle position sensor (TPS) signal wire for input values. These run on 5 volts and usually operate in a range from 0.5 to 4.5 volts. Once open and closed throttle positions have been calibrated in the ECU, this voltage is converted into a percentage between 0 and 100 percent and is displayed in the software.

The throttle body is opened and closed by way of a cable that is connected to the accelerator pedal. When the throttle is closed, the computer reads a low voltage signal. When the throttle is wide open, the computer reads a high voltage signal. In other words, the voltage signal changes relative to throttle position about 0.5 volts at idle and about 4.5 to 5 volts at wide-open throttle. This informs the computer of necessary speeds and/or acceleration.

Ignition Systems

The direct/distributorless ignition system (DIS) uses a control module that is part of the coil assembly and connecting wires to replace the ignition distributor. In a waste spark system, as it is commonly called, a spark plug is attached to each end of the induction coil secondary winding.

Each coil of the system fires two plugs at the same time in two companion cylinders. The pistons in these cylinders will reach TDC at an identical time. The cylinder at TDC on the compression stroke is the event cylinder, while the cylinder at TDC on the exhaust stroke or TDC overlap is the waste cylinder. When the coil fires, both spark plugs fire at the same time to complete the electric circuit.

Crankshaft Position Sensor

The purpose of the crankshaft position sensor (CKP) is to provide a signal to the ECU that can be used as a reference to calculate RPM. This signal tells the ECU that the engine is cranking and/or running. It also identifies cylinder position for sequential fuel injection and ignition and on systems using the sequential coil-on-plug (COP) ignition.

The CKP sensor is used in conjunction with a special crankshaft pulley that uses a reluctor wheel with 36 teeth with one missing tooth, or 36-1. It has a tooth every 10 crank degrees. This crank trigger is needed for DIS wasted spark application and COP systems.

The CKP sensor signal is needed for the engine to start. When the engine cranks, the ECU looks for an

The crankshaft position (CKP) sensor is found in electronically controlled fuel-injection systems, and it is used to determine injector and spark operation. It can be a Hall-effect switch (solid-state silicone chip dependent on a magnetic field to give a signal to the ECU) or a magnetic pickup type of sensor. (Photo Courtesy the Dub Shop)

The CKP sensor is located in front of the crankshaft pulley. The CKP sensor works with a 36x reluctor wheel. The reluctor wheel is mounted on the crankshaft pulley. A reluctor is reluctant, or unwilling, to allow a magnetic path, so it aids in the generation of an electrical signal to the ECU. (Photo Courtesy the Dub Shop)

An ignition system called coil-on-plug (COP) or coil-near-plug (CNP) is available from the Dub Shop to have a sequential ignition system to match the sequential fuel-injection system. (Photo Courtesy the Dub Shop)

RPM signal from the CKP sensor. The Dub Shop offers its version of a CKP sensor called the Mini Cam Sync. It will be needed when using sequential fuel injection, sequential spark, or sequential fuel and spark.

This sensor provides one sync pulse to the ECU just before number-1 is at TDC on the compression stroke. This happens before the crankshaft pulley missing tooth passes the CKP sensor. When the pulse from the CKP sensor is received by the ECU and then the missing crankshaft tooth is seen, the ECU then knows to start the sequential cycle, firing each injector or plug in the firing order starting with cylinder number-1.

Camshaft Position Sensor

The main purpose of the camshaft position sensor (CMP) if used is to provide the ECU with a signal that helps determine where number-1 or

the starting point is in the engine firing order 1-4-3-2. The ECU provides the power feed for the CMP. The ECU uses this signal for basic control of the COP ignition control circuit and the fuel injectors.

Coil-On-Plug Ignition

Coil-on-plug (COP) ignition uses one induction coil for every plug. This technique is called coil-by-plug, coil-near-plug, or coil-over-plug ignition. COP eliminates the use of plug wires that can cause misfires and be a source of EMI or electromagnetic interference that may cause problems to some computer signals. The ECU directly controls the operation of the ignition coil timing of the spark.

Fuel Injection Fuel Pump

The use of an ECU in electronic fuel injection pretty much requires the use of an electric fuel pump

because a steady, controlled supply of fuel is needed over a mechanical unit. The Dub Shop sells the Walbro inline fuel pump that works well with its other fuel-injection components. This particular fuel pump can handle most engines over 400 hp in either a normally aspirated or turbocharged/ supercharged engines. If a different fuel pump is selected, make sure that it is compatible with the engine management computer (ECU).

Injectors

Fuel is delivered to the engine by way of the fuel injectors. The ECU controls the fuel injectors. The fuel injector is provided a continuous supply of pressurized fuel by a fuel pump. As the fuel injector solenoid becomes energized by being grounded by the ECU, it injects the pressurized fuel into the intake manifold. The computer controls fuel flow by pulse

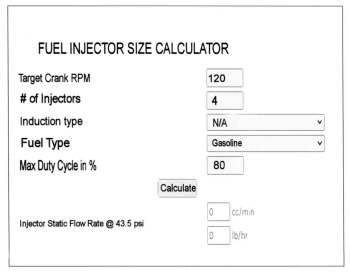

FUEL INJECTOR SIZE CALCULATOR

Target Crank RPM	120
# of Injectors	4
Induction type	N/A ˅
Fuel Type	Gasoline ˅
Max Duty Cycle in %	80
	Calculate
Injector Static Flow Rate @ 43.5 psi	0 cc/min
	0 lb/hr

Use the injector calculator provided on thedubshop.com/choosing-your-injectors. This is found in the fuel-injection tech section under choosing your injectors. Results are based on target horsepower and induction-type maximum duty cycle. (Photo Courtesy the Dub Shop)

width modulation of the injector "on time." The on time of the injector is determined by a combination of the inputs. The Dub Shop provides an online injector calculator to determine what size injectors to use.

An injection system can be set up to be either simultaneous (also called bank injection) or grouped injection, where half of the fuel injectors are in a group that are pulsed simultaneously. In a 4-cylinder VW engine, there are two cylinders per group. There is one injection pulse per power cycle.

With grouped injection, one cylinder gets the injection pulse right before the intake valve opens, and the other cylinder gets the injection pulse about 180 degrees before the intake valve opens. In a sequential injection system, the injectors operate in engine firing order sequence.

The crankshaft position sensor along with a camshaft position sensor are used to determine when to open the injectors and fire the spark plugs on when using sequential fuel, sequential spark, or sequential fuel and spark.

EFI kits and options are listed in the next section.

Forced Induction

Naturally aspirated (NA) engines rely only on an atmospheric pressure of 14.7 psi to push the air-fuel mixture into the combustion chamber. The piston compresses this mixture before ignition to increase the force of the burning due to the expanding gases caused by their ignition. The greater the compression of the air and fuel gas mixture, the greater the power resulting from combustion. A higher compression ratio means higher thermal efficiency or the portion of the heat supplied to the engine that is turned into work. As the compression ratio increases, the expansion ratio also increases, thus thermal efficiency increases.

When a turbocharger or super-charger is added, the volumetric efficiency is greater than atmospheric pressure because air-mass flow of the engine is increased due to the increased pressure. The intake valve timing on a four-stroke cycle engine determines if the engine is actually supercharged. If the cylinder air pressure at the start of the compression stroke is higher than atmospheric, then basically the engine is super-charged. The degree of supercharging is directly related to the actual cylinder air pressure charge. The amount of force an air-fuel charge produces when it is ignited is largely a function of the charge density.

The density of the air-fuel mixture can be increased by adding more air pressure using a supercharger or turbocharger. These are mechanically or gas-driven air pumps that will use more air pressure to compress the air-fuel mixture, making it denser. When the density of an air-fuel mixture is greater, so is its weight or mass. Engine horsepower is directly related to the weight or mass of an air-fuel charge combusted within a

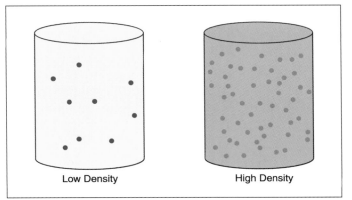

Low Density   High Density

Density is the mass weight of a substance in a given amount of space. The greater the density of an air-fuel charge that is forced into a cylinder, the greater the force it produces when it is ignited—and the greater the engine power. As more fuel and air is stuffed into an engine cylinder, the combustion charge becomes more powerful, and the engine produces more power and torque.

given time period. The amount of additional air pressure is called boost, and this is the value that needs to be known and be able to measure and regulate.

Boost is the air pressure developed in a supercharger or a turbocharger. Boost increases the air mass for a certain engine displacement. In a Roots-type supercharger, the air ratio is consistent with engine displacement throughout the speed range. Supercharger boost in a Roots Blower will not be consistent due to the fact that at lower speeds there is leakage because there is time for the leakage between the supercharger case and the rotors that leads to a loss in boost.

An increase in boost pressure will increase the pressure pushing or sucking the charge into the cylinder. Turbocharging can have draw-through or blow-through systems, so the pressure is more on the top or vacuum on the bottom of the charge.

When the boost pressure is greater, the compression and expansion ratios will be greater. For example, if the compression ratio is 8:1, a smaller amount of boost pressure can be used. Static compression is the

compression ratio that was built into the engine. Compression ratio is the ratio of the cylinder volume at BDC to the volume at TDC. The effective compression ratio is the ratio after adding the boost pressure and is what the engine gets while running. It is influenced by cam timing, intake boost pressure, connecting rod length, and volumetric efficiency.

In the Compression Ratio Based on Boost Pressure table, I listed the engine static compression ratio in the left column. Then, the very top row shows the boost pressure that is going to be run. The values in the columns below that boost pressure are the resultant effective compression ratio. Wallace Racing has an effective compression ratio on its website (wallaceracing.com).

Regarding boost pressure, I recommend not going over 7 to 8 psi for any street build. On a street build, ACE Performance Engines recommends running about 10-psi boost with E85 (85-percent ethanol and 15-percent gasoline) gasoline without an intercooler. This is because E85 has an octane rating of 108, where regular gasoline is 87. If using a modern EFI system such as Fuel-

Tech or the Dub Shop's MegaSquirt and reducing the timing advance to keep engine temperature at the safe level, the motor should develop about 340 bhp at the flywheel.

Mario Valletta concurs with me on a street build with boost kept from 7 to 12 psi. These builds typically do not use an intercooler with that boost pressure. The intake air temperature must be kept at a reasonable level.

If using an intercooler on the VW build, then 15 to 20 pounds of boost will work. Race builds usually start at 14 to 15 psi. Using this boost pressure, you would be able to double an NA engine's horsepower because you are putting twice the air into the engine. If the engine is a robust build with a strong bottom end and good breathing, 30 to 40 psi is what Mario Valletta of the Dub Shop tells me he hears in the race groups.

Supercharging

The supercharger is an engine belt-driven air pump that supplies air pressure greater than 14.7 psi into the intake manifold to boost engine torque and power by compressing the charge. A supercharger provides

Compression Ratio Based on Boost Pressure

| Static Compression Ratio | Boost Pressure (PSI) | | | | | | | | | | | |
	2	4	6	8	10	12	14	16	18	20	22	24
6.0:1	6.8:1	7.6:1	8.4:1	9.3:1	10.1:1	10.9:1	11.7:1	12.5:1	13.3:1	14.2:1	15.0:1	16.6:1
6.5:1	7.4:1	8.3:1	9.2:1	10.0:1	10.9:1	11.8:1	12.7:1	13.6:1	14.5:1	15.3:1	16.2:1	18.0:1
7.0:1	8.0:1	8.9:1	9.9:1	10.8:1	11.8:1	12.7:1	13.7:1	14.6:1	15.6:1	16.5:1	17.5:1	19.4:1
7.5:1	8.5:1	9.5:1	10.6:1	11.6:1	12.6:1	13.6:1	14.6:1	15.7:1	16.7:1	17.7:1	18.7:1	20.8:1
8.0:1	9.1:1	10.2:1	11.3:1	12.4:1	13.4:1	14.5:1	15.6:1	16.7:1	17.8:1	20.1:1	20.0:1	22.1:1
8.5:1	9.7:1	10.8:1	12.0:1	13.1:1	14.3:1	15.4:1	16.6:1	17.8:1	18.8:1	21.1:1	21.2:1	23.5:1
9.0:1	10.2:1	11.4:1	12.7:1	13.9:1	15.1:1	16.3:1	17.6:1	18.8:1	19.8:1	22.4:1	22.5:1	24.9:1
9.5:1	10.8:1	12.1:1	13.4:1	14.7:1	16.0:1	17.3:1	18.5:1	18.5:1	20.9:1	23.6:1	23.7:1	26.3:1
10.0:1	11.4:1	12.7:1	14.1:1	15.4:1	16.8:1	18.2:1	19.5:1	19.5:1	21.9:1	24.8:1	25.0:1	27.6:1
11.0:1	12.5:1	14.0:1	15.5:1	17.0:1	18.5:1	20.0:1	21.5:1	23.0:1	24.5:1	26.0:1	27.5:1	29.0:1

an increase in power without the turbo lag associated with turbochargers. However, because superchargers are engine-driven, they take horsepower away from the engine to operate; thus, they are not as efficient as a turbocharger.

Superchargers operate on the positive-displacement principle, which means they work at a constant flow rate regardless of the exit pressure. They can operate with or without internal compression. Centrifugal or spiral-type superchargers have internal compression like a water pump. The Roots-type supercharger does not have internal compression.

Roots-type superchargers were named for Philander and Francis Roots, two brothers from Connersville, Indiana, who patented the design in 1860 as a type of water pump to be used in mines. Later, it was used to move air on the two-stroke-cycle Detroit diesel engine

LOBE

A supercharger is basically an air pump driven mechanically by the engine. Gears, shafts, chains, or belts from the crankshaft can be used to turn the pump, which means that the supercharger pumps air in direct relation to engine speed.

and other supercharged engines. The Roots-type supercharger is called a positive-displacement design because all of the air that enters is forced through the unit.

The Roots-type supercharger found on racing VW bugs uses twisted blade rotors that turn in the opposite direction to each other. The gap between these rotors helps to determine the boost pressure. The pressure ratio (i.e., the pressure before compression to the pressure after compression of a mechanical supercharger) does not depend on its rotation speed. However, the volumetric flow (volume of air) is dependent on blower rotational speed.

If the engine and the blower have the same speed ratio, a bigger blower that has more volume will make more boost than a smaller one on the same size engine. If the engine displacement increases, boost will decrease if the blower speed and blower size remain the same. With a specific blower size and a given size engine, boost may be increased by running the blower faster by using a gearset to overdrive the blower. Of course, it can be decreased by running it slower.

Turbocharging

Approximately 20 percent of an engine's power is used by a mechanically driven supercharger. A turbocharger is a centrifugal supercharger connected to a turbine drive wheel, which is located in the engine exhaust path. Wasted exhaust gas is reclaimed to perform work because combustion heat energy lost in the engine exhaust (40 to 50 percent) is used to operate the turbocharger. A turbocharger's main advantage over the engine-driven supercharger is that it does not drain engine power.

When the engine turns at low speed, both exhaust heat and pressure are low and also the turbine is about 1,000 rpm, which is a low speed. Due to this low speed, the compressor doesn't turn fast enough to develop any boost pressure. The air simply passes through it, and it operates as a naturally aspirated engine.

As engine speed increases, both exhaust heat and flow increases, causing the turbine and compressor wheels to rotate faster. Since there's no brake and really little rotating resistance on the turbocharger shaft, the turbine and compressor wheels accelerate because the exhaust heat increases. An engine running at full power will have turbocharger speeds between 100,000 and 150,000 rpm.

Intercooler

The intercooler is used to reduce the temperature of the air after it has passed through a turbocharger but before entering the intake manifold. Compressing a gas adds heat to it and raises its temperature. When the air going into the intake manifold is cooled, it becomes tighter and denser to achieve more power. It is basically a radiator for hot air, and passing air through it cools the air and makes it denser.

If your build is for a racing application, using 15 to 35 pounds of boost will work. You will need to install an intercooler to keep the air temperature within reason. Neither CB Performance, EMPI, Air Cooled, or Scat sells intercoolers or turbochargers.

Alligator Performance offers the BladeRunner GT Series Intercooler (part number AFE-46-20011).

Boost Control

Superchargers and turbochargers will increase the pressure, pushing

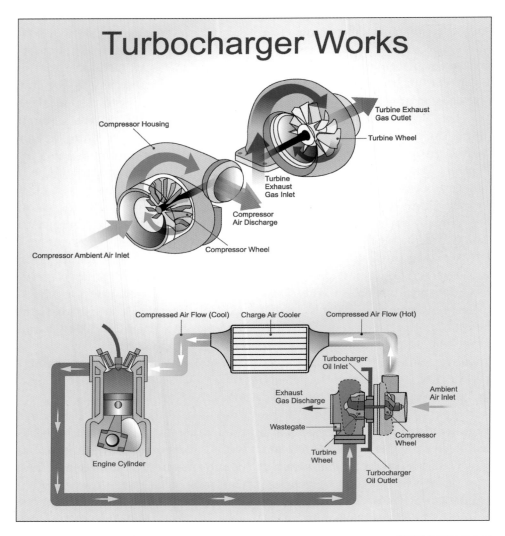

Turbocharger Works

Compressor Housing

Turbine Exhaust Gas Outlet

Turbine Wheel

Turbine Exhaust Gas Inlet

Compressor Air Discharge

Compressor Wheel

Compressor Ambient Air Inlet

Compressed Air Flow (Cool)

Charge Air Cooler

Compressed Air Flow (Hot)

Turbocharger Oil Inlet

Ambient Air Inlet

Exhaust Gas Discharge

Wastegate

Compressor Wheel

Turbine Wheel

Turbocharger Oil Outlet

Engine Cylinder

A turbocharger looks much like the centrifugal pump used for an engine water pump. Hot exhaust gases flow from the combustion chamber to the turbine wheel through the exhaust system. The gases are heated, and they expand as they leave the engine. The expansion of hot gases against the turbine wheel's blades forces the turbine wheel to turn—not the force of the exhaust gases. (Graphic Courtesy Shutterstock)

In a typical turbocharger, the exhaust from the engine turns the turbine on the left side more than 100,000 revolutions per minute. The turbine is connected by a shaft to a compressor located on the right side of the turbocharger. The compressor blades draw air from the air-filter housing and force it into the intake manifold to provide extra power. (Photo Courtesy Shutterstock)

An intercooler is also called an air-to-air cooler because it cools the air using air to reduce air temperature for forced induction (turbocharged or supercharged) systems to improve volumetric efficiency. This is done by increasing intake air density through nearly constant pressure cooling.

When the wastegate is closed, all of the exhaust travels to the turbocharger. When a specified boost amount develops in the intake manifold, the wastegate valve opens. As the valve opens, most of the exhaust flows directly out the exhaust system, bypassing the turbocharger. (Photo Courtesy Shutterstock)

air into the intake manifold engine beyond 14.7 psi. This increased pressure forces more air into the combustion chamber over what would normally be forced in by atmospheric pressure to provide a heavier charge with greater mass. This increased charge increases engine power.

The amount of boost or intake manifold pressure can be measured in either pounds per square inch (psi), inches of mercury (Hg), BAR, or atmospheres. The higher the boost (pressure), the greater will be the horsepower. Other factors must also be considered when increasing boost pressure: as boost pressure increases, the temperature of the air also increases and as the temperature of the air increases, combustion temperatures also increase, which increases the possibility of detonation.

To prevent over-boost and engine damage, some turbocharger systems use a wastegate. The wastegate is a bypass valve at the exhaust inlet to the turbine, which can allow all of the exhaust into the turbine or route part of the exhaust past the turbine, back into the exhaust system.

With less exhaust flowing across the vanes of the turbocharger, the turbocharger decreases in speed and boost pressure is reduced. When the boost pressure drops, the wastegate valve closes to direct exhaust gases back over the turbocharger vanes, again allowing the boost pressure to rise. The wastegate is the pressure control valve of a turbocharger system.

Draw-Through or Blow-Through Setup

You will need to decide on either a draw-through or blow-through setup. Neither a blow-through or draw-through system is a quick bolt-on road to big power. However, they do open up the doors of forced induction to carbureted bugs.

With a blow-through setup, the turbocharger feeds the carburetor. The exhaust gases spin the exhaust side turbine, then the compressor side turbine blows through the carburetor. For this, the carburetor needs to be set up properly.

A standard NA engine carburetor setup may not deliver enough fuel to match the compressed air coming from the turbocharger. The engine may not run well. So, consider a draw-through system, where the turbocharger is placed after the carburetor. This way, rather than the carburetor feeding the engine, it's actually feeding the turbocharger. The compressor turbine draws in the cold air and fuel, and then delivers it to the engine. This is an effective method of getting power, but the addition of fuel within the turbocharger can shorten its life. The Weber IDA or the Dellorto DLRA are used with a draw-through turbocharger.

It would be much better to use electronic fuel injection, where the fuel is injected into the engine at a high speed and a high pressure in a blow-through configuration. These systems will require some planning and lots of fabrication and tuning. Yet, when done correctly they will give a build some much-needed boost and horsepower.

Installation

Supercharging in a VW air-cooled engine should only be used for robust off-road or racing builds. I strongly suggest using EFI instead of carburetors. These builds must have a strong bottom end with H-rods and a counterweighted forged crankshaft along with the right heads and camshaft for good breathing.

Turbocharging can be applied to a mild build along with robust racing and off-road builds. If you are a good fabricator who also knows how to weld, you can fabricate your own unique turbo or supercharged bug. However, if you are a "put together nuts and bolts" type of builder, go for the kit approach. I will list what kits and components are available in the build section to follow.

Off the shelf turbocharger systems are available from CB Performance, the Dub Shop, and Low Budget Turbos at 714-639-4BUG. There should not be any reliability concerns regarding these turbochargers because they have proven to be reliable. If building a high-performance engine over 200 bhp, it will need high-octane gasoline. The components needed for a bug supercharger setup are available from the Dub Shop, and I will list them in the build recommendation section. These systems will require a compatible fuel system whether it is a blow-through or draw-through system.

Build Recommendations

More power means more speed, so it is necessary to upgrade the braking system.

With a turbocharger comes more heat. Make sure to install gauges to measure the temperature, oil pressure, air-fuel ratio, and boost level so that you do not destroy your engine. With an electronic fuel-injection system, safeguards are available for a boosted engine.

Turbocharging will deliver a 50-percent boost in power for an air-cooled engine, so upgrade the clutch and add driveline supports.

There are only two available aftermarket superchargers: AMR500 Mini-Roots and the Judson centrifugal supercharger. The Judson unit is completely different from a Roots blower and is not a positive displacement unit like the Roots blower. It is a centrifugal supercharger that is belt driven by the crankshaft. It compresses the air-fuel mixture from the carburetor using four sliding vanes located on an eccentric rotor. As the rotor spins, the vanes are thrown outward from centrifugal force to seal against the wall of the supercharger. This action pressurizes the air-fuel mixture and pushes it into the intake manifold. The result is that the volume of air/fuel is increased. This is a draw-through system using a carburetor. This unit was built for older 36- and 40-bhp engines.

EFI Kits

With more air, the engine will need more fuel. Fuel burned without air becomes smoke. If a vehicle is fuel injected, the smallest size injectors offered by the Dub Shop will support a good bit of boost. The Dub Shop provides an online injector calculator to determine what size injectors to use. If your car is not fuel injected, it might be something to consider instead of carburetion on a turbo build.

The Dub Shop EFI kit contains everything you need to install EFI on your build:

The carburetor works by the atmospheric pressure differential, so make sure that it is in an environment in which it can match the pressure of the turbocharger. A shroud or cover may need to be manufactured for the carburetor, where the pressure can be stabilized. (Photo Courtesy ACE Performance Engines)

- Complete wire harness
- Intake manifolds
- Injectors you selected
- TPS
- MAP sensor
- IAT sensor
- Head temperature sensor
- CTS for blower
- Hall sensors (CKP sensor)
- Reluctor pulley
- Ignition coil(s)
- Fuel pump, filter, pressure regulator and 5/16-inch hardline
- O_2 sensor: needs to be bung welded into the exhaust and sized for the sensor and the routing of its wiring.

The VW FuelTech FT450 EFI kit for all air-cooled engines includes the following:

- FT450 ECU Digital Dashboard and data logger
- Fuel injection
- Integrated dashboard with data acquisition, power management, and boost controller
- Flex fuel sensor

The Haltech EFI system from Gene Berg contains the following:

- ECU
- Harness for a 4-cylinder VW horizontally opposed engine
- Air temperature sensor
- Oil temperature sensor
- TPS
- Relays
- Installation disk, serial download cable, and instruction manual

Joe Blow fuel-injection kits include the following:

- EFI ECU
- CKP sensor
- Head temperature sensor

Turbocharger Kits

Turbochargers require a whole new exhaust, but a supercharger does not. Provide the right location for the supercharger and belts and pulleys to drive it. EMPI, Air Cooled, and Scat do not sell turbochargers. Turbochargers do not work well with excess backpressure, 1½ inch work well for mild builds and $1^5/_8$ inches for higher boost applications. You can even go to 2 inches.

Kawell Racing Engines builds draw-through turbocharger systems for street builds without problems when the boost pressure stays within the 7- to 8-psi range.

CB Performance (part number 7169) is a complete turbocharger kit for about $1,800. It contains most of what is needed to turbocharge a bug. It includes all of the plumbing and exhaust plus the turbocharger unit (part number 7489 T03/T04) with a 0.63 A/R exhaust housing, turbine wheel, compressor housing (0.70 A/R), and a 59-mm compressor wheel. Hoses and clamps along with either EFI or the right carburetors for the build will still need to be purchased.

An inexpensive turbocharger kit is available from Low Budget Turbos. It offers a complete turbo kit like it was a factory installed unit. It offers kits for all years and can custom make one to fit any build.

Supercharger Kits

For a high-performance build, install one of the following systems:

A Dub Shop AMR500 Mini-Roots supercharger features the following:

- EFI system from the Dub Shop, FuelTech, or Haltech
- Supercharger Roots blower (part number AMR500), refurbished

The AMD450 mini Roots-type supercharger unit uses the traditional twisted-blade rotors that turn in the opposite direction of each other. This is the most common supercharger used on VW air-cooled engines, and it is sold in kit form by Joe Blow Superchargers and the Dub Shop. (Photo Courtesy the Dub Shop)

- Mexican alternator stand
- AMR500 mounting bracket
- AMR500 six-rib serpentine pulley
- AMR500 hardware pack
- AMR500 gasket set
- AMR500 supercharger oil

A Joe Blow superchargers kit features the following:

- AMR500 side-draft kit
- Budget AMR500 kit: Designed for use on 1,600-cc upright engines and using a JB S&S carburetor and standard serpentine drive

Any racing build with a turbocharger or supercharger requires an intercooler. Alligator Performance offers the BladeRunner GT Series intercooler (part number AFE-46-20011). Other intercoolers are available from Derale Performance and Banks Power (the Techni-Cooler system).

Nitrous Oxide

Nitrous oxide (N_2O) is boost in a bottle that can provide performance

---

Shown is the AMD450 mini Roots-type supercharger location on a Type 1 upright engine with a single serpentine drive belt. This installation uses an electronic fuel-injection system with a single throttle body. There are more elaborate systems using dual throttle bodies. (Photo Courtesy the Dub Shop)

without adding a supercharger or turbocharger along with more carburetion. It is a colorless, non-flammable gas. Nitrous oxide has 2 nitrogen atoms and 1 oxygen atom with about 36 percent of the molecular weight in oxygen.

When nitrous oxide is injected into the very high heat of combustion, the nitrogen bond is broken and its molecules split into nitrogen and oxygen, creating an instantaneous increase in oxygen. This means that more oxygen is available to mix with more fuel during combustion to make more power.

Nitrous oxide is a made gas because, even though both nitrogen and oxygen are in the atmosphere, they are not combined into one molecule. They also require heat and a catalyst to be combined. Nitrous oxide requires 11 pounds of pressure per degree of Fahrenheit to condense it into its liquid form.

Nitrous oxide is stored in a pressurized storage container and must be installed at an angle so that the pickup tube lays in the liquid. The discharge or front end of the nitrous oxide system (NOS) storage bottle should be toward the front of a VW build.

Dry Nitrous Oxide Injection

A dry nitrous system increases the pressure to the injectors by applying nitrous pressure from the solenoid assembly directly into the intake, which increases fuel flow.

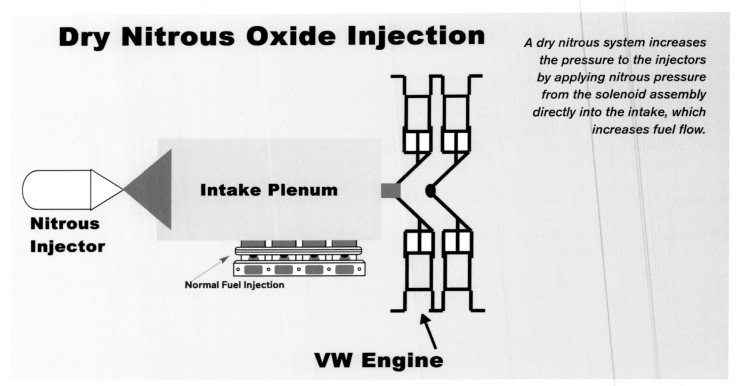

Nitrous Injector

Intake Plenum

Normal Fuel Injection

VW Engine

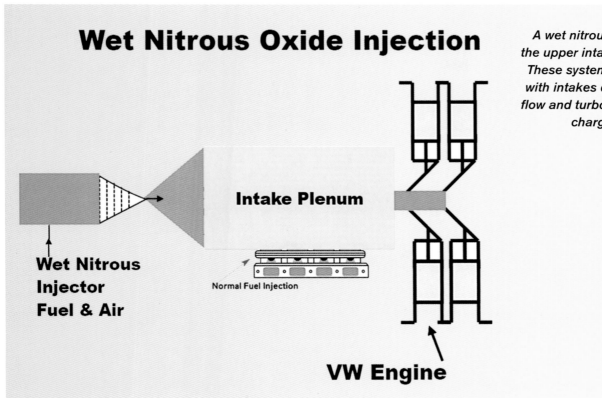

Wet Nitrous Oxide Injection

A wet nitrous system makes the upper intake wet with fuel. These systems are best used with intakes designed for wet flow and turbocharged/super-charged applications.

Wet Nitrous Injector Fuel & Air

Intake Plenum

Normal Fuel Injection

VW Engine

There are three types of nitrous systems: dry, wet, and direct port.

Dry System

In the dry system, nitrous oxide is injected into the intake manifold using a separate solenoid injector. A dry nitrous system means that the fuel required to make additional power with the nitrous oxide will be introduced through the fuel injectors. Fuel makes more power and nitrous lets you burn more fuel. This keeps the upper intake dry of fuel.

The pressure to the injectors is increased by applying nitrous pressure from the solenoid assembly when the system is activated. This causes an increase in fuel flow, just like turning up the pressure on a garden hose from half to full.

Wet System

The second type of nitrous kit is called a wet nitrous system because a carburetor plate system is included that adds nitrous oxide and gasoline at the same time. It is placed about 3 to 4 inches ahead of the throttle body for fuel-injected applications or just under the carburetor with a plate system.

Direct-Port System

The third type is the direct-port, or fogger, nitrous system, which injects the nitrous oxide and gasoline directly into each intake port. This fogger system adds the nitrous and gasoline together with a fogger nozzle. The fogger nozzle is a solenoid valve that mixes and meters the NOS and fuel to each cylinder.

This is the more powerful and accurate of the three systems due to the addition of the fogger nozzle into each intake runner. It also has the ability to use stronger solenoid valves along with a distribution block that injects nitrous and fuel to the nozzles by way of connecting tubes.

Nitrous Oxide Kits

CARiD sells the following four nitrous oxide kits for VW air-cooled engine builds:

- ZEX: wet nitrous system
- Nitrous Express: EFI sport compact nitrous system
- Nitrous Express: Hitman wet nitrous system
- NOS: drive-by-wire wet nitrous kit

Summit Racing sells the following nitrous oxide kits for VW air-cooled engine builds:

- Nitrous Express (NX) 20001-15
- Nitrous Express (NX) 20001-00
- Nitrous Express (NX) 20001-12

EXHAUST SYSTEM AND COOLING SYSTEM

As stated in Chapter 1, various forms of bolt-on horsepower can be added to an engine build, including an exhaust system with less airflow restriction that allows the engine to breathe better. The stock muffler along with the heater boxes in a 1,600-cc engine were designed for about 50 bhp.

The stock muffler does a good job of keeping the noise down, but there is a big restriction on flow to keep that noise down. There are bolt-on performance-based exhaust systems that remove that restriction and are better-flowing mufflers to keep safe from the noise police. These systems are available from EMPI, JBugs, JEGS, the Dub Shop, Gene Berg Enterprises, Scat Enterprises, John Mayer, etc.

The use of the exhaust system that breathes better or allows more exhaust to exit the engine can add up to 2 to 3 more horsepower in a stock VW air-cooled engine. That is approximately a 6.5-percent power improvement. When a Stinger exhaust or a 4-into-1 collector box exhaust system is added, the increase for a stock VW engine jumps up as much is 5 hp for an almost 11-percent increase in power.

A 4-into-1 system is four exhaust pipes, one from each exhaust port going into one exhaust collector box. Most of the exhaust systems available for VW air-cooled engines use pipes (headers) that are around 32 to 40 inches long. These header lengths work well with Super V engines and those with added carburetion, electronic fuel injection, and higher compression and displacement.

4-into-1 Merged Exhaust Systems

A 4-into-1 VW exhaust system uses a collector box at the end of where the header pipes merge. It allows a tuned header length to increase engine power by developing more vacuum applied to each combustion chamber. The collector increases the exhaust gas flow out of the engine, developing more

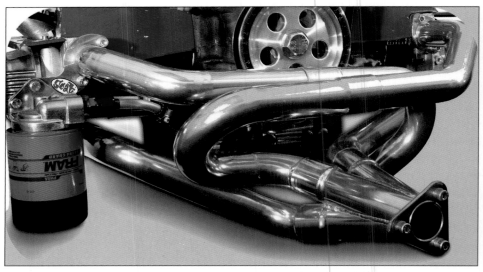

A collector box is located at the end of where the header pipes merge. It increases the engine exhaust gas flow and increases the engine's output. (Photo Courtesy Scat Enterprises)

horsepower. The short branches of traditional exhaust manifolds offer minimal scavenging. Scavenging is the draw off of the exhaust gas, having the inertia of the gas create a low-pressure region that aids the companion cylinders during blow down.

The collector box connects the cylinders that allow a discharge pressure wave to enter the neighboring exhaust pipe. The pressure wave then splits, with one wave going to the collector while the other wave returns to the initial open exhaust port. If the lengths of the pipes are right, the heartbeat will arrive toward the top of the exhaust period and can suck out the residual exhaust gas from the bore.

The sizes of the first tubes, header, and collector length all affect the system performance. Typically, an air-cooled engine should use $1^3/_8$- to $1^5/_8$-inch-diameter header pipes about 32 to 40 inches long from each cylinder going into a collector box. It then connects to a muffler and then through a 6-inch-long pipe that has at least a 50-percent larger cross-sectional area than the collector box.

The size of the first header tubes should support the diameter of the valve scavenge area. However, the flange of the pipe should meet with the exhaust port face within the plate. It's normal for the outside port to be larger than the valve seat.

Some engine builders believe that the larger area of this junction reduces exhaust back-pressure. Many off-the-shelf VW systems are marketed as being of equal length, but there may be a variation within the primary tubes. The cross-section of the pipe must be large enough to evacuate the swept volume of the cylinder and small enough to keep up

a high velocity. A high-RPM engine would support a larger-diameter primary tube. This can be a function of shorter evacuation time combined with higher piston speed. These exhaust systems are mass-produced, so you will need to accept what's going to fit. If doubtful, choose a smaller-diameter primary tube.

Technically, increasing the length of the collector will broaden the scavenging wave. A smaller-diameter collector places emphasis on the expansion wave at the open end of the pipe where it reaches atmosphere (open) or the system (closed). This suggests that a short-length, large-diameter collector will produce more low- to mid-range horsepower, while a protracted collector will increase high engine-speed scavenging.

If the camshaft profile is significantly changed, the tuning effect of the exhaust becomes more important. Mild camshafts with minimal overlap produce lower cylinder pressures at the tip of the exhaust stroke. Camshafts with a lot of overlap will be sensitive to the tuning effect and will require some trial and error or use of the Dynomation 6 software suggested in Chapter 2 to see what will work for the best performance. Downstream of the collector box, the exhaust pipe should be 50 percent larger than the diameter of the first tube.

I found a formula in the *Scientific Design of Exhaust and Intake Systems* book that provides a good idea of how long the individual headers should be. I am not saying you need to use it; it is just an example of how exhaust valve size would affect header length.

A good length based on my calculations is about 39 inches. Determine how long the exhaust tube

The book titled Scientific Design of Exhaust and Intake Systems (Engineering and Performance) 3rd Edition by Philip Hubert Smith, Phillip H. Smith, and John C. Morrison has helpful information regarding your exhaust system.

should be by using the following the simple formula from that book. For example, if the build was a mild stock engine using the standard bore of 85.5 mm with the standard stroke of 69 mm with 32-mm exhaust valves and a 276-degree-duration camshaft, the exhaust header length should be 39 inches long.

$$P = \frac{ASD^2}{1,400d^2}$$

A = Camshaft duration (276 degrees)

S = Stroke in inches (69 mm converted to 2.72 inches)

D = Bore in inches (85.5 mm converted to 3.67 inches)

d = Exhaust valve port diameter in inches (32 mm converted to 1.26 inches)

So:

$$\frac{276 \times 2.72 \times 11.33 \ (\text{which is } 3.67 \ \text{squared}) = 8,506}{1,400 \times 1.88 \ (1.37 \ \text{squared}) = 2,632}$$

The answer is 3.23 x 12 = 39 inches (3.23 feet is converted to inches by multiplying by 12).

In calculations, the exponents, or the numbers to be squared, must be calculated before the multiplication or division. The rule if you remember was PEMDAS, which means the order is parentheses, exponents, multiplication, division, addition, and finally subtraction. PEMDAS stands for: Please Excuse My Dear Aunt Sally.

Sadly, none of the aftermarket companies tell you how long the headers are. To determine length, measure them using a cloth tape measure.

Header Size

I recommend that the header inner diameter be close in size to the exhaust valves. For example, 35-mm exhaust valves use a $1^3/_8$-inch exhaust system, 42-mm exhaust valves use a $1^5/_8$-inch system, and 44-mm exhaust valves use a 1¾-inch system. I have seen large-valve heads using the $1^5/_8$ sizes.

CB Performance, Scat, and Gene Berg Enterprises offer competition system header pipe exhaust systems in 1¾, $1^7/_8$, and 2 inches. Gene Berg Enterprises offers a custom build exhaust using $2^1/_8$-inch header pipes.

The general rule for header size is to use 1½ inch for builds up to 2 liters, and $1^5/_8$ inch for builds greater than 2 liters. These sized systems with merged collector boxes are all available from the major aftermarket suppliers. However, some may not be true merged systems that help scavenge or suck out the exhaust gas. Non-merged exhaust systems are sometimes called extractor exhaust systems. I would not use glass-pack muffler systems because they do little

This 4-inch Monster long muffler has a straight-through path that more than doubles the stock flow. A straight-through muffler with radial silencing chambers around a flow tube uses a series of different-sized holes. Large holes on the entry side cancel low-frequency sounds, while the exit side uses smaller holes for high-frequency wave weakening. (Photo Courtesy Scat Enterprises)

If you are building a street machine in a cold climate, keep the heater box heating system for the heater and defrost functions. (Photo Courtesy Scat Enterprises)

to improve flow, but they do sound cool.

Mufflers

The OEM mufflers are claimed to be too restrictive compared to most aftermarket systems. It does do a good job of noise reduction from 600 to 6,000 rpm. The chambers inside a stock muffler take the exhaust gases and route them around several baffles designed to reduce noise. However, this does create large amounts of backpressure.

A longer muffler with less restriction due to a larger tube diameter is the way to go if this build is for the street. For example, use a Corvair muffler or the Bugpack muffler at the end of a performance 4-into-1 system instead of a Stinger. The most popular muffler has been the single or dual quiet muffler system.

Heater Boxes

If you live in a very warm climate such as Southern California or Florida, you may be able to do away with the heater boxes. The inside diameter of the exhaust pipe flowing through the heater boxes was not designed to flow more exhaust gas than the stock 50-bhp engine. So, if you are in the situation where you need the heater boxes, purchase a better-flowing one, such as a Dansk heater boxes. These European heater boxes have larger inner diameter tubing, and they are also lighter than stock.

EMPI offers heater boxes for Type 1 and Type 2 under part numbers 3255, 3256, 7320, and 55-7320. Scat and most of the other firms only offer the standard heater boxes. I have seen some modification older non-fresh air heater boxes from the older 40-bhp

engines built before 1962 by using large diameter header pipes.

If heating is not an issue, replace the heater boxes with J-pipes or use a performance or competition type exhaust system that installs in place of the heater boxes by directly connecting to the rear exhaust ports. My

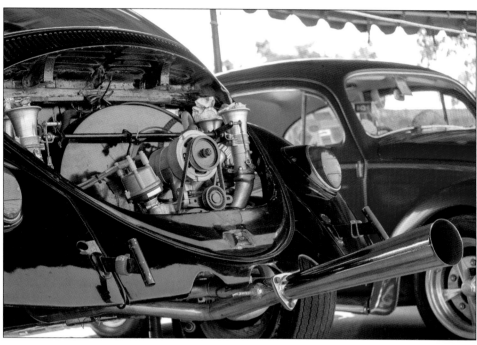

A Stinger exhaust system is a 4-into-1-type setup with four pipes: one of each cylinder going into a collector box and out a tapered funnel-shaped tailpipe. (Photo Courtesy Shutterstock)

Straight stacks will peak, which means that they may provide a big power boost at a tuned RPM but may also detract from performance at other engine speeds. At one time, Formula racers required straight stacks, but they are no longer required. (Photo Courtesy Scat Enterprises)

recommendations are in Building an Exhaust System section of this chapter.

Open Exhaust Stingers

Stinger exhaust systems are very popular systems among drag racers. If these systems are installed instead of a muffler there will usually be an increase in horsepower through most of the RPM range, but they are very noisy. However, if you merely remove the muffler without bolting in some kind of extension onto a 4-into-1 systems, the bottom-end performance will most likely suffer.

Building an Exhaust System

You might believe that this would be easy, but there are factors that have to be considered in the building of a tuned exhaust system. Consider the bore, stroke, exhaust valve duration of the camshaft, and the exhaust port diameter. These factors will affect the speed of the exhaust gas out of the engine.

Base 1,600-cc Mild Street Build

Anytime you change from the stock exhaust system so the engine can breathe more freely, induction systems and ignition timing changes will be needed to get better performance on mild and stock builds. For the mild street build using a stock 1,600-cc engine, this build would have had a three-angle valve job and modifications to the Solex 34 PICT-3 carburetor along with an ignition upgrade. Several bolt-on systems to increase horsepower are listed below.

EMPI

It is possible to go from the standard heater boxes to the Dansk heater boxes under EMPI part numbers 3255, 3256, 7320, and 55-7320. EMPI also offers the GT exhaust system with the Quiet Muffler under part number 3414 for a Type 1 and Karman Ghia 1,300 to 1,600 cc.

Scat

Scat offers Euro 2-Tip Tri-Mil exhaust (part number 55153-Euro-Cer Ceramic), Black Euro 2-Tip Tri-Mil exhaust (part number 55153-Euro-Blk), and 4-Tip GT extractor system (part number 55153).

Gene Berg Enterprises
- Part number GB 903 (for 50-hp 1,300/1,500/1,600-cc sedan with single muffler)
- Part number GB 903DP (same as part number GB 903 with dual mufflers)
- Part number GB 907 (for the 50-hp Type 2)
- Part number GB 908 (for 50-hp Karmann Ghia using a collector and single muffler located under the bumper)
- Part number GB 912H (header and GB 973A muffler)
- Part number GB912 (for a Type 2; includes a collector and single muffler for off-road, muffler under back bumper)
- Part number MAT 932HB-L (Flanged 1½-inch heater box - left [no fins])
- Part number MAT 932HB-R (Flanged 1½-inch heater box - right [no fins])
- Part number MAT 933HB-L (1⅝-inch finned heater box – left)
- Part number MAT 933HB-R (1⅝-inch finned heater box – right)

CB Performance

The high-performance 1⅝-inch ID heater boxes (left and right) (part number 3682) are available.

Street-Use Performance Build

This is a mild build that has been upgraded to a 1,776-cc or 1,904-cc build with larger valve heads, mild performance camshaft, and an enhanced carburetion or electronic fuel-injection system. If you live in a cold climate and it's for street use, I recommend changing the heater boxes from the standard to the Dansk heater boxes under EMPI part numbers 3255, 3256, 7320, and 55-7320. My recommendations for street performance exhaust systems are as follows:

Scat

Buggy Master Exhaust Systems are available for Type 1 engines. The system includes a quiet muffler and comes with heater boxes under part number 55232 or is ceramic coated under part number 55232C.

EMPI

The Sideflow exhaust system is available for Type 2, 1968–1971 engines. It uses 1½-inch tubing featuring a true 4-into-1 merged collector. The mounting flanges are thick, and it includes a black quiet muffler. It comes complete with gaskets and hardware. Systems are available that clamp to bolt-on heater boxes EMPI part numbers 3255, 3256, 7320, and 55-7320.

The stainless-steel Extractor & Stinger for Type 1 and 2 engines uses 1⅜-inch header tubing. The three-bolt muffler flange is centered, and the flange is at the 1 o'clock position with elongated holes for muffler alignment. This system can be used with heater boxes. Part numbers 3767 S/S (extractor only) fits Type 1 and Type 2 from 1,300 to 1,600 cc. Part number 3477 is for the Stinger only.

Gene Berg Enterprises
- Part numbers GB 971A-2M and GB 971A-2SM for street mufflers
- Part number MAT 932HB-L: Flanged 1½-inch heater box - left (no fins)
- Part number MAT 932HB-R Flanged 1½-inch heater box - right (no fins)
- Part number MAT 933HB-L: 1⅝-inch finned heater box - left
- Part number MAT 933HB-R: 1⅝-inch finned heater box - right

CB Performance

CB Performance offers a wide variety of exhaust systems:

- CB part number 3500 Streetster Hideaway exhaust system is available for use with Dansk heater boxes under EMPI part numbers 3255, 3256, 7320, and 55-7320
- CB part number 3644 1½-inch Flanged Pro-Flow Street system comes complete with better flowing heater boxes for better performance
- From Gene Berg, CB Part numbers GB 971A-2M and GB 971A-2SM (street mufflers)

High-Performance Racing and Off-Road

This is a high-performance build that has been upgraded to an engine over 2 liters using large valve, ported and polished high-performance heads, high-performance camshaft, dual carburetion, or electronic fuel-injection system. It can also be equipped with a supercharger or turbocharger.

Heater boxes are rarely found on these builds because these are high-performance systems. These exhaust systems are for all racing applications and off-road systems. My recommendations for high-performance exhaust systems from the following vendors are as follows:

EMPI
- EMPI offers a sideflow exhaust system for Type 1 applications using 1½-inch header tubing into a 4-into-1 merged collector. It has thick connection flanges and a quiet muffler if needed. It comes with gaskets and hardware.
- EMPI Sideflow merged exhaust system (part number 3485) with 1½-inch tubing features tig welding and thick header flanges. This system includes a black quiet muffler with stainless-steel tip. This is a competition system and does not use heater boxes.
- EMPI Sideflow exhaust system for Type 1 engines (part number 3263) with 1⅝-inch tubing and a 4-into-1 merged collector. The mounting flanges are thick, and it includes a quiet muffler, if needed. The kit includes gaskets and hardware. This is a competition system and does not use heater boxes.
- EMPI's Buggy Dual Stack Exhaust for Type 1 engines (part number 3373) is an exhaust system that does not use heater boxes or mufflers, as it is for off-road or racing. The system features 1⅜-inch tubing.

Gene Berg Enterprises

Gene Berg offers high-performance exhaust systems for

builds up to 7,500 rpm for racing and off-road competition engines.

- Part numbers GB 932S, GB 933S SW 27#, GB 934 SW 28#, GB 935 SW 29#, GB 936 SW 30#, GB 937 SW 33#, and GB 938 SW 34#. These systems come with a stinger and header pipes from cylinders-1 and -3 to the exhaust header and stinger. These exhaust systems use slip joints on the number-2 and -4 head pipes to allow for a proper fit and to clear any oil pump and filter combinations.
- Part number GB 932 is a 1½-inch competition system that comes with a merged collector and will not clear the thermostat.
- Part number GB 932M is a 1½ merged sedan system. It comes with a single high-flow muffler, if needed (#GB 971A), header (#GB 932), and all installation hardware.
- Part number GB 932S is a 1½-inch competition system with a merged collector and stinger. This system will not clear the thermostat.
- Part number GB 933 is a 1⅝-inch merged header only.
- Part number GB 933M is a single muffler if needed for a merged 1⅝-inch system.
- Part number GB 933S is a 1⅝-inch competition sedan system with a merged collector. The system comes with a stinger.
- Part number GB 934 is a 1¾ competition sedan system with a merged collector. Number-1 and -3 headers do not clear factory shrouding with a thermostat.
- Part number GB 934SL is a 1¾-inch competition sedan system with a merged collector.

It comes with the stinger. The number-1 and -3 headers do not clear the thermostat.

- Part number GB 935S is a $1^7/_8$-inch competition sedan system with a merged collector. It comes with a stinger and three-bolt flange. This system does not clear the thermostat. It works with Berg Dynosoar and Superflow heads. This exhaust system was designed to develop BHP in the 5,500- to 9,000-rpm range.

- Part number GB 936S is a 2-inch header pipe competition sedan system with a merged collector. The system comes with a stinger and three-bolt flange. It works with Berg Dynosoar and Super-flow heads. This exhaust system was designed to develop BHP in the 5,500- to 9,000-rpm range.

- Part number GB 937S is a $2^1/_8$-inch header pipe competition sedan system with a merged collector, three-bolt flange, and stinger. This system is for cylinder heads with large valves using at least a 40-mm exhaust valve. This exhaust system was designed to develop BHP in the 6,000- to 10,000-rpm range. Berg says this will be a custom order.

Scat
- The Merge Sidewinder exhaust system uses $1^5/_8$-inch tubing with 3/8-inch-thick flanges with a Dynomax-type muffler for all Type 1 engines (part number 551SW-SS).

- EMPI sells a Dual Python universal exhaust system for Baja Bugs, Sand Rails, and Trikes. It fits Type 1 engines and works with single or dual carburetor kits. It is a straight-stack design. Heater boxes are not used and two

A $1^5/_8$-inch-diameter merge sidewinder exhaust system is available that uses a $1^5/_8$-inch mandrel-bent 16-gauge tubing that has 3/8-inch-thick tubing walls and a flange-mounted Dynomax-type muffler to the header pipes. These are available from Scat (part number 551SW-SS) or EMPI (part number 3479). (Photo Courtesy Scat Enterprises)

Baja-style exhaust systems use a merge collector that allows the exhaust from each of the four pipes to merge together gradually at the collector for greater horsepower. Heater boxes cannot be used. The merge collector goes straight up like a stack. (Photo Courtesy Scat Enterprises)

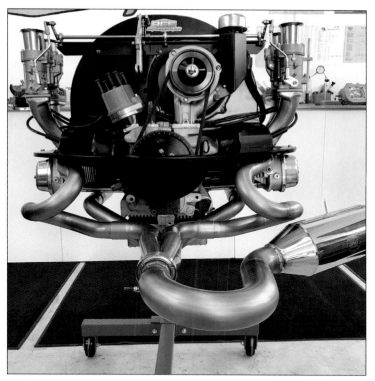

Headers are also called collector boxes, and they are designed to enhance the evacuation of exhaust gases from the combustion chamber and cylinder. This enhances engine performance by increasing the scavenging effect of the exhaust system, thereby drawing more exhaust gas from the cylinder. By increasing the evacuation of the exhaust gases from the cylinder, the incoming air-fuel mixture does not become diluted, and power output increases. (Photo Courtesy ACE Performance Engines, Stefan Rossi)

- Dual Merge QP Muffler, Type 1 SCQ-2C (part number SCQ-2)
- Single Hide-A-Way Muffler SCQ-HIDE-CER (part number SCQ-HIDE)

CB Performance

CB offers the following performance systems:

- $1^7/_8$-inch Full Merged Exhaust with Stinger (part number 3668). Heater boxes cannot be used.
- 2-inch Full Merged Exhaust with Stinger (part number 3669). Heater boxes cannot be used.
- $1^3/_8$-inch Full Merged with Fat Boy Quiet Muffler (part number 3674). Heater boxes cannot be used.

models are offered: black mufflers with chrome tips full stacks (part number 55010) or ceramic coated mufflers (part number 55011)

- Racing Baja Merge Exhaust for Type 1 and 4 with $1^5/_8$-inch tubing, and 5/16-inch machined sealing flanges. Merge collector design adds 10 to 15 percent more horsepower.

Racing Type 1 merge-type systems for Type 1 and 2 engines come with headers and mufflers. Various individual parts are offered:

- $1^1/_2$-inch Merge Header SC112C (part number SC112)
- $1^5/_8$-inch Merge Header SC158C (part number SC158)
- $1^3/_4$-inch Merge Header SC134C (part number SC134)
- 2-inch Merge Header SC200C (part number SC200)
- Stinger Merge Muffler for T1 SCQ-SC (part number SCQ-S)
- Stinger for 2-inch Merge Header SCQ-SCL (part number SCQ-SL)
- Single Quiet Muffler SCQ-1C (part number SCQ-1)

Engine Cooling

Head temperature is an air-cooled engine's biggest enemy. Head temperature is responsible for more damage than many other failures, and it is not often found as the failure issue. This is a reason the fuel induction system must match the requirements of the VW air-cooled engine build. The specific fuel delivered to

If your build is for high performance, consider using the Bergmann 911–style fan shroud (Scat part number 25085). The Bergmann 911–style shroud kit uses a serpentine belt and a balanced 12-blade fan along with a high-output alternator. (Photo Courtesy ACE Performance Engines, Stefan Rossi)

Make sure to install the cylinder deflector tin for maximum airflow over the cylinders. Clean-flowing cooling vanes must be around the cylinder head for maximum cooling through the head and around the intake ports. Some performance cylinder heads, such as AA Performance and CB Performance, use a second full cooling fin on the head. (Photo Courtesy ACE Performance Engines, Stefan Rossi)

the engine is responsible for near 50 percent of the cooling.

Back in Chapter 3, I discussed using the doghouse shroud to move the oil cooler out of the cooling fan flow path. The doghouse shroud used with the internal engine oil cooler adapter places the oil cooler outside of the cooler fan area for better cooling. That is because when it was alongside the fan, there was not enough airflow over the cooler. Regarding the lubrication system, for oil cooling management, increase the sump size and use a larger oil pickup.

Heavy-Duty High-Output Cooling Fan

The VW forced-air cooling systems use sheet metal shrouding to direct air over the heads, cylinders, and oil cooler. On later 1,300- to 1,600-cc engines, thermostat-controlled cooling was provided by a bellows-type air flap under each side of the engine. These thermostat flaps open when

the temperature of the air under the cylinders reached 205°F.

Earlier engines were controlled by an air throttle ring on the blower fan outlet and not recommended for any builds. Make sure the thermostats are installed and working. You

definitely do not want cooling air to escape before it has done its work in cooling the engine.

When installing the tin shrouding, make sure of the following: to plug any opening in the sheet metal; the spark plug seals are installed; and the heater box openings, if used, are securely connected to the heater hoses.

The cooling fan is an often-overlooked component of the air-cooled engine. Bent or cracked fins, worn hub, or out-of-round fans can cause damage to an engine from overheating. The cooling fan is driven by the crankshaft pulley belt through the generator/alternator at 1.8 times engine speed, depending on the pulley diameter. The standard pulley size was 6¾ inches.

A power pulley can be installed that has a diameter of 5¾ inches to turn the cooling fan faster. The later-style factory fans were wider than the earlier types but still compatible with the Type 1 and Type 2 Doghouse fan shrouds. For the all-out racing machine, consider using the Ram-Air Porsche Fan Shrouds and a large fan.

The engine compartment seals that are against the firewall must be tight because they keep hot air from the cylinders and exhaust from getting into the engine compartment. The cooling fan will not suck in any of this hot air. EMPI and Scat sell firewall kits. (Photo Courtesy Scat Enterprises)

ENGINE BUILDS

I have done a considerable amount of research on potential engine builds using the tremendous number of available components and information from aftermarket suppliers. I built performance VW 1,600-cc engines back in the 1970s when I was work-ing for Volkswagen Atlantic in Valley Forge, Pennsylvania, and I worked with a person who built Super V engines for racing.

If you are building a stroker and using radical parts, I suggest building a mockup engine and then taking measurements to make sure that nothing will blow up. There is a lot of information available on engine builds. The builds in this chapter are from personal experience and builders I have contacted.

Common Rebuild Materials

Permatex Aviation Form-a-Gasket is a good choice of sealant for the oil pump and can also be used for the case halves. However, be warned of it getting brittle and cracking, causing an oil leak. I use Permatex Ultra Lube on the assembly of all internal parts. You will also want to use moly lube on the camshaft and lifters.

Build 1: 1,600-cc Bolt-on Horsepower

This build adds exterior components and removes the cylinder heads for a valve job, porting, and possible increase in compression ratio. We are not disassembling the short-block. This is a stock 1,600-cc engine with an 85.5-mm bore, 69-mm-stroke crankshaft, and dual-port heads.

This build uses the following components and processes:

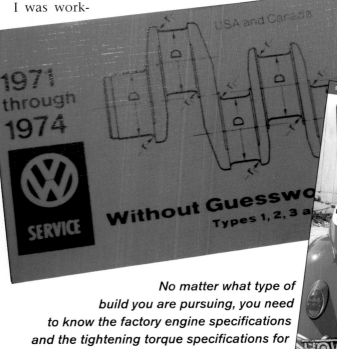

No matter what type of build you are pursuing, you need to know the factory engine specifications and the tightening torque specifications for the entire engine assembly. A good source for this old information is the Volkswagen Without Guesswork *book, which was originally supplied by the Volkswagen company in Germany. Unfortunately, these sometimes can be a little difficult to find. You can also find assembly specifications in the CarTech book* VW Air-Cooled Engines: How to Rebuild 1961–2003 *by Prescott Phillips.*

I use Permatex Ultra Grey gasket maker high-torque sealant on the case halves on all builds. I find that this sealer, because of its silicone base, tends not to crack as opposed some of the other sealers.

You can bolt on horsepower in the form of components such as better-flowing exhaust system and heater boxes. This, along with stock-carburetor jetting modifications and minor head changes, can provide an 11-percent increase in horsepower.

Remove the cylinder heads and complete the three-angle (30-45-70) valve job and the porting shown in Chapter 2. While the heads are off, measure the combustion chamber and do a minor fly cut to increase the compression ratio. The standard compression ratio on a 1,600-cc Type 1 was 7.3:1. Use the process from Chapter 2 to measure and raise the compression ratio to 8:1.

Remove the 34 PCIT-3 Solex carburetor and perform the modifications suggested in Chapter 7. Use larger main and air correction jets and check for full throttle opening, porting the carburetor, and install-

Coat all main bearings with Permatex red Ultra Slick engine assembly lube. Install the upper camshaft shaft bearing inserts to the case and the lower crankshaft bearing inserts to the case if you are using Chevrolet-style split crankshaft bearings.

ing an improved-flow air cleaner or velocity stacks.

Upgrade the exhaust system to one with better flow, such as upgrading from the standard heater boxes to the Dansk heater boxes. Install a better-flowing exhaust system from EMPI, Scat, Gene Berg, or CB Performance. There will be an 11- to 12-percent increase in horsepower (from 50 to 56 bhp).

Build 2: 1,776-cc Engine

To build a 1,776-cc engine, use a 90.5-mm cylinder and pistons set with a stock 69-mm stroke crankshaft. The 90.5 mm is a very common upgrade bore-size piston cylinder set from the standard 85.5 mm used in the standard 1,600-cc engine. It also has the same cylinder wall thickness as a stock 85.5-mm cylinder. I recommend using an eight-bolt flywheel for this build or any serious horsepower increase.

Base 1,600-cc Stroke and Bore Displacement									
	Bore (millimeters)								
	83	85.5	87	88	90.5	92	94	96.5	101.6
Stroke 69 mm STD	1,493	1,585	1,641	1,679	1,776	1,835	1,914	2,019	2,237

1,776 Stroke and Bore Displacement									
	Bore (millimeters)								
	83	85.5	87	88	90.5	92	94	96.5	101.6
Stroke 69 mm STD	1,493	1,585	1,641	1,679	1,776	1,835	1,914	2,019	2,237

2,110-cc Stroke and Bore Displacement									
83	Bore (millimeters)								
	85.5	87	88	90.5	92	94	96.5	101.6	
Stroke 82 mm (Stroker)	1,775	1,883	1,950	1,995	2,110	2,180	2,275	2,399	2,659

This build requires the following components and produces approximately 109 bhp:

- Mahle 90.5-mm pistons and cylinder matched set
- Eight-dowel Scat forged and counterweighted crankshaft
- Eagle 120 camshaft
- Stock rebuilt dual-port heads with three-point performance valve job
- Offset manifolds
- Weber IDF dual carburetors using a 28-mm main Venturi
- Solid cam followers
- 30-mm oil pump with mini sump and external filter
- Bosch 009 distributor with PerTronix electronic ignition upgrade
- Stock fuel pump check at a 5-psi output
- $1^5/_8$-inch exhaust system using Dansk heater boxes

Build 3: 2,110-cc Engine

Let's walk through building the 2,110-cc engine based on the

H-beam rods are used on robust high-horsepower builds because they are light with high strength due to their forged chrome steel construction. The caps used a fillet radius to reduce the amount of clearance required on stroker applications and were sleeved to the rod to eliminate cap shifting. (Photo Courtesy ACE Performance Engines, Stefan Rossi)

The 2,110-cc engine build used a split bearing at the number-3 main bearing due to the stresses associated in that area and because of its more robust design. Many aftermarket companies sell these bearings. (Photo Courtesy ACE Performance Engines, Stefan Rossi)

Straight-cut or spur timing gears were used on this build. When installing the camshaft timing gear to the crankshaft timing gear, align the two dots on the crank gear with the single dot on the camshaft timing gear. Also, use a dial indicator to check the backlash between the timing gears. (Photo Courtesy ACE Performance Engines, Stefan Rossi)

1,600-series engines, which is a classic stroker engine.

Starting with the case, no extensive machining was done because a new EMPI Bubble Top case was selected. It is possible to buy a cheap Chinese-made case from AA Performance. The case must be notched for the longer stroke. This case was machined to fit the 90.5-mm cylinder and piston sets. It also came with the 8-mm head stud case savers. A new cam plug was installed with flat side toward the flywheel using Permatex Gasket Maker. The plug kit came from EMPI.

This build used an 82-mm stroker crankshaft that has counterweights for good balance. There are many places to buy this crankshaft; take look in the source guide and use whatever fits your budget. However, make sure that it is a forged crank.

This build used H-beam longer connecting rods dues to the long stroke made with forged 4340 chrome molybdenum steel, such as Scat H-beam 5.5-inch or longer connecting rods with ARP 2000 bolts. The standard Volkswagen connecting rod measures 5.394 inches.

Split bearings were used in this build at number-3. Assemble the case without the crankshaft and camshaft to check clearance on the main and camshaft bearings. Check bearing clearances with the bearings installed in an assembled torqued-to-specifications case using sealer without internal components. Measure ID and compare with camshaft and crankshaft OD measurement. Clearance specs can be found in the *Without Guesswork* book. Assemble the new connecting rods to the crankshaft and use Plastigauge to check the bearing clearances. When tightening the rod bolts to specifications, I would also use a stretch gauge

2,165-cc Stroke and Bore Displacement									
	Bore (millimeters)								
		83	**85.5**	**87**	**88**	**90.5**	**92**	**94**	**96.5**	**101.6**
Stroke	**78 mm (Stroker)**	1,688	1,791	1,855	1,897	2,007	2,074	2,165	2,282	2,529

to make sure that the bolts do not stretch beyond 0.005 to 0.006 inch. During case assembly, this build used nuts with a seal, and the bevel spring washers have the concave side down with Permatex to form a gasket on them and flat side up.

Also make sure that the split bearings do not rock in the case and the dowel pins line up for case assembly. Dowel pin holes in bearings face toward the flywheel. Install the bearing halves in the top case half. Use angular notched lifters for the best lubrication, and install them using engine oil.

CB Performance heads with spring package and 70-degree-cut valves were used on this build along with 0.080-inch copper head gaskets with the flat side up toward the cylinder and roller rocker arms. The cylinder deck height was checked, and no barrel spacers were needed.

The Dub Shop electronic fuel-injection system was used with all components (ECU, injectors, sensors, intake manifolds, throttle body, and wiring harness) from the Dub Shop.

The Dub Shop complete turbo-charger setup was installed. Horsepower is now in the 150-plus-bhp range.

Build 4: 2,165-cc Engine

This build uses one of the larger piston and cylinder sizes at 94 mm. It started with a Scat Killer case that was machined for the 78-mm stroker crankshafts and sized to fit the

Components for the 2,165-cc high-performance, high-displacement build were laid out prior to assembly. These included a Berg case and big valve heads, dual Weber IDA carburetors, CB Performance spur cut timing gears, and King Racing bearings. (Some components in the photo were not used for this build.) (Photo Courtesy ACE Performance Engines, Stephan Rossi)

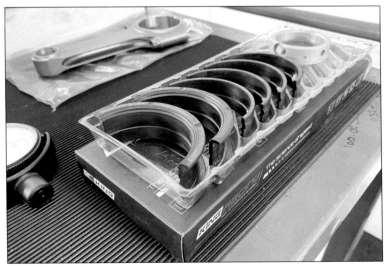

The King Performance Chevrolet split main bearings were used for all main bearings with the number-1 position bearing being solid. I recommend these type bearings for a robust 2,165-cc engine build. (Photo Courtesy ACE Performance Engines, Stephan Rossi)

Check bearing clearances with the bearings installed in an assembled and torqued-to-specification case using sealer without internal components. (Photo Coutesy ACE Performance Engeines, Stephan Rossi)

94-mm cylinders at the bottom. It has the 8-mm case savers built in for the 8-mm case studs. This is an oversquared high-RPM engine, so the Scat H-beam connecting rods are rated up to 9,000 rpm. Brake horsepower is in the 150 to 200 range.

This build requires the following components:

- 78-mm Scat stroker Volkstroker Pro-Drag Flange crankshaft
- Chevrolet-type split main bearings for all main bearings with a solid bearing at number-1
- Eagle camshaft (part number 6087) with an FK-87 grind
- CB Performance 044 Super Mag CNC round-port cylinder heads (40-mm intake and 35-mm

exhaust valves)
- CB Performance Pauter machine billet roller rocker arm kit with a 1.3:1 rocker ratio
- Holley Electric Red Fuel Pump
- Dual Weber IDA carburetors on Gene Berg (part number LA INTAKE012) 40 x 37.5-mm welded intake manifolds

Build 5: 400-bhp Engine

The displacement of this build is 2,276 cc, and it was built by Ray Mejia of Los Angeles, California.

This build develops 400 hp and is made up of the following components:

- Type 1 magnesium case
- 82-mm Bugpack flanged crankshaft with 411 Chevrolet journals and split bearings
- 5.5-inch Scat H-beam rods with 0.200-inch pins
- Mahle cylinders (not cylinder sets)
- 94-mm Wiseco pistons
- SLE camshaft special grind
- Straight/spur-cut timing gears
- Street Eliminator cylinder heads with 44-mm intake valve and 37.5-mm exhaust valve using PSI springs. They were polished by Ray Mejia with final machining done by Brothers Machine Shop along with the head studs.

2,276 Stroke and Bore Displacement									
	Bore (millimeters)								
	83	85.5	87	88	90.5	92	94	96.5	101.6
Stroke 64	1,385	1,470	1,522	1,557	1,647	1,702	1,777	1,872	2,075
69	1,493	1,585	1,641	1,679	1,776	1,835	1,914	2,019	2,237
74	1,602	1,699	1,760	1,800	1,904	1,968	2,054	2,165	2,399
78	1,688	1,791	1,855	1,897	2,007	2,074	2,165	2,282	2,529
82	1,775	1,883	1,950	1,995	2,110	2,180	2,276	2,399	2,659
84	1,818	1,929	1,997	2,044	2,161	2,234	2,332	2,457	2,724

To find the bearing clearance, measure the outer diameter of the crankshaft bearing surface and subtract this value from the outer diameter of the bearing installed in a case torqued to specification. (Photo Courtesy ACE Performance Engines, Stephan Rossi)

- Compression ratio set at 8.4:1
- Rocker arms are Scat 1.25:1 ratio
- Custom-made intake system using a single 50-mm-opening throttle body
- RC550 fuel injectors
- CB Performance intake manifolds
- CB Performance 30-mm oil pump with full-flow oil system
- Scat 1.5-quart sump with billet sump plate
- EMPI breather box
- The Dub Shop Hall-effect CKP sensor with a traditional distributor
- Turbonetics T3/T4 turbocharger
- Turbo Smart Comp-Gate 40 wastegate
- Custom-made exhaust system with $1^5/_8$ header tubing, ceramic coasted with oxygen sensor bung, and Magnaflow muffler, built by Ray Mejia.
- Ron Lummis Engineering flywheel
- Ron Lummis Engineering REV-6 racing clutch
- Bernie Bergmann fan shroud

The engine build by Ray Mejia was featured in **HotVWs** *magazine in October 2019. This engine developed 400 hp. It is installed in his 1956 oval-window Type 1.*

CHAPTER 9

Torque Specifications

Fasteners	Ft-lbs	Nm	Size Diameter x Pitch (mm)
Connecting Rod Nuts	22–25	30–34	9 x 1
Connecting Rod Cap Screws	32	43	9 x 1
Crankcase Nuts (8 mm)	14	19	8
Crankcase Nuts (12 mm)	18	24	12 x 1.5
Cylinder Head Nuts (8-mm stud)	18	24	8
Cylinder Head Nuts (10-mm stud)	23	31	10
Rocker Shaft Nuts	14–18	19–24	8
Heat Exchangers at Head	14	19	8
Muffler Clamp Bolts	7	9	6
Intake Manifold Nut	14	19	8
Preheat Flange Nut	7	9	6
Oil Pump Nut (M6)	9	12	6
Oil Pump Nut (M8)	14	19	8
Oil Drain Plug	25	34	14 x 1.5
Oil Strainer Nut	5	7	6
Oil Cooler Nut	5	7	6
Oil-Filler Gland Nut	40	54	–
Flywheel Gland Nut	235	319	28 x 1.5
Clutch-to-Flywheel Bolt	18	24	8 x 1.5
Spark Plugs	22–29	30–39	14 x 1.25
Engine-to-Transmission Nut	22	30	10
Crossmember Bolt (M8)	18	24	8
Crossmember Bolt (M10)	29	39	10
Generator Pulley Nut	40–47	54–64	12 x 1.5
Fan Nut	40–47	54–64	12 x 1.5
Crankshaft-to-Flywheel Bolt	253	343	–
Crankshaft Pulley Bolt (Type 1)	29–36	39–49	20 x 1.5
Crankshaft Pulley Bolt (Type 3)	94–108	127–146	20 x 1.5
Crossmember to Body	18	24	8
Sump Screen Nuts	5	7	–

SOURCE GUIDE

AA Performance Products
1080 E. Edna Pl.
Covina, CA 91724
626-333-5555
aapistons.com

Air Cooled
379 W. 6500 S.
Murray, UT 84107
801-453-1906
aircooled.net

Aircooled Vintage Works
P.O. Box 603
Cardiff, CA 92007
858-354-4942
aircooledvintageworks.com

Airhead Parts
1770 N. Ventura Ave.
Ventura, CA 93001
1-800-927-2787
airheadparts.com

Alligator Performance Intercoolers
11783 N. Warren St.
Hayden, ID 83835
208-719-7400
alligatorperformance.com

Appletree Auto
800-433-2521
appletreeauto.com

Automotive Racing Products
1863 Eastman Ave.
Ventura, CA 93003
1-800-826-3045
arp-bolts.com

Banks Power
546 S. Duggan Ave.
Azusa, CA 91702
1-800-601-8072
bankspower.com

BorgWarner
1849 Brevard Rd.
Arden, NC 28704
1-800-787-6464
borgwarner.com

CARiD.com
1 Corporate Dr.
Cranbury, NJ 08512
1-800-505-3274
carid.com

CB Performance Products, Inc.
1715 N. Farmersville Blvd.
Farmersville, CA 93223
1-800-274-8337
cbperformance.com

Chirco
9101 E. 22nd St.
Tucson, AZ 85710
1-800-955-9795
chirco.com

Dune Buggy Warehouse
2610 Bobmeyer Rd.
Hamilton, OH 45015
513-868-9543
dunebuggywarehouse.com

The Dub Shop
17239 Tye St. SE, Suite E
Monroe, WA 98272
206-414-8456
thedubshop.com

EMPI (US headquarters)
301 E. Orangethorpe Ave.
Anaheim, CA 92801
1-800-666-3674
empius.com

Fuel Tech
27601 Bella Vista Pkwy.
Warrenville, IL 60555
1-800-666-9688
fueltech.net

Gene Berg Enterprises
1725 North Lime St.
Orange, C A 92865
714-998-7500
geneberg.com

Heritage Parts Center
47 Dolphin Rd.
Shoreham-By-Sea
BN43 6PB
United Kingdom
heritagepartscentre.com/us/
    volkswagen

JBugs
1338 Rocky Point Dr.
Oceanside, CA 92056
1-800-231-1784
JBugs.com

JEGS Performance
101 Jegs Pl.
Delaware, OH 43015
1-800-345-4545
jegs.com

Joe Blow Superchargers
P.O. Box 2105
Hilton Plaza
South Australia 5033
45 860 391 553
joeblow.me

John Maher Racing
Unit 3 The Pier
Leverburgh
Isle of Harris
HS5 3UB
United Kingdom
44 1859 520797
johnmaherracing.com

Kawell Racing Engines
78 Miller Loop Rd.
Friendship, TN 38034
731-677-2160
davekawellracingengines.com

LJ Air Cooled
426 N. Barranca Ave. #5
Covina, CA 91723
626-625-5223
ljaircooledengines.com

Mid America Motorworks
2800 N. 3rd St.
Effingham, IL 62401
1-800-500-1500
mamotorworks.com

MoFoCo Enterprises Inc.
4170 N. Lydell Ave.
Milwaukee, WI 53212
414-963-1020
mofoco.com

Moore Parts Source
714-666-6688
mooreparts.com

Scat
1400 Kingsdale Ave.
Redondo Beach, CA 90278
310-370-5501
scatvw.com

S&S Aircooled Parts and Accessories
747 S. State College Blvd., Suite 70
Fullerton, CA 92831
714-886-7636
ssaircooled.com

RockAuto
6418 Normandy Ln., Suite 100
Madison, WI 53719
608-661-1376
rockauto.com

SoCal Imports
6831 Paramount Blvd.
Long Beach, CA 90805
562-633-4979
socalautoparts.com

Summit Racing
1200 Southeast Ave.
Tallmadge, OH 44278
1-800-230-3030
summitracing.com

Stinger Performance Engineering
5560 Meadow Sweet Ln.
Shawnee, KS 66226
stinger-performance.com

Texas Aircooled
6031 Hwy. 6 N. #165-249
Houston, TX 77084
713-467-2373
texasaircooled.com

The VDub Factory
4279 NE 36th Ave.
Ocala, FL 34479
352-620-8007
thevdubfactory.com